CAST DOWN

EARLY AMERICAN STUDIES

Series editors:
Daniel K. Richter, Kathleen M. Brown,
Max Cavitch, and David Waldstreicher

Exploring neglected aspects of our colonial,
revolutionary, and early national history and culture,
Early American Studies reinterprets familiar themes
and events in fresh ways. Interdisciplinary in character,
and with a special emphasis on the period from about
1600 to 1850, the series is published in partnership with
the McNeil Center for Early American Studies.

CAST DOWN

Abjection in America,
1700–1850

Mark J. Miller

PENN

UNIVERSITY OF PENNSYLVANIA PRESS

PHILADELPHIA

Published by
University of Pennsylvania Press
Philadelphia, Pennsylvania 19104-4112
www.upenn.edu/pennpress

Printed in the United States of America
on acid-free paper
1 3 5 7 9 10 8 6 4 2

Library of Congress Cataloging-in-Publication Data
ISBN 978-0-8122-4802-9

CONTENTS

From Roses to Neuroses

Early in the thirteenth century, a monk in Assisi, Italy, tried to quell his lust through a severe self-mortification of the flesh. Tormented by desire, he ran out into the snowy winter night and threw himself into a wild rose bush, whose thorns cured him of his passion. Then, miraculously, despite the cold, the roses began to bud and bloom. Their blossoms, which had been white, were now flecked with red. Seven centuries later, when psychologist Theodor Reik recounted this story of St. Francis in his 1940 treatise *Masochism and Modern Man*, he took care to distinguish religious martyrdom from sexual masochism. According to Reik, the sexual masochist uses pain to create sexual excitement while the martyr's pain atones for sexual excitement. Martyrdom, Reik concludes, is a form of what he calls "social masochism" governed by a "sublimated form of masochistic feeling."[1] The martyr, inspired by accounts of religious suffering and guided by "bishops, churchwardens, and the community" at large, participates in a social ritual governed by what Reik calls the church's "increasing striving for 'publicity.' "[2] Religious publicity—the circulation of ideas in print, speech, or manuscript form—generates the martyrological desire that then sustains the church. In the supposedly secular modern age, Reik drolly observes, it is not roses but neuroses that arise from the willed experience of redemptive suffering.[3]

This study charts the conceptual continuity that lies between Reik's roses and neuroses. Following Reik's suggestion that church publicity played a key role in shaping the desire for suffering, *Cast Down* focuses on the uses of abjection—the desire for religious suffering—during two periods of rapid transformation: first, the 1730s and 1740s, when new models of publication and transportation enabled eighteenth-century transatlantic Protestant religious populism, and, second, the 1830s and 1840s, when liberal reform movements emerged from nonsectarian religious organizations. In the eighteenth and nineteenth centuries, abjection helped organize a constellation of affective states, behaviors, and ideologies that contributed to the development of the modern notion of masochism but cannot be contained within the bounds of its current definition. Many twentieth-century psychoanalysts, including Reik, understood masochism as an outgrowth of or point of origin for sexuality. Social theorists, psychologists and theologians (often the same people) in the eighteenth and nineteenth centuries laid the groundwork for this notion by mixing earlier, religious notions of suffering with emerging conceptions of gender and race.[4] This period of mixing older and new ideas, from early modern to modern, is at the center of my study. The groundwork was laid by early modern Puritan and Quaker converts who developed practices of self-regulation and identification that contributed to modern notions of interiority and the liberal humanist subject. These converts also narrated the disappearance of a sinful "individual" self and appearance of a gracious self stripped of "personality" and inseparable from the divine. Following these developments within Protestant experience and theology, the eighteenth and nineteenth centuries witnessed a broader cultural shift in the social meaning of religion, rank, and visible markers of sex and cultural difference. These concepts were supplemented and, in some cases, supplanted by the development of gender and race as internal characteristics or aspects of personality.[5]

The resonance of abjection in colonial American and U.S. culture is due, in part, to the concept's deep religious roots. Abjection has a long history in the spiritual traditions of the peoples of the book, for whom it takes shape through complaints of misery or vileness (e.g., "zalal" in Eikhah 1:11) used to cement oppositional identity, to console and discipline readers and listeners, and to otherwise structure rituals of purification or sanctification. Derived from the Latin *abiectus*, literally meaning "cast down" or "throw away," the term was first applied in classical antiquity to classes of people whose ongoing ceremonial and institutional marginalization allowed the imperium to function.[6] The term accrued a positive connotation as performances of abjection, such as ancient Christian rituals of circumcision, were used to manage the threat of abject classes by celebrating, incorporating, and containing their practices.[7] Moreover, behaviors or characteristics abjected by others were adopted for self-definition, as when terms of derision and ridicule ("methodist," "quaker," "black") were reclaimed for use as a means of self-identification. The ambivalence of abjection—its positive and negative connotations—appears in cognates such as the Greek καταβάλλω, which, as an 1841 Boston lexicon has it, connotes both "to throw down" and "to lay, as foundations."[8]

Abjection is characterized by this twofold ability to suspend the marginal in the center of society and to transform the terms and processes of marginalization into means of public self-instantiation.

Cast Down is primarily concerned with religious discourse's historical and symbolic development of abjection in relation to race. Discourses of abjection paved the way for and sometimes complicated the development of race in both sectarian religious publics and the reformist publics that developed out of sectarian organizing. New notions of gender and race often supported social practices otherwise called into question by Enlightenment concepts of universal rights and subjectivity.[9] They did so by transforming the meaning of race, first through a scientific biologism and later with a Romantic emphasis on social difference, spiritual complexity, and psychological depth. One American exemplar of this process is Thomas Jefferson. His articulation of Enlightenment freedoms in his 1782 *Notes on the State of Virginia* coincided with both a scientific "suspicion" that African Americans' low social status was grounded in biological difference and a traditional religious admonition that the sin of slavery would result in divine judgment against the nation as a whole.[10]

In my study, abjection is separable into at least three distinct elements: exclusion from civic or church recognition, psychological depression, and internalized low status. These elements can function separately but more often work together in unexpected ways. For example, writing in 1833, Pequot Methodist William Apess reminded his "brethren in the ministry" that his Indian "brethren," stranded on New England's reservations, are "the most mean, abject, miserable race of beings in the world." Here, Apess's pride in his marginalization from an evangelical mainstream takes shape through racial self-abnegation. His portrait of low racial status attempts to shame his more elite interlocutors by juxtaposing biblical and modern scientific notions of family, spiritual abjection, and racialized abjection.[11]

Abjection's frequent connection to race in early nineteenth-century writing suggests the two terms' ideological mobility and interconnection. When abjection was explicitly conjoined with race, abjection's deep religious history helped structure a gradual movement from class- to race-based accounts and rankings of difference.[12] For example, a series of late eighteenth-century English colonial letters, reprinted in Philadelphia in 1819, described servants in Calcutta as alternately an "abject class" and an "abject race."[13] Religion also lent an air of continuity to what were actually new ideas about inherent racial difference percolating in popular discourse. When the term was used in a

more modern, racial form, it was most often associated with Africans and
enslavement. In 1812, the Rev. Thomas Scott, in an essay republished in several Anglican and other house organs, encouraged all Christians to pray for
"the poor African slaves . . . that abject race."[14] More taxonomic accounts employed the term "abject" as an ostensibly objective descriptor to help rank
different racial subgroups. For example, an 1834 account of Oceania's "minor
nations" in London's *Foreign Quarterly Review* opined that one "race will be
found more abject, miserable, and mischievous, than the lowest of the yellow
race."[15] This merely descriptive use of abjection unmoors the concept from a
religious basis and rejects possible social origins for racial difference in favor
of attributing racial abjection to prior conditions, such as biology.

On the other hand, even when discussing "abject Africans," evangelical
writers well into the nineteenth century resisted the taxonomic divisions
instituted by scientific racism. For example, although early nineteenth-
century white evangelical colonizationists agreed with the practical conclusions of Jefferson's scientific racism, they still described African American
inferiority as contingent on social circumstance rather than inherent. As
one 1828 Connecticut evangelical colonizationist tract has it, "The free co-
loured population . . . are, and, *in this country*, always must be a depressed
and abject race."[16] Evangelicals' insistence on social circumstance is creditable
to their enduring belief in a monogenetic creation in the face of scientific
evidence in favor of polygenetic human origins. One Presbyterian minister's
1847 tract promoting the colonization of Australia, for example, asserted that
even the "abject race" of Paupauans were still of "one blood" with the Europeans.[17] Some went further. Quaker abolitionist Anthony Benezet, in a post-
Revolutionary letter reprinted in an 1826 issue of the abolitionist *African
Repository*, posed abjection as a condition separate from race. Benezet began
by offering a monogenetic account of African Americans as "our fellow creatures of the African race" before noting that it was suffering alone that placed
African Americans in an "abject situation." Rather than treating African
Americans as social outcasts, Benezet suggests, their abject status actually
"gives them an additional claim to pity."[18] In sum, while abjection's connotation of absolute destitution made the term valuable as a descriptor in the
construction of modern racial taxonomies, these uses could not escape the
term's religious origin and ambivalence.

As the above examples indicate, large-scale ideological shifts in the meaning of religion and race were often made in incremental steps. This attenu-
ated process allowed for tremendous amounts of what might appear to be,

from our vantage point, contradiction or ideological confusion. Indeed, popular discussions of religion and race, rather than simply disseminating authoritative moral or scientific conclusions, were grounded in cultures of performance, citation and reprinting that offered multiple religious, political, scientific, rhetorical, and other appeals. In this context, the religious rhetoric of abjection participated in the creation of new and wide-ranging racial norms while also allowing and sometimes even encouraging participants in evangelical discourse to depart from those emerging norms. Put another way, the rhetoric of abjection in the eighteenth and nineteenth centuries helped construct, consolidate, and reify racial difference. At the same time notions of abjection and eroticized accounts of differences in power demonstrated a competing tendency toward the dissolution or disordering of racial difference well into the nineteenth century.[19] The tension between consolidation and dissolution is thrown into sharp relief in work that places disparate images, scenes, and narratives of suffering and abjection cheek by jowl, thereby highlighting contradictions in racial ideologies. This combination of censure and qualified permission was part of a larger process in which desire and identity were reproduced and contested through speech, writing, and embodied practice.

Jefferson, Apess, Lang, and others conjoin, to various degrees, Enlightenment scientific rationality and religious warning in ways that might seem, at first, unusual. In part, then, my work here is to identify and interpret the widespread combination of early modern and modern notions of the self, the divine, and community, especially the endurance of religion in modern developments of race. Religion remained central to notions of the self in the eighteenth and nineteenth centuries. Most important, religion participated in a larger shift in the power of suffering to license speech and writing within religious bodies and in more public evangelism.[20] The mystical or supernatural charge that bodily suffering held in the early modern era was increasingly derided in the eighteenth century, and Enlightenment humanitarianism, premised on a notion of rational and free public discourse, similarly chipped away at martyrology by making expressions of desire for suffering morally suspect.[21] Ascetic forms of suffering retained their capacity to license speech and leadership among Quakers, Methodists, Baptists, and some smaller sects. More generally, though, authoritative religious speech, including speech that engaged sentimental appeal, was increasingly linked to rational, empiricist Enlightenment discourse grounded in ascetic self-control.[22] Many religious communities harnessed the power of sentiment to institutionalize white male control. Leaders of established evangelical movements criticized the affective power of some forms of bodily suffering to sanction authoritative speech while increasing the affective power of other forms of suffering, especially long-distance travel, that were least hazardous for men who appeared white. As such, they resembled scientific communities that subjected sentiment to rationality while creating racially and sexually exclusive fora within which sentiment could flow freely.[23]

My notion of abjection emphasizes historical forms of religious suffering grounded in earlier notions of body, mind, and desire. It also draws on more recent theories that emphasize discontinuity and unexpected recurrence.[24] For example, my account of abjection's role in the construction of race complements a long line of feminist anthropological and psychoanalytic criticism that sees abjection as central to processes of group, individual, and psychic formation.[25] It is also informed by subsequent women-of-color feminism and queer of color critique, which show how abjection can be used to create, sustain, and contest racial, sexual, and gendered identities.[26] The spiritual, social, and political uses of abjection in religious discourse inform and complicate some psychoanalytic constructions of erotic suffering. For example, psychoanalytic treatments of "Christian masochism" tend to see early Christian and medieval martyrologies as *loci classici* of religious suffering, ignoring later religious forms. This approach becomes problematic when psychoanalytic approaches analyze early modern forms of suffering through modern models of body and mind in which sexual subjectivity is organized around libido, genitalia, and object-choice.[27] Genre is also crucial to broadening our sense of religious abjection. Julia Kristeva's foundational account of abjection, for example, describes modern literature as a "substitute" for "the sacred," but reading literature in the context of eighteenth- and nineteenth-century conversion narratives, religious periodicals, and abolitionist newspapers reveals a far more dynamic relationship between the literary and the sacred. These other genres often credit the sacred for effecting personal, social, and political change.[28] While the rise of psychoanalysis at the end of the nineteenth century helped reframe desirable suffering and abjection as sexual rather than spiritual, this transformation was part of a longer conversation about representations of suffering that continued to include religious voices and concerns.[29]

Finding the balance between historicist practice and theoretical insight is vital to my project. When used in conjunction, historicism and theory are complementary.[30] So, while most historical studies of eighteenth-century eroticism and pleasurable suffering rightly emphasize their incommensurability with later psychoanalytic concepts such as masochism, there are threads of connection between them; following those threads across the centuries allow us to ask new questions of early American writing and performance. How, we might ask, have eighteenth- and nineteenth-century texts and writers helped create material, intellectual, and emotional conditions of possibility for sexological and psychoanalytic taxonomies? How were social, psychological, and public processes transformed in the process?

These broad investigatory questions were inspired by the specific historical problem raised by Reik's focus on publicity in his distinction between roses and neuroses. What exactly did happen when miracles of transformation—the winter bloom of the rose, the flight of a dove from a martyr's mouth—faded from Christian accounts of redemptive suffering? Many such instances of disappearance may be traced to sixteenth-century debates about the Eucharist, in which Protestant reformers disavowed God's direct contravention of natural law. Mainstream English Protestant exegesis maintained that miraculous transformation was only a symbol or representation of the true miracle, God's salvation of the soul from sin. In the English literary tradition, the most significant disappearance of miracles of transformation from scenes of suffering occurred in John Foxe's four editions of the *Book of Martyrs* (1563–83). Foxe's portraits of Protestant martyrs draw on a pagan tradition of noble death and a medieval Judeo-Christian tradition of joyful suffering.[31] No roses bloom when Foxe's martyrs are tortured, but neither do they become neurotic. In an early modern Protestant ideological framework, physical transformations cannot signify martyrdom's miraculous power. Instead, martyrs are men and women whose faith allows them to experience feminizing, abjecting torture and yet produce bold, masculinized speech (or, less often, eloquent silence in the face of demands to speak).[32] In the lavish illustrations from the *Book of Martyrs*, virtually every martyr has their palms pressed together or hands upraised and mouth open, as if in prayer. Many of the larger cuts illustrating specific accounts of martyrdom featured speech banners with pious messages emanating from the martyrs' mouths. The spectacular violations, tortures, and burnings for which the *Book of Martyrs* is justly famous worked hand in glove with more quotidian scenes of speech in suffering. In the episode that ended Foxe's 1563 edition, the "godly Matrone" Gertrude Crokehay, jailed in Amsterdam for allegedly being an Anabaptist, "declar[ed] . . . her faith boldly, without any feare" and found herself quickly freed. Foxe thereby connects these everyday declarations of faith to more spectacular public acts of dissenting speech.[33] Whether at home, in court, or on the scaffold, dissenting speech reverses the disabling political and emotional intent of jailing, public burning, and other spectacular punishment. Dissenting speech moves an audience of observers, readers, and other witnesses to the Protestant cause.[34]

Print accounts of torture, operating through serial acts of compilation, publication, circulation, discussion, revision, and republication, played an important role in Protestant self-definition by multiplying the power of witnessing. The *Book of Martyrs* itself thematized this value of print, describing oral and textual engagements with martyrdom as central to dissenting religious subjectivity.[35] Foxe's famous 1576 account of Bishop Nicholas Ridley's botched burning helps illustrate the larger pattern. As Foxe writes, Queen Mary's executioners tied Ridley and his fellow "Oxford Martyr" Hugh Latimer to the stake and lit the kindling beneath their feet. Latimer, attempting to encourage Ridley, told him to "plaie the manne"; dying "manfully," Latimer prophesied, would transform their burning into a vehicle for Reformation by lighting "suche a candle [as] shall neuer be put out."[36] Latimer burnt up quickly and died but Ridley, in ironic fulfillment of Latimer's prophecy, was tortured by a fire of "euill makyng." Gruesomely, Ridley "burned cleane all his neather partes, before [the fire] once touched the vpper," with Ridley praying piously all the while. Ridley's mutilated but speaking body came to embody martyrological abjection, becoming, as one critic has it, a site "of pity recuperated as . . . defiant strength."[37] Indeed, Foxe insisted that emotional response could transform such suffering into a spiritually and socially redemptive experience. "[S]urely," Foxe wrote, "it moued hundredes to teares, in beholdyng the horrible sighte. For I thynke there was none that had not cleane exiled all humanitie and mercie, whiche would not haue lamented to beholde the furie of the fire so to rage vpon their bodies." Here as elsewhere, Foxean martyrology constructs Protestant subjectivity around the sympathetic public response ("teares, in beholdyng") to the martyr's manly will to suffer ("plaie the manne") a sensational, feminizing physical violation ("burned cleane all his neather partes") caused by an intemperate Catholic desire ("the euill makyng of the fire").[38] In elaborating and sometimes eroticizing a discourse of embodied agony as the basis for Protestant martyrological public subjectivity, Foxe hoped to vindicate Protestantism by presenting Marian martyrs as the true heirs to the Christian legacy of redemptive suffering.[39] Public accounts of suffering, rendered in highly gendered, often sexual, and subtly imperial terms, take on the once-miraculous capacity to signify faith.

During both the execution and the public circulation of execution narratives, representation and mediation play a crucial role. Foxe and his book inherit the martyr's primary duty to help transform violence into a vehicle for sustaining communities of dissent.[40] Indeed, the *Book of Martyrs* became so important to nonconformists that Bishop Laud refused to license a new edition in the early seventeenth century.[41] Ridley's burning, in particular, became something of a touchstone for all sorts of dissent; it was excerpted and reprinted with surprising frequency in theological and popular magazines until the mid-nineteenth century, though its meaning shifted dramatically.[42] In short, despite the royal imprimatur on Foxe's work and its orthodox support for church and king, the logic of Foxean martyrdom, in which suffering forms the basis for dissenting speech and publication, ensured that martyrology became central to new modes of dissent in England and its Atlantic colonies.

Atlantic martyrology was informed by many different colonial practices and dreams of empire.[43] These, in turn, would be crucial to martyrology's contributions to the later development of race. As Protestant martyrological traditions crossed and recrossed the Atlantic, they were reflected and refracted through the practice and fantasy of colonial enterprise. Sensational representations of suffering in English, French, and Dutch translations of Bartolomé de Las Casas's *Brevissima Relación* (1552) were of special importance.[44] One of Foxe's collaborators translated the first English edition of Las Casas, and the depictions of suffering in the *Book of Martyrs* share a common representational language with English and other Protestant translations of Las Casas's work.[45] The dialogue between martyrology and English colonial strategy hinges on the translations' different treatment of English and Indian suffering. The parallels between Spanish Catholic torture of Indians and English Catholic torture of Protestants offered an irresistible point of connection for English Protestant partisans. However, English translators broke martyrology's link between suffering and speech by flattening Las Casas's careful use of Arawak, illustrating physical violations even more graphically, and presenting Indian suffering without accompanying Indian speech acts or spectatorial Indian communities of witness.

The political value of denying Indian martyrdom is clearest in *The Teares of the Indians* (1656), a propagandistic English translation by John Phillips for his uncle John Milton, Cromwell's erstwhile censor and then-Secretary of Foreign Tongues. Phillips's preface, addressed to Cromwell, describes the "cry of [Indian] blood ceasing at the noise of Your great transactions, while you arm for their revenge." In this miniature colonial drama of sound and force, English valor alone can mute Indian suffering.[46] In contrast to Foxe's martyrs, whose sensational suffering formed the basis of dissenting subjectivity, Phillips's flayed, dismembered, and dead Indians cry out only for English vengeance before being quieted by English force.[47] In separating English witnessing from Indian suffering, *Teares* hollows out the rhetoric of martyrdom to promote English imperial expansion unchecked by Indian presence. Phillips's insistence on English witnessing and vengeance helped lay the groundwork for later racial distinctions between bold white sacrifice and the mere abjection of Indians and Africans.

Martyrology's power as a vehicle for religious and political dissent became more fractured in the late seventeenth and eighteenth centuries, when Protestant martyrology began to compete with Counter-Reformation martyrological accounts of colonial suffering and Indian conversion. French representations of Indian suffering in New France were relatively generous, as they allowed Native converts' spiritual trials to confirm Native faith.[48] Authorities in colonial New England were less generous, increasingly using martyrology as a bludgeon against dissenters, Indian tribes and competing colonial powers.[49] Puritan leaders represented Quakers, Indians, and their mutual ally, witches, as effectively torturing the colony.[50] The gendered and proto-racial dimensions of Foxean martyrological rhetoric posed special challenge to the colony's self-fashioned patriarchs. On one hand, martyrology's link to dissent was so strong that we can detect both disgust and a hint of admiration, or possibly fear, in John Winthrop's 1646 account of Mary Oliver's punishment. Oliver, as though embracing Latimer's admonition to "plaie the manne," took her court-ordered whipping "without tying and . . . with a masculine spirit, glorying in her suffering."[51] Martyrological rhetoric also helped Cotton Mather defend his colony's conduct to London and, he hoped, to heaven. Figuring the colony as peculiarly persecuted, Mather hoped to defray God's anger at the colony's failure to treat not only "wild" Indians but even "African slaves . . . as those that are of one Blood with us [and] have Immortal Souls in them."[52] Martyrological discourse was also central to English colonizers' practical and spiritual understanding of dissent and colonial violence. The colony's Quakers and other organized dissenters also proliferated martyrological accounts of their treatment.[53] Perhaps in response to the socially destabilizing effect of martyrological discourses, late seventeenth- and early eighteenth-century editions of the *Book of Martyrs* actually moved closer to *The Teares of the Indians* by including only the most graphic scenes of torture. These streamlined editions, whose popularity may also speak to their growing consumption as pornography, minimized the capacity of martyrdom to justify dissent while allowing for new connections between dissent and other forms of suffering.[54]

Foxe's proto-racial, gendered notions of the martyr's suffering would resound in accounts of religious suffering during the transatlantic revivals of the 1720s and 1730s, named, by a later generation of revivalists, the Great Awakening. These revivals were constituted by an incredibly diverse body of texts and practices, including some models of conversion that once again granted social or physical weakness the ability to license religious speech and writing. In New England, these models of conversion helped corrode Congregationalist hierarchies of speech and deference, eventually resulting in the broadening of New England's "speaking aristocracy," the class of men who spoke and published on social, political, and theological issues.[55] During the revival itself, written and spoken accounts of affective conversion, including the affective experience of personal sin and abjection, allowed for even more disruptive forms of expression. In the manner of St. Francis, socially marginal converts described an intense internal sense of abjection to legitimate their public religious speech and writing.[56] Revival conversion narratives recounted individuated, internal experience, but they did so largely through textual surfaces (including written, spoken, or otherwise embodied performances) that explicitly encouraged imitation.[57] The predictable teleology and formulaic rhetoric of conversion narratives contained some of the resulting threat to social order. Nevertheless, variations within the genre allowed converts to test the limits of public speech.

Abjection was crucial to the development of revivalist affect out of, and sometimes in opposition to, martyrological suffering. The key difference between the speech of Foxean martyrs and that of revival converts lies in the shift from an external torturer to an internal or supernatural tormentor. Where Foxean martyrology emphasized a "manful" will to suffer, many revival converts described their intensely affective experience of abjection, permeability, and rupture, an experience that historians have identified as feminized in that culture. Moderate revival leaders such as Jonathan Edwards defended converts' extreme affective sense of abjection and grace as the products of an internal awareness of personal sin and God's sublime perfection. Revivalist expressions of intense affect are rooted in the Puritan use of textual methods of self-examination, including expressions of self-hatred and annihilation, designed to minimize a "personal" identity associated with sin. Revivalism integrated the public performance and expression of abjection into detailed life narratives that circulated more widely than the ritualized formulae that had been prerequisite to church membership. This integration and circulation allowed performances and expressions of abjection to take on new social and psychological importance.

Nicholas Ridley's burning and Jonathan Edwards's affective conversion are two of six scenes of abjection that help sketch out this book's movement from Foxe to Freud. Each scene illustrates a discrete moment of public subject-creation. Chapter 1 considers the eighteenth-century management of abject affect through the limited circulation of the conversion narrative, epitomized by Edwards's account of weeping in a closet. The second chapter moves into the early nineteenth century and evaluates the creation of an Indian public subject through temperate ascetic self-control, focusing on Pequot William Apess's writing and preaching in New York's reformist Methodist churches. Chapter 3, illustrated by the branded hand of white abolitionist Jonathan Walker, considers the mid-nineteenth-century creation of visibly white public subjects through martyrological narrative. In Chapter 4, a German child's erotic reading of *Uncle Tom's Cabin* links political and erotic negotiations of "perversions" of sympathy in the aftermath of the revolutions of 1848. Finally, my epilogue, focused on the vulnerability of *Moby-Dick's* cabin boy Pip, considers the value of "child pets" and "tea boys" in eighteenth- and nineteenth-century developments of race and religion.

Collectively, these chapters describe religious abjection's direct and indirect contributions to race. Direct contributions include explicit textual linkages of abjection and race, while indirect contributions include racialized discussions of affect, interiority, publicity, and spectacle. Indirect contributions constitute the majority of the accounts of exclusion from civic or church recognition, psychological depression, and internalized low status on which my study is focused. Religious discourses of abjection participated in the racialization of the concept by using it to help construct race as a social reality ostensibly grounded in objective physical, mental, emotional and other differences. Though these religious uses of abjection were more spiritually than sexually erotic, they offered a vast reservoir of material available to pornographic and other explicitly sexual readings because of their social prominence and powerful affective charge. Indeed, the line between religious and pornographic representations of abjection blurred whenever evangelical reformers began to operate in nonsectarian public spheres, especially as evangelical material was taken out of a sectarian interpretive community in attempts to "sacralize" the public sphere as a vehicle for reform. In these moments, reformers spoke and wrote to such a wide audience and incorporated such a range of material into their work that abjection's affective charge bled into neighboring categories of desire and signification.

This brief outline suggests some of the ways in which literary-historical readings of eighteenth- and nineteenth-century religious and reformist writing intersect with philosophical, theological, and theoretical discussions of abjection. Before turning to my first chapter, I want to lay out the larger discursive field in which these key debates play. As Reik's account of religious publicity recommends, attending to this larger discursive field will help ground an eighteenth- and nineteenth-century literary history of religious abjection, erotic suffering, and the place of suffering in a hitherto under-recognized part of the history and theory of the public sphere.

One of the most heralded eighteenth-century figures in debates about publicity, suffering, and politics is Edmund Burke. His account of sublimity in his *Enquiry into the Origins of the Sublime and Beautiful* (1757) takes up the same connections between aesthetic and political problems of interpretation and consensus that would come to preoccupy his later work on social revolutions. Looking at Burke, we can address two familiar questions from the less familiar perspective of my book's premises and aims. First, how do Burke's aesthetic concerns relate to his description of "public spirit" as arising "from private reflection upon public affairs and from their public discussion" in salons and print?[58] Second, how is this aesthetic dimension connected to Burke's treatment of race and gender in his *Enquiry*, as well as his subsequent writing on the American, French and Haitian revolutions?

Burke, in his famous distinction between two species of feeling, the sublime and the beautiful, proposes that the former is caused by sympathy for pain, the latter by sympathy for pleasure. Recent histories of pleasurable pain have focused on Burke's description of spectatorial delight as a source of erotic pleasure; as later chapters will elaborate, several early accounts of masochistic desire eroticize the sort of absolute, arbitrary power of the master that nineteenth-century abolitionists outlined in their reports on the Southern slave system.[59] Seeing Burke's aesthetics as wedded to his politics sheds new light on his contribution to the history of abjection and helps us examine existing critiques of publicity and the public sphere in the context of religious discourse.

In the *Enquiry*, Burke proposes that pleasure is derived from the presence of beauty, while "delight" is a sublime sensation that "accompanies the removal of pain and danger."[60] Some degree of "removal," in other words, is a prerequisite to delight: spectators find pain or danger "delightful" only when it is kept "*at certain distances*, and with certain modifications."[61] In structuring his account of spectatorial delight, Burke reverses gendered and racialized contexts of seeing. He places spectatorial delight in a political context by aligning sublimity with monarchial power while associating pity with the revolutionary spectator's terror at the power of weakness. Burke makes an implicit connection between the pleasure of beauty and terror in the French Revolution's reversal of hierarchies of rank, race, and gender. He begins by attempting to evoke a delightful sort of terror by recounting the "few hours" of "torments" suffered by Robert Damiens, "the late unfortunate regicide" whose protracted public torture, though "inflicted" by "justice," received extensive and sometimes critical coverage in English magazines earlier that year.[62] Burke insists that the torture itself, as well as laudatory representations of torture such as his own, performs the moral work of the sublime by reinforcing hierarchy through a display of awesome force. In Burke's account, the witness's sympathetic experience of Damiens's pain is enjoyable not primarily because of pity for suffering but rather sympathy with his terror at the sublime power (the king) causing the pain. As in much Gothic and sensational fiction, the spectator's pleasure in sublime terror is meant to be anti-revolutionary and anti-republican.

Finding beauty in the abject entails political risk. Pity is dangerous because it fails to guard against revolutionary, republican terror.[63] The Haitian and French revolutions provoked Burke's bitterest denunciations when terror inverted hierarchies of rank, race, and gender.[64] In aesthetic terms, this political reversal was possible because the seeming weakness of the Haitian and French rabble deluded elite spectators and lulled them into submission. Burke describes this power of weakness as the terror of the beautiful, epitomized, in the *Enquiry*, by a woman's "neck and breasts," wherein a "deceitful maze" of swells and curves produces, in the spectator, an "unsteady eye."[65]

Beauty's apparent weakness is the source of its strength, for, as Frances Fergu-son remarks, it "is always . . . robbing us of our vigilance and recreating us in its own image." Pity may therefore result in "death and defeat—loss of collective liberty" if not prevented by an invigorating experience of the sublime.[66]

Burke's *Reflections on the Revolution in France* (1790) guards against pity's threat by deploying a sublime image of Versailles as "polluted by massacre, and strewn with scattered limbs and mutilated carcasses."[67] Crucially for my study, Burke's condemnation of the Jacobinic mob works by developing eighteenth-century religious languages of public censure, including anti-revivalist accounts of evangelical "enthusiasm." Burke represents the Jacobinic mob as a sensational catalogue of abjection, a montage of "horrid yells, and shrilling screams, and frantic dances, and infamous contumelies, and all the unutterable abominations of the furies of hell, in the abused shape of the vilest of women."[68] Republican revolutions, like the *Enquiry*'s beautiful woman, overcome monarchial power by a deceit that belies the reality of abject disorder. Burke's terms here closely resemble the much earlier denunciations of evangelical Protestant revivalism. Anglican missionary Charles Brockwell, writing in 1742, denounced a revival in Salem, Massachusetts, by claiming that it caused "Men, Women, Children, Servants, and Nigros" to utter "groans, cries, screams, and agonies" and perform "ridiculous and frantic gestures" until, at the height of frenzy, they become "Exhorters." Like Brockwell, Burke attempted to curb popular speech by associating it with bodily abjection, linking the publicity of the poor with variously illicit sensations to suggest that they ought to be excluded from recognition by church or state. Rather than demonstrating a historical arc from Enlightenment religious to secular dissent, Burke's and Brockwell's shared language of abjection speaks to the common origins and ongoing dialogues between them. This shared language of abjection also indicates how paradigms of race and gender that are now most often considered in exclusively secular terms had religious resonance and implication.

For all his conservatism, Brockwell's greater engagement with religious discourses of abjection lets him grant abject figures more room for public speech. Both Brockwell and Burke end their scenes with figures who publicly deceive (exhorters and prostitutes, respectively), but Burke reverses Brockwell's trajectory between publicity and sensation. While Brockwell traces the emergence of cacophonous public speech and hearing out of a dense panoply of abject sensation, Burke's portrait of cacophonous urban poverty ends in an infernal vision of sexual abjection. Historically, within religious communities that granted abjection a spiritual and moral value, people or groups associ-ated with abjection were able to leverage that association to access the pulpit and other privileged sites of communication. This was especially true when communities associated with abjection were developing in opposition to po-litical elites or other religious groups.[69] The eighteenth and nineteenth centu-ries witnessed a transformation of the relationship between dissenting religious speech and abjection that re-imagined these abject associations as interior characteristics. Such interior states remained linked to abjection even as attempts to disconnect suffering from dissent created different align-ments between them.

Burke's treatments of revolutionary and enthusiastic public expression were central to Jürgen Habermas's account of plebian publicity. In *Structural Transformation of the Public Sphere* (1963), Habermas credited Burke for for-mulating and legitimating the concept of public opinion by grounding the concept in private reflection upon, and public discussion of, public affairs.[70] However, Habermas's carving out of eighteenth-century European rational-deliberate political publics from other incarnations was trebly haunted. It was haunted in advance by Great War intellectuals who saw publics as phantoms dependent on sovereign authority to check internal violence.[71] It was haunted from the left by theorists of hegemony, who, working in dialogue with Schmittean analysis, cast doubt on several of Habermas's key claims: the sep-aration of rational discourse from ideology; the public's politically opposi-tional character; and the universal rational subject.[72] And finally, Habermas's public sphere was haunted by the ephemeral, poetic quality of his own ac-count of plebeian publicity.

This final haunting is the most fruitful to dwell upon, as it lets us consider Habermas's work in light of more recent critiques and, particularly, in light of this book's innovative historicization of abjection. In the preface he penned for *Structural Transformation*'s first publication, Habermas echoes Brockwell and Burke in describing a short-lived plebeian public sphere as essentially an "illiterate" bourgeois public "stripped of its literary garb" ("*die ihr literarisches Gewand abgestreift hat*").[73] This phrase has served as a point of entry for working-class, feminist, and African American critiques of *Structural Trans-formation*'s flawed premises upon a notion of universal subjectivity.[74] Such critiques often highlight the public sphere's Janus face. One is productive, constituting and nurturing a public subject. The other is a negative space of abjection, silencing, and social death, conceptualized in the eighteenth and nineteenth centuries as private and resulting in sub- or counter-public forms.[75]

These and other critiques of Habermas tend to pose resistance or oppositionality as characteristic of such sub-, counter-, or otherwise alternative publics.[76] More congenial to my notion of abjection is the concept of vestibulary publicity. This concept is derived from Hortense Spillers's account of vestibulary culture in her 1987 "Mama's Baby, Papa's Maybe: An American Grammar Book." Spillers's essay, though essential to black feminist and queer of color critique, has not been adequately integrated into discussions of the public sphere. Published two years before the English translation of *Structural Transformation* that unleashed much U.S. critique of Habermas, "Mama's Baby" seems less defensive about the Marxist humanism that would be so roundly attacked in 1989 and is perhaps more fluid as a result. Spillers's essay uses abolitionist narrative as a way to recall histories of slave suffering that remained unrecognized in political, legal, deconstructive, feminist, and psychoanalytic criticism. Spillers describes the manner in which eighteenth- and nineteenth-century doctors created scientific, abolitionist, and simply public knowledge by "profitabl[y] 'anatomizing'" injured, ill, or disabled slaves. Such slaves bore "in person the marks of a cultural text" that was literally written on and by their body.[77] The knowledge embodied in anatomized slaves, Spillers writes, irretrievably splits society into a mainstream "culture," including medical, scientific, and other rational-critical debate characteristic of the public sphere, and a "cultural *vestibulary*," including the slave and his or her knowledge and desires.[78] Spillers's cultural vestibulary encompasses subaltern or "infamous" speech, accessible only via traces left on public speech, as well as conflicted or corrupted spheres of publicity that arise alongside those traces.[79] The vestibule—architecturally, the room between the entry and living space; medically, a cavity before the entrance to another, often more important structure; poetically, a space of transition, at the threshold, *in limine*—is an abject space, between the inside and outside. The varieties of abjection are created and contested in material structures, including publics, that produce embodied differences in health, safety, labor, speech, writing, and so on.

Spillers's architectural referent clarifies the vestibulary public's interstitial but not necessarily resistant character. As an eighteenth- and nineteenth-century architectural element, the vestibule managed different publics and the boundaries between public and private spaces. Describing Thomas

Jefferson's eccentric vestibule at Monticello, for example, critic Duncan Faherty writes that the space's ostensible edificatory republicanism belies its
function as a performative space that "ripples with a complex notion of public and private."[80] The most notable feature of Jefferson's vestibule was its
staircase. Modeled after new private staircases in France, the staircase's steep
narrowness frustrated movement between floors, and its obtuse location hin-
dered even the imagination of a host family's symbolic descent and circulation among guests.[81] Of course, design is not the same as use, and Jefferson's
daughters recorded their complaints as they struggled against his design.
Struggle takes on another dimension for the enslaved, who had less access to
writing and for whom the vestibule was a workplace. Some of those enslaved
by Jefferson eventually established alternative religious spaces and publics.
Peter Fossett, for example, founded a Baptist church that posthumously honored Fossett with a photograph in its own vestibule, and Fossett also lever-
aged his early association with Jefferson to tell his story in the public sphere.[82]
Most of the enslaved left only traces of their struggles. In some sense, these
traces appear in Jefferson's other architectural innovations. The lack of easy
circulation between floors, for example, was dependent on Jefferson's development of complementary systems—from dumbwaiters and revolving cup-
boards to subterranean slave quarters and tunnels—that minimized the
visibility of the enslaved while still allowing for labor and surveillance.[83] The
innovations do not appear in the vestibule, but the vestibule's unique design
depended on their presence.

   Like Jefferson's vestibule, vestibulary publicity *assumes* a troubled, contested function within state, religious, or other power, as well as within itself.
The vestibulary public joins, *avant la letter*, with critics of a rational-critical
public sphere who help us understand how power adheres in bodies, texts,
and publics. As such, the vestibulary public reveals the trace of those most
marked by abjection, as well as the structuring principles of abjection—of
inclusion and exclusion—that underlie all similar structures. Under some
conditions, the vestibulary public may also work like a pressure valve, allowing or failing to allow for the ideal function of the public and private. Because
the vestibulary public poses neither a necessarily oppositional (public/coun-
terpublic) nor a hierarchical (super/subpublic) relationship, it avoids some of
the pitfalls associated with narrow notions of hegemony and thereby anticipates more recent reconceptions of publics as "performative commons" or,
alternately, disavowals.[84]

   We can further illuminate the discursive field surrounding Americanist debates about publicity by considering how vestibulary publicity reveals a gap between Habermasian pronouncements on rational-critical debate and the nuances of Habermas's work. These gaps begin with Habermas's early account of the nonrational communicative powers of language. Spillers's poetic incorporation of the metaphor of the vestibule into a dense but wide-ranging textual analysis resembles *Structural Transformation*'s evocative description of the plebian public as "stripped of its literary garb." Habermas's most influential terms are rational social-scientific in tone, but the generally wry and lively quality of his prose lends an irony to his use of this phrase, which smacks of the cultural elitism that marked Habermas's Frankfurt school mentors. This redolence surely encouraged critics to pounce on the phrase as a solecism revealing the sexualized and gendered frameworks of Habermas's conception of public debate. We might peer, alongside those critics, beneath the bourgeois public to see the plebian public, with its penny press and theaters of sensation, as an obscene violation of bourgeois norms. But Habermas wrote the introduction just as he was distancing himself, geographically and intellectually, from Frankfurt and its notions of "the identity of domination and reason." We therefore have some reason to read the phrase as a catachrestic meta-commentary on his *Habilitationsschrift* itself.[85] In this alternate reading, Habermas's "stripping" of "literary garb" is, like Spillers's vestibule, a poetic, self-referential, and perhaps self-critical gesture at enduring connections between print, clothing/investment, erotic violence, and performance. Calling the plebian public "stripped" (*abgestreift*) connotes its undisguised, more essential character and also gestures at eighteenth- and nineteenth-century religious and revolutionary rhetorics of disclosure.[86] This stripped public, as Habermas notes, achieved significant benchmarks in circulation and organizing.[87] Rather than being excluded from political economy, the plebian public, as later literary historians would discover, flowed directly from the seventeenth-century publics that arose from within cultures of printing, petitioning, and other excitations of controversy in broadly circulating print and oratorical culture, satisfying print capitalism's profit motive without being markedly bourgeois.[88] The plebian public flourished in eighteenth-century popular English colonial and U.S. evangelical print culture, much of it organized around public orations and the distribution of inexpensive or free print material.[89] Habermas's own subsequent reappraisals of the dialogue between religion and rationality also address the importance of religious dissent in the long Enlightenment, confirming that "Enlightenment rationality" began as a style of religious debate.[90] Ultimately, in the wake of two generations of revisionary scholarship on the mutual development of popular and "proper" literature, as well as Habermas's own movement away from a dialectic and unified notion of historical process, the "stripped" plebian public appears as an important part of the loosely jointed networks of print, oration, and organizing in which religious discourses of abjection flourished and were transformed.[91]

Well before his recent encounters with religion, Habermas subtly reframed his analysis of religious publicity by crediting E. P. Thompson's 1963 *Making of the English Working Class* for his reconsideration of nonbourgeois publics.[92] Thompson's influence on Habermas has implications for my work on religious abjection in two competing ways. Thompson's generous evaluation of working-class religious organizers has been inspirational to my work, but Thompson was also one of the first to employ psychoanalytic rhetoric to pathologize religious discourses of suffering. As part of his attempt to moderate celebratory accounts of Methodism's influence on labor organizers, Thompson proposed that, if English Methodism was a "nursing-ground" for labor, the nurse was a cruel one. Working-class Methodists gained experience in economic and political organizing by struggling *against* Methodist rules and leaders as much as by working with them.[93] Methodist publicity, Thompson concluded, partook of "pathological aberrations of frustrated social and sexual impulses" driven by a "perverted eroticism . . . by turns maternal, Oedipal, sexual, and sado-masochistic"; its "authentic language" was one "of sexual sublimation streaked through with masochism."[94] In short, for Thompson, sadomasochistic perversion was the internal psychic mechanism that stoked, and was reciprocally stoked by, the economic engine billowing out religion's ideological smokescreen.

Thompson's diagnosis of pathological religious masochism was for some time the abject within my own project. Its exemplification of a vexed scholarly engagement with religion made Thompson's work hard to embrace.[95] Why would Thompson, whose measured evaluations of working-class organizing made him vital to Habermas's reevaluation of the plebian public sphere, criticize English Methodism in such violently normalizing psychosexual terms?[96] Whatever its origin or intent, Thompson's language is deeply rooted in the history of public debates about religion in the seventeenth and eighteenth centuries. More specifically, it is a specimen of critique (quite familiar to Thompson himself) casting religious emotion as a form of erotic perversion.[97] Following the seventeenth-century imagination of "sodomite" Quakers, or *Gangraena*'s delicious denunciations of schismatic "libertinism," eighteenth-century religious dissenters' secular competitors for public attention cast doubt on their piety by associating religious emotion with an uncontrollable, often feminized, sexual desire orchestrated by religious elites.[98]

We can condemn the tenor of Thompson's critique, then, while finding in it a germ of insight. The vocabulary of submission in eighteenth-century evangelical texts helps frame erotic submission in broadly affective terms. This broader framework can help expand the horizons for contemporary queer readings of masochistic sexuality, as eighteenth-century evangelical negotiations of power, publicity, sex, and gender inform embodied and imagined pleasures in both the past and the present. Sexuality develops through a contradictory process of proscription and approbation, and the rhetoric of pleasurable suffering in eighteenth-century Protestant dissent could have simultaneously displayed an identification with Christ's suffering and at the same time contributed to the transformation of sexual perversions. The commonsense reading of Moravian and Methodist hymns as, in historian Phyllis Mack's words, "more plausibly . . . an identification with Christ's redemptive suffering than . . . an unconscious sublimation of genital sex" corrects Thompson's reductive psychoanalysis but should not exclude the possibility that the hymns might provide another sort of erotic charge for either Methodist adherents or their critics.[99] Moravian and Methodist identifications with Christ's suffering were, indeed, labeled perverse by hostile popular, theological, and scholarly publications. Methodism's innovations in public evangelism also make Thompson's claims about Methodism's capacity to effect psychological change more plausible. In the eighteenth-century Atlantic world, Methodism's popularity was grounded in its unprecedented success in reaching and shaping a public. Like many Protestant evangelical sects, Methodism attracted adherents by cultivating a religious "sense" capable of hearing its messages "aright"; Methodism was particularly successful in its use of the sensual experience of the camp meeting, small group worship, hymn singing, exhorting, preaching, and many new forms of publishing and reading. Eighteenth-century Methodism thereby extended, in new public contexts, the sixteenth- and seventeenth-century rituals of abjection, including conversion processes of self-regulation and identification, that grounded and attempted to transcend the (sinful) modern self. When heard "aright," these public practices claimed to ameliorate the effects of what Habermas terms "cultural differentiation," bridging the growing divides between sexual, spiritual, and economic rhetoric.[100] Heard wrong or circulating in the wrong context, this rhetoric could also lead to new perversions. These two outcomes may not be as distinct as either Thompsonian skeptics or the faithful would prefer. As Chapter 1 will show, the work of Jonathan Edwards and other eighteenth-century revivalists offers an affective alternative to the spectatorial delight imagined by Methodism's critics, employing the racial and gendered tropes of suffering during conversion in different ways.

CHAPTER 1

Conversion, Suffering, and Publicity

What did it mean for a congregational minister in New England to write of his desire to be "emptied and annihilated; to lie in the dust, and to be full of Christ alone"?[1] This famous passage from Jonathan Edwards's "Personal Narrative" (c. 1739) offers a fruitful point of departure for tracing the connections between religious abjection, conversion, and protean theories of masochism in the eighteenth century. Edwards's treatment of abjection is determined, to a large degree, by his concern for the public perception of the revival and his own place within it. Though often contrasted to "old light" moderates, Edwards intended to harness the disruptive potential of revival affect. This is especially true of the moments of apparent perversity that arise from the extremity of Edwards's religious sentiments. Looking at Edwards's expressions of religious abjection in a revivalist context helps us see how they are constituted by the interplay between "personal" emotional experience and public political exigency. Revivalism also helps us flesh out discrete intellectual, textual, and historical connections between Edwards's religious practice and masochism's established Enlightenment philosophical basis.

The affective or inward turn in eighteenth-century revivalist publicity, as well as the strong links between Scotland and New England, points to the crucial role of theories of sentiment in structuring Edwards's accounts of affective conversion. Although historian J. G. Barker-Benfield noted more than twenty years ago that eighteenth-century sensibility and evangelism were "two branches of the same culture," subsequent accounts of sympathy, eroticism, and pleasure have attended to the former at the expense of the latter.[2] Studies of the interdependence of pornographic and humanitarian depictions of slave suffering, for example, rely overwhelmingly on Adam Smith's account of sympathetic feeling to define the relationship between sympathizer and sufferer. While Smithian accounts of sympathy fold neatly into accounts of sadism, I assert a clearer line connecting masochism to the sorts of evangelical affective religious practices that Smith and Burke, following Shaftesbury, condemned as forms of religious enthusiasm. Eighteenth-century "enthusiastic" revivalist affect, speech, performance, and publicity wove together evangelical affect and Enlightenment sympathy to generate abject sensation and stimulation.

Evangelical discourses of abjection offer a unique window onto scholarly debates about publicity outlined in the Introduction. Suffering and abjection in revivalist epistemologies of conversion participated in the public creation of a modern subject in the eighteenth-century Anglo-Atlantic world. Subsequent chapters will draw on these revivalist epistemologies of conversion to trace the irregular development of race and gender in the early nineteenth century. In the eighteenth century, the evangelical public was constituted by a body of believers who, at least in theory, transcended sectarian, familial, local, national, linguistic, or imperial affiliations. The evangelical public contributed to the development of the bourgeois public sphere but, like other publics, depended on a more recursive relationship between speech, performance, and writing for its success and mobility.[3] From the perspective of Shaftesbury and other primarily secular Enlightenment figures, eighteenth-century Protestant evangelical discourse as a whole engaged the nascent propositions of rational-critical publicity at an oblique angle, alternately adapting, criticizing, or troubling its methods. Most importantly, Protestant evangelical thinkers in Scotland and the Americas described rational public debate as itself dependent on God's grace or other forms of divine dispensation or intervention. Divine dispensation could be encouraged through affective religious performance, including performances of abjection. This evangelical public was still dependent on slavery, silencing, or marginalization, but could credit those problems to sin or divine absence. The religious rhetoric of abjection might therefore be seen as an apology, an atonement, or an excuse for the failure of the gracious community to achieve its ideals, as well as a performance of the impossibility of those ideals.

As Michael Warner writes, Edwards's most famous revival sermon, "Sinners in the Hands of an Angry God," offers an "expressive language for power and abjection" that outdoes all "secular equivalents," including sadomasochism and Foucauldian analysis, in its antihumanist "displace[ment]" of affect and its wedding of "pleasure and obliteration" in the gap between the abject, sinful speaking self and God's irresistible, sovereign will.[4] Eighteenth-century evangelical publicity, as Warner has more recently observed, cannot be separated from "secular equivalents" in the period.[5] In the eighteenth century, revivalist affect, speech, performance, and publicity wove together Puritan and Enlightenment sympathy to generate abject sensation and stimulation. Edwards offers an unusual, perhaps unique, engagement with Puritan and Enlightenment Common Sense empirical philosophies that link suffering, education, subjectivity, and social order.

By virtue of his education at home and at Yale, his wide correspondence, and the culture of visitation characteristic of eighteenth-century New England, Edwards was influenced by a spectrum of moral philosophy and theology much like that available to his contemporaries in England and Scotland, including faculty psychology and Common Sense philosophy.[6] He was also influenced by a Puritan mode of sympathy that helped cohere a transatlantic dissenting community.[7] Puritan sympathy was distinguished by its narrower scope as well as its rhetorical emphasis on a discourse of humiliation designed to "soften" proud hearts.

In an instrumental sense, "Sinners in the Hands of an Angry God" was part of Edwards's long campaign to convert his auditors and readers to a "lively" sense of Christianity by offering an intensely affecting portrait of personal sin and divine perfection. It was also somewhat atypical, as many of his sermons emphasized Jesus' love and God's grace. Edwards's work in another genre, the conversion narrative, is more centrally concerned with the matrix of abjection, embodied accounts of divine encounter, affective erotics of suffering, and public subject formation. Literary critics and historians have long compared Edwards's conversion narrative to earlier Puritan narratives. With origins in biblical accounts of Paul's conversion, Augustine's *Confessions*, and casuistical manuals for self-examination, Puritan narratives developed practices of self-regulation and identification that contributed to modern notions of interiority at the center of liberal humanist subjectivity. In dialectical fashion, Puritan narratives also provide points of resistance to that subject by narrating the disappearance of a sinful individual self and invoking a gracious self, stripped of personality and, in various ways, inseparable from the divine.[8]

Studies of 1740s revivalism as a transatlantic phenomenon, as well as the conversion narrative as a popular genre enabling the publicity of the colonial dispossessed, offer two new avenues of approach. Edwards's use of the conversion narrative in his 1737 *Faithful Narrative* engaged earlier Puritan and contemporary English and Scottish theories of sentiment and sensation to defend revival conversion, excite intense religious feeling, and resist theological accommodations to free will that would eventually lead to the development of a liberal subject.[9] Edwards's accounts of conversion offer something quite distinct from the "delicious" pain of Enlightenment sentimental narrative. The latter depends upon the sympathizing spectator's imaginative bridging of the emotional, economic, or social distance between himself and the suffering object of pity while also, as many critics note, maintaining and sometimes reinforcing that distance. For Edwards, conversionistic sympathy encourages the spectator's imitation and repetition of the process of conversion, including the convert's sensational experience of suffering, humiliation, and intense, sometimes unbearable abjection.

Over the course of the revivals in New England, performances and narratives of conversion became public sites for recording and contesting norms of bodily behavior. Conversion transformed the relationship between affect, bodily performance, publicity, and emerging notions of racial and gender difference. Like most of his fellow revivalists, Edwards departed from seventeenth-century Puritan models of conversion by rejecting the methodical, preparationist model of "particular steps" and instead grounding conversion in a sensational experience of affect and sentiment, notions crucial to the development of masochism and the liberal subject for whom masochism could be a perversion.[10] Under some conditions, affective conversion, rather than the longer process of sanctification or traditional criteria such as civility, community election, age, rank, or education, became the most important qualification for authoritative public religious speech and performance. Understood as the embodied and textual performances of an interior affective experience, conversion authenticated the emergence of a gracious self and sometimes enabled the publicity of more marginal members of colonial society.

The *Faithful Narrative* attempted to manage revivalism's disruptive effects but was taken up and transformed in the evangelical public in unexpected ways. Edwards's so-called "Personal Narrative" of his conversion redoubles its attention to the revivals' connection between affect, performances of abjection, and disruptive publicity. Unpublished in his lifetime, his "Personal Narrative" describes a remarkably modern subject, marked by an affective experience of interiority, delighted by the thought of being subsumed, pierced, and otherwise abjected, and promoting the tearful performance of suffering and grace. To be sure, previous generations of converts and their ministerial amanuenses had narrated periods of heightened emotion, bodily suffering, and mental or spiritual self-dissolution. Indeed, revival-era disputes about the nature of converts' affective experiences and performances of bodily harm or weakness reprise sixteenth-century Catholic-Protestant debates about the boundary between the suicide's sin and the martyr's redemptive suffering.[11] Those debates, centered on the value of suffering for salvation, generated John Donne's poetic accounts of the redemptive quality of an imagined violent and erotic integration with the divine.[12]

Because several critics have identified the eroticization of a painful union with God in women's midcentury revival conversion narratives, it may be tempting to read Edwards's accounts of tearful suffering and joy as elaborations of a prototypically feminine masochistic eroticism.[13] He developed those erotics to promote a Calvinist model of conversion that could negotiate the distant but emerging philosophical and theological challenge posed by liberal humanism and the more immediate threat of competitive, itinerant, "compulsive" evangelism epitomized by the celebrated George Whitefield. Edwards's "Personal Narrative" frustrates the conversion narrative genre's contribution to the development of a modern liberal subject by insisting on the uncertainty of grace and limiting the public authority granted to the gracious self. In short, while the spiritual erotics in Edwards's conversion narratives may resemble masochistic desire, Edwards's portrait of the convert's affective sense of abjection and annihilation as intensely desirable resists the emergence of a liberal humanist subject for whom those desires would be perverse by incorporating affective interiority into a carefully controlled speaking subject.

Edwards also denied other aesthetic and philosophical principles that would be necessary preconditions for psychoanalytic masochism. Edwards's later treatises on revival and conversion specifically respond to Shaftsbury's critique of enthusiasm and demand for a rational evaluation of affect, moving in a different direction from Edmund Burke's later construction of the liberal subject in the flight from sublime terror. Edwards also complicates what Julia Kristeva describes as the generation of speech out of the *jouissance* of introjected abjection and helps illuminate what more recent accounts of abjection discuss as masochistic self-shattering.[14] Edwards's constellation of affective states, behaviors, desires, and scenarios, in other words, may have contributed to the development of early masochisms but does not remain within even those fluid boundaries. Instead, it points to one of the many ways in which affective experiences, performances, and accounts of suffering have been used to construct political identifications, subjectivities, and behaviors prior to the invention of masochism.

Sex in the Evangelical Public

Edwards's exploration of some theological and philosophical underpinnings of an affective experience of powerlessness, self-abnegation, and self-destruction was grounded in the evolving relationship between sentiment, affect, bodily performance, and publicity in eighteenth-century transatlantic evangelical revivalism. The most innovative elements of 1730s and 1740s revivalism arose from elaborations of performances of religious feeling in oratory, letters, and print. Revivals in Europe, England, Scotland, New England, and the southern and mid-Atlantic colonies were as diverse in their etiology and processes as their geographic scope suggests but were connected by publications, itinerant performances, and lay practices endorsing intensely affective worship styles.[15]

Some of the promise of, and resistance to, revivalism would have been familiar to earlier generations of English and colonial Puritans. Dissent in England and New England was itself a creature of transatlantic colonial print culture.[16] Seventeenth- and early eighteenth-century ministers regularly wrote and preached about humiliation and abjection to tame the hot, moist, sanguine character of the less pious by stimulating cold, dry, earthy melancholic passions.[17] The periodic rise and fall of public piety had been a recurring, somewhat ritualized feature of the religious landscape in Scotland, England, and New England for decades.[18] For much of the eighteenth century, English and colonial cartoonists, novelists, balladeers, and playwrights associated revivalism with the excessive sensuality of poor or "rustic" young women, Indians, and sexual deviants.[19] Like Shaftesbury, they condemned revivalists for exciting a range of dangerous affective states under the cover of morality.[20] George Whitefield's itinerancy, meteoric celebrity, and fundraising success made him a lightning rod for such attacks. Among the earliest was an erotic 1740 pamphlet speculating at length about the nature of the "secret Sin" Whitefield mentions in his conversion narrative. The pamphlet excerpts and recontextualizes Whitefield's language of intense religious feeling to describe the devil "working [Whitefield] up" until he was "*bleeding with the Excess.*" It toys with the possibilities of maternal incest, bestiality, sodomy, and service as the devil's bottom (sex with "the Devil . . . always uppermost") before concluding it was likely the sin of "Onan": masturbation was held to weaken the eyes, and Whitefield had a severe squint.[21] Thirty years later, at the other end of Whitefield's career, *Town and Country* magazine offered a more genteel parody of "Dr. Squintum's" imagined marriage to "Parrawankaw," an Indian princess in America who converted, bore him many children, and became a Methodist preacher.[22] Unlike the progressive social critique mounted in French anticlerical erotica, these and other parodies attack, in comfortably bawdy registers, the slippery appeals of affective revivalism to young women, the poor, slaves, Indians, prisoners, prostitutes, sodomites, and those guilty of other sexual sins.[23] Although Edwards and Whitefield offered distinct models of conversion and converted subjectivity, as I will discuss below, these parodies reflect fears of the influence and porosity of a transatlantic revival culture that Edwards's *Faithful Narrative* had an important hand in shaping.

Opposition to revivalism in New England was generally less obscene, but American critics shared their English contemporaries' distaste for affective revivalism's appeals to the colonial dispossessed. As in England, the criticism, though implicating theological difference, was less concerned with doctrine than style of worship.[24] Affective revival in New England pressured hierarchies of speech by encouraging public behaviors and performances that were considered sick or "Distempered," lazy, rude, immoral, and menacingly linked to riot, slave revolt, Catholic influence, and Indian attack.[25] Anticipating later Anglican critiques of Methodist "noise" and irregular movements, New England critics used classical hierarchical psychology privileging rationality and humoral models recommending balance to condemn revivalist demagogues' excitement of "hot," "animal," bodily passions and encouragement of irregular bodily performance, including loud religious exhortation. They focused on behavior that circumvented or corrupted vertical hierarchies of speech and horizontal, collegial relationships between established ministers.[26]

Anti-revivalist furor overstated the revivals' immediate effects on social order, if not their later influence.[27] What critics denounced as exhortation and frenzy was revivalism's stuttering, experimental, contradictory, and often self-defeating proliferation of new forms of social organization and identity, less concerned with hierarchies of rank determined by public election or education and more concerned with self-management and various sorts of difference.[28] The revivals broadly participated in this shift by engaging gentler models of suffering, sentiment, and individual responsibility for spiritual development that would eventually come to include responsibility for sexuality.[29]

Eighteenth-century revivalist ministers in New England developed earlier models of conversion by promoting itinerancy, affective styles of worship, the wide distribution of periodicals and books, and the use of newspapers, broadsides, and other inexpensive formats. Edwards and some other established ministers in New England embraced revivalism to foster church membership and increase their pastoral and collegial influence. By focusing on individual emotional relationships with God and using direct, intense expressions of religious feeling, revivalist ministers also promoted religious practice by members of groups often marginalized in English colonial worship, including young women, free blacks, the indentured and enslaved, and members of neighboring tribes such as the Delaware.[30] These more marginal members of colonial society used English associations of femininity, heathenism, and incivility with abjection and bodily corruption to develop forms of public religious expression that helped them create oppositional gender or racial identities.

Faithful Narratives, Social Religion, and "Feminine" Suffering

Edwards's descriptions of Northampton's 1734–35 "season of awakening" were swept up into the burgeoning evangelical public, where they helped establish performances of intense religious affect as legitimate bases for evaluating conversion. Their history of publication and circulation offers an early example of the evangelical public's structuring, moderation, and unpredictable dissemination of revival conversion performances.

Edwards's descriptions were shaped by an English imperial and global Christian imaginary, as well as local concerns in Northampton, Boston, and London.[31] His earliest recorded narrative of the revival appeared in a letter to Benjamin Colman, pastor of Boston's urbane, theologically liberal Brattle Street Congregational Church. Colman's accounts of Connecticut Valley revivals in Boston's secular *New England Weekly Journal* had contributed to sensational rumors of back-country religious fervor, and Colman had asked Edwards for a more edifying narrative.[32] Satisfied, Colman forwarded Edwards's letter to London dissenters Isaac Watts and John Guyse, who shared the news with their congregations and requested additional details. Edwards quickly obliged with a longer letter that Colman abridged and published in Boston before sending on to London. Watts and Guyse "corrected" and published that longer letter by subscription for their congregations as *A Faithful*

Narrative of the Surprizing Work of God in the Conversion of Many Hundred Souls in Northampton (1737). It was quickly reprinted for profit, publicly advertised, and distributed in London, Edinburgh, Glasgow, and Boston, with translations in German and Dutch, becoming a handbook for midcentury revivalism and establishing Edwards's authority on the "marks" of conversion.[33]

Edwards had, since his college days, dreamt of publishing in London, but he may have been surprised by the transformation of his work in the emerging evangelical public sphere.[34] Reflecting a widespread concern for the disappearance of local traditions in the face of growing transatlantic trade, Edwards began his longer letter by attributing Northampton's lack of "corrupt[ion] with vice" to its "distance from seaports," but his own influence and reputation depended on his narrative's transformation and commodification in those same routes.[35] The *Faithful Narrative*'s popularity was due to its timeliness—its status as "news"—and its narrative format, which could offer striking portraits of converts' religious affections. These conversions became something of a *succès de scandal*. Watts and Guyse, wary of endorsing such "raised affections," had repeatedly asked Colman for "some other minister in New England" to publish an account. Elsewhere, Watts, citing the "reproaches we sustain here, both in conversation and in newspapers," explained they were obliged to "make some alterations of the language, lest we together with the book should have been exposed to much more contempt and ridicule."[36] What remained was "surprizing" enough: the narrative justified converts' vivid imagination of hell as a "dreadful furnace," of "blood running from [Christ's] wounds," and a rapturous sense of Christ's "beauty and excellency." Despite insisting that no converts had visions with "bodily eyes" or espoused innovative doctrines, dress, or styles of worship, the *Faithful Narrative* endorsed converts' performances of bodily weakness, including fainting, collapse, and near death, as a holy "sinking" under the "sense of the glory of God" or "divine wrath" until God nearly "dissolved their frame."

Edwards agreed that "there are some things in it that it would not be best to publish in England"; he took special care to condemn lay preaching by pairing the urge to preach with the urge to commit suicide, declaring both "strange, enthusiastic delusions."[37] But Edwards may have been more troubled by Watts and Guyse's promotion, in their extensive editorial apparatus, of a simpler model of converts' sense of grace, or "new light." Edwards's own model preempted critics who claimed that revival simply excited embodied "animal" passions by using faculty psychology and other Enlightenment theories connecting body and mind through sense and feeling. His account of conversion further distinguished between "natural" affections, such as sympathy, and "gracious" affective responses. As Edwards explained in a 1733 sermon descriptively entitled "A Divine and Supernatural Light, Immediately Imparted to the Soul by the Spirit of God," strong affections about the things of religion were no proof of grace: "A person by mere nature . . . may be liable to be affected with the story of Jesus Christ . . . as well as by any other tragical story . . . as well as a man may be affected with what he reads in a romance, or sees acted in a stage play."[38] Such natural affect, initiated by reading romances or seeing plays, could be evaluated rationally on the basis of its beneficial effect on the body and mind. In contrast, gracious affect, "imparted" by the "indwelling" of the Holy Spirit, could produce harmful affections and yet remain beneficial.[39] As in Edwards's typological practice, the affective experience of the gracious convert reveals earthly effects to be "images or shadows" of the "Excellency" of divinity.[40]

As this tension between Edwards and his editors suggests, the *Faithful Narrative*'s layers of ministerial comments, notes, revisions, and counterrevisions tried to manage and stabilize the meaning of revival conversion but tended to highlight and possibly contribute to the multiplication and proliferation of meaning.[41] This tendency is clearest in Watts and Guyse's introductory attempt to forestall criticism of Edwards's two exemplary converts, a young woman and a girl whose conversions were almost entirely grounded in affective realizations of sin and grace, without any rational basis or sustained postconversion good works. In the postmillennial framework shared by many revivalists, converts who were young, female, poor, or "heathen" held special value as heralds of Christ's return and the world's end. These converts' greater propensity to bodily weakness, corruption, and sin made their conversion more remarkable but also more suspect, especially if their conversion included "impressions on . . . imaginations" or visions. Edwards characterized this problem as one of narrative. "[S]ome weaker persons," Edwards wrote, "in giving an account of their experiences, have not so prudently distinguished between the spiritual and imaginary part."[42] Edwards's own conversion narrative addressed this suspicion by insisting on strict Calvinist limits to grace and describing "weaker" converts as easily corrected by his ministerial guidance. Edwards's conversion narrative also dramatized this process of correction by narrating one young woman's slow, agonizing silencing by disease and death, invoking affective conversion within a highly sentimental framework designed to moralize and moderate readers' responses.

The narrative thereby extended a ministerial tradition of adapting women's sacred speech and performance for use by evangelical men, making confessions of guilt and displays of "inarticulate ecstasy and self-silencing" the most acceptable styles of women's public revivalist worship in New England.[43]

In England, though, and increasingly in New England as well, women's "inarticulate ecstasy and self-silencing" loomed in the shadow of Revolution-era female prophecy, ecstatic religious practice, and sacred violence.[44] Watts and Guyse, rather than defending Edwards, bowed out. Stating only "we must allow every writer his own way," they deferred to Edwards's authorial privilege even as they undermined its basis in sound judgment, a compliment Edwards returned when he rewrote their introduction for his 1738 Boston edition.[45] Other revivalists with access to print made more concerted efforts to transform Edwards's account; John Wesley published an edition meticulously pruned of Calvinism, distributing it widely among his followers and sending it to every Anglican bishop. In its various published forms, the *Faithful Narrative*'s affective conversions broke free of Edwards's limitations on lay speech and salvation. Edwards's evocation and defense of affective conversion take shape through a traditional ministerial structuring and management of female preaching and performance, but conversion narratives after the *Faithful Narrative*, refracted through other revival practices, opened affective experiences and performances to further reinterpretation by a range of editors, readers, and listeners who helped produce new communities that challenged existing hierarchies of speech. In this and other ways, the popularity and power of the *Faithful Narrative* depended on its transformation by the evangelical public.

This process of transformation would come to be typical of the 1740s evangelical public, in which evangelical communities of letters, contributions to secular periodicals, and book publishing increased and were augmented by new evangelical periodicals in London, Glasgow, Edinburgh, and Boston. The periodicals, consisting largely of letters from British Dissenters, traveling missionaries, itinerants, and settled colonial ministers, offered news of "extraordinary" affective religious performances, including fainting, visions, trances, and ecstatic speech.[46] In the American colonies, such performances incorporated immigrant and creole English women's spiritual practice as well as traditional spiritual practices from Welsh, Scottish, Dutch, Native American, African, and other communities variously marginalized and constrained.

Accounts of converts' "feminine" performance sometimes cover over these multiple cultural influences on revival practice, in part because the language of revival conversion was structured by the sexed norms of Puritan religious performance.[47] Conversion had been a cornerstone of Puritan social organization since the 1630s, when Puritan communities on both sides of the Atlantic began requiring accounts of religious experience for church membership and voting rights within the church. Sixteenth- and seventeenth-century New England Puritans often spoke or wrote and recited their accounts of conversion in front of congregations they hoped to join, with ministers occasionally recording and publishing those accounts. They usually described conversion as a movement from knowledge of sin to conviction, faith, mortification and penance or spiritual combat, and true but imperfect assurance of salvation. Well into the eighteenth century, Puritans and other dissenters emphasized the uncertain nature of assurance, often operating within a preparationist model in which conversion was one step in a spiritual journey charted along an emotional circuit running from anxious doubts about salvation to assurance and back to doubt.[48]

In both England and the colonies, seventeenth-century Puritan men's conversion narratives idealized willing submission to divine and earthly authorities by invoking biblical tropes of women's submission and servants' loyalty filtered through the *Pilgrim's Progress*, other popular nonconformist narratives, and contemporary spiritual biographies.[49] In a long mystical theo-erotic tradition, Puritan ministers established their fitness to lead by figuring themselves as "nursing fathers," maternally devoted to their divine charges, and "brides of Christ," desiring erotic union with divinity.[50] Thomas Shepard's journal, for example, records his need to "desire Christ and taste Christ and roll myself upon Christ" or "lie by him and lie at him," though often, as he wrote in his *Autobiography*, "Christ was not so sweet as [his] lust." For Shepard and others, conversion was an uncertain, circular process in which doubt and grace intertwine in a drama of competing desire. Even when "the Lord made himself sweet to me and to embrace him and to give myself unto him," Shepard wrote, "yet after this I had many fears and doubts."[51] The Puritan glorification of openness to God as typically feminine engaged the one-sex model of gender that also predominated in contemporary medical and philosophical traditions, so that, as Elizabeth Maddox Dillon observes, this "sexualized rhetoric" articulates "power differentials that did not necessarily inhere in bodies."[52] Lower forms of bodily lust, marked as female, figure the higher desire for union with the divine.

The revivals participated in this shift away from this one-sex "feminine" model of piety broadly but unevenly. As New England's economy and society became more closely integrated with England's in the late seventeenth and early eighteenth centuries, the ideal of erotic "female" subjection and servants' loyalty lost ground among many men and wealthier women in favor of "gentler ideas of piety and suffering" appropriate to those virtuously brought up. In more prosperous towns, sermons, which often reflected a consensus of community ideals, moved toward the English post-Restoration latitudinarian norm of rationality and persuasion and emphasized Jesus' love rather than God's wrath.[53] Though continuing to evoke emotion, they abandoned erotic "female" piety as a master trope for human relationships with God.[54] In other ways, though, the revivals resisted the shift away from the one-sex model, describing conversion as divine impregnation and insisting on the convert's humiliation and suffering.[55] In the late eighteenth and nineteenth centuries, gentler notions of suffering became more narrowly associated with middle-class whiteness and female difference.[56]

In New England, these changes in notions of race, gender, and sexuality were precipitated or accompanied by the separation of conversion from church membership and church membership from civil privileges.[57] With fewer legal inducements to encourage full membership, established ministers in New England leaned more heavily on rhetorical and ritual techniques such as open communion. Solomon Stoddard was a public champion of these techniques, which helped corrode the link between the conversion narrative and religious or civil privileges. Edwards eventually attempted to restrict communion and reinstate the conversion narrative as a requirement for full membership—a fiasco precipitating his 1749 dismissal—but for most of the 1730s and 1740s, he embraced Stoddard's use of rhetorical and personal means of persuasion to evoke and manage conversion.

The transformation of Edwards's narrative in the evangelical public chipped away at traditional Reformed limits on grace and thereby transformed the meaning of Edwards's converts' suffering, which, even as it incorporated newer sentimental modes, was firmly rooted in earlier notions of sex, bodily control, and ministerial and community oversight. Edwards's pastoral interest in reinstating conversion as a means of reasserting ministerial control was shaped, in part, by his inability to maintain traditional ministerial and community regulation of sexuality.[58] Edwards insisted that conversion demanded public accountability for a range of bodily behaviors, including religious performances, sex, and other erotic practices, that could only be addressed within a gathered congregation of the faithful.

The controversy over conversion, sex, and publicity that led to Edwards's 1749 dismissal was, in some way, prefigured in the *Faithful Narrative*'s accounts of conversion as a substitution of gracious affective practice for "licentious" bodily practice. Edwards's innovative incorporation of sentiment into his conversion narrative participated in the wider attempt to attract "gentler" converts, but he embedded sentimental conversion in earlier models of conversion, such as Shepard's and St. Francis's, directed at controlling a broad array of fleshly lusts. The *Faithful Narrative* begins by describing the salutary effect of small-group "social religion" on young people overly fond of "licentiousness," "night-walking," tavern drinking, "mirth and company-keeping," and other friendly or erotic practices outside church or family. One of the "greatest company-keepers," a young woman, offered Edwards her conversion narrative, and "News" of her conversion "seemed to be almost like a flash of lightning, upon the hearts of young people." The "licentious" convert shared her narrative with "many" others, who "went to talk with her, concerning what she had met with." They formed vanguards of young converts, not unlike Wesley's early bands, who led a "general" revival encompassing all ages and ranks of European creoles and immigrants, "several Negros," and neighboring Indians.[59] Even after the revival cooled, Edwards wrote to Colman in 1737 that converts did not "return to ways of lewdness and sensuality."[60]

Edwards's "flash of lightning" offers a key into the new importance and challenges of performances, narratives, and published "News" of conversion. It also reminds us of the difficulty with reading eighteenth-century revival practice as either sexual or purely spiritual and therefore outside the bounds of the erotic. The flash or dart of lightning on the heart was a traditional Reformed trope for the convert's sense of God's power. Traceable to Augustine's "light of confidence" and subsequent rejection of fleshly "lusts," this metaphorical "flash" moved conversion away from older, visionary experiences of revelation such as Paul's "great light" from heaven.[61] Seventeenth-century Puritans followed Augustine in using the phrase to signal moments of assurance, while Edwards and other revivalists specifically associated it with the new perceptual capacity (the "Divine and Supernatural Light") granted to converts. The *Faithful Narrative* characterizes lay performances and accounts of conversion as *themselves* imbued with this divine power, implicitly justifying print publication as an extension of that process. At the same time, by obscuring Edwards's role in spreading the news of her conversion, it imagines evangelical publicity as a disembodied emanation into an empty field.

Standing as the *Faithful Narrative*'s first individual account of conversion, the "licentious" convert helps establish the meaning and significance of the book's subsequent sentimental conversions, which also attempt to describe affective revivalist speech, organization, and performance as a substitute for illicit sexual practice.

Like many revival conversion accounts, the *Faithful Narrative* could be read as a case study of sublimation, with the important qualification that it explicitly promotes the substitution of embodied, affective "social religion" for illicit sexuality associated with problematic lay religious expression. Social religion, which was evoked, guided, and promoted by Edwards but modeled and dependent on women's speech, conversation, and organizing, was crucial to Northampton's shift from illicit erotic activity outside the bonds of marriage to intense spiritual feeling inside the bonds of faith.[62] Edwards's two exemplary converts, delineated through new sentimental models of female piety, lapse into silence, while the "licentious" convert, delineated through older models of bodily lust and corruption, undergoes a moral transformation and achieves an important role in promoting social religion. Rather than straddling a cultural-historical boundary after which point sublimation can occur, sentimental narrative extends and continues an older model of converted selfhood in which fleshly lusts are replaced by embodied affective social performances of faith as part of the process of forming an evangelical public.

Letters, Tears, and Being "Swallowed Up in Christ"

In a preface to Edwards's 1738 Boston edition of *A Faithful Narrative*, four Boston ministers took special note of Edwards's claim for the salvific work of conversion narrative. "There is no one thing that I know of, that God has made such a means of promoting his work amongst us," Edwards wrote, "as the news of others' conversion." Why, then, did Edwards leave his own conversion narrative unpublished?[63]

In New England, the circulation of conversion narratives in the emerging evangelical public extended and magnified the existing conflict between the established church's dual roles as, first, a gathered congregation of the faithful and, second, an instituted means to grace. As only the gracious, predestined by God, were called to convert, to whom did the narratives speak? What public roles and responsibilities did conversion entail, especially ministerial conversion? Edwards's own conversion narrative, first published after his death as the "Personal Narrative," presents a reticulated response to the disruptive consequences of affective conversion by intervening in the genre's association of embodied performances of conversion with authoritative public religious expression.

Edwards likely composed the letter in which his narrative appeared around 1740, just as he was emerging as a leading moderate colonial revivalist.[64] Facing increasing sectarian division and public skepticism about revival, his narrative responded by incorporating the intense physicality, self-doubt, and circularity characteristic of more marginal converts' narratives but locating them in a more entirely affective register. Edwards's rhetoric of self-abjection may therefore be understood as part of a larger public strategy authorizing intense performances of bodily suffering, increasing revivalist converts' autonomy from some "gentle" norms of public behavior by encouraging greater self-control and attention to rank in public religious expression. Edwards's attention to rank would also include a refusal to enter into the wide, less distinguishable, and more unstable sorts of address encouraged by fully capitalized print narratives of conversion and the various versions of the *Faithful Narrative.*[65]

Edwards follows Puritan conversion precedent by narrating the repeated erasure of a sinful "personality" but diverges by depending more entirely upon affect and sensation, or what Myra Jehlen and Michael Warner identify as a "perverse pleasure" in the "sentiment of annihilation and abjection."[66] Part of Edwards's greater "perversity" lies in his narrow scope and lyrical account of sense and perception. While the *Faithful Narrative* followed the effects of conversion on a community of believers, exemplifying young women whose conversions were calculated to generate salvific public affect or sentiment, Edwards's conversion narrative focuses on his highly individuated psyche and embodied affect. Because Edwards's narrative seems so modern in its descriptions of psychic interiority and eroticized individual affect, his embrace of abjection appears psychologically and sexually perverse. Edwards's apparent perversity is magnified by his composition of the narrative for the edification of a young acolyte, his future son-in-law. As part of a letter from an established minister to a younger man, the narrative is explicitly didactic, located in the immense body of eighteenth-century English advice literature calculated to control the passions of unmarried men.[67] Constructed as an exemplum to confront the exigencies of the revival, Edwards's conversion narrative intervenes in the genre's support for disruptions of hierarchies of speech and publication, registering subtle shifts in the meanings of sex and rank.

Edwards's representation of the relationship between his own affective state, his affective performance, his authorial self, and his ministerial role attempts to limit the disruptive potential of revival performance. He begins by outlining a two-stage process of conversion to the doctrine of predestination, first a rational "conviction" and then an affecting, "*delightful* conviction." Echoing his earlier sermons on the "new light," Edwards attributes his "delight" to his new affective capacity or disposition toward God brought about by his reading of scripture. To illustrate his divinely implanted sense, Edwards disperses metaphors of light and taste in Baudelairean profusion, describing God's sovereignty as "an exceedingly pleasant, bright and sweet doctrine" and even, in carefully couched terms, his sense of what "seem'd to be, as it were, a calm, sweet cast, or appearance of divine glory, in almost every [natural] thing." Chronicling another series of affecting scriptural readings, Edwards describes his growing awareness of personal sin through formulaic expressions of personal abjection, including his "extreme feebleness and impotence" and his heart's "innumerable and bottomless depths of secret corruption and deceit."[68]

Edwards illustrates his increasingly affective sense of his own sin and God's sovereignty by introducing the metaphor of violent bodily incorporation with Christ. These violent images become his narrative's primary trope for explaining his affective experience of personal abjection and divine power. Incorporation replays the Puritan ideal of erotic submission to Christ in a more abstract, affective, and explicitly violent key. Edwards begins by expressing his desire to be "swallowed up in Christ" and "have [Christ] for my head, and . . . be a member of his body." These phrases apply the metaphor of corporate or church embodiment (Christ as "head" of the church) to his own soul and perhaps gesture toward a "swallowing up" of rational thought in the soul's victory over death. Then, compounding the metaphor of bodily incorporation, Edwards invokes the metaphor of grafting, imagining himself as a plant "cut entirely off from his own root" and forced to rely entirely on God, "grow[ing] into, and out of Christ." His tropological account of bodily incorporation with Christ returns to a narrative description of embodied affective performances of an increasingly abstract and comprehensive sense of sin and God's grace. To magnify the sinner's essential unwillingness to submit to the divine and the irresistible, sovereign power of God to compel not only submission but also joyful submission through a desirable violence,

Edwards amplifies the violence of these images and applies them to rational thought. Alternately absorbed and penetrated by the divine, Edwards was freed from "thought and conception," swept up in a "flood of tears, and weeping aloud" for "about an hour," and filled with competing desires "to be emptied and annihilated; to lie in the dust, and to be full of Christ alone" as well as to be cast into a pit so deep that only the "piercing eye of God's grace" could reach him.[69] These phrases, drawn from scriptural figures for the influence of grace, were commonplaces in Puritan spiritual autobiography and New England ministerial guides to conversion such as Stoddard's *A Guide to Christ*.[70] By introducing these expressions into a narrative form and using them to mark internal affective shifts in sense and sensation, Edwards imbues them with a greater affective power.

Edwards's rhetoric of abjection resembles revival conversion narratives by women, the poor, and Native and African Americans, which tended to be more embodied and continued the older Puritan model of conversion as a recursive or sometimes unfinished process. The most remarkable narratives are visionary and deeply uncertain, only hinting at progress toward self-assurance. A brief 1754 narrative by Montauk Temperance Hannabal, recorded by Samson Occom, concludes with Hannabal's description of a "Swoun" in which she "found [her] Self into great Darkness" with a voice guiding her to "Something" like "a Pole . . . Put over a Deep hole."[71] Narratives by European creole and immigrant women are similarly recursive, if usually more assured, describing spiritual development as an embodied battle with Satan and theoerotic absorption or penetration by Christ. Connecticut farmwoman Hannah Heaton, in a 1741 narrative, writes that she "thot [she] felt the devil twitch [her] clothes" and "whisper" suicidal urges "in her ear." Naming and drawing on her experience at sermons by Gilbert Tennent and George Whitefield, Heaton described one revival in which "many were crying out" and she "thot the flor [she] stood on gave way." Suddenly resigned to her fate, she "thot I see iesus with the eyes of my soul stand up in heaven a louely g[o]od man with his arms open ready to receive me his face was full of smiles he loockt white and ruddy and was iust such a saviour as my soul wanted."[72]

Edwards's wife, Sarah Edwards, offered a more abstract but similarly erotic sense of floating or swimming like "a mote of dust" in God's "stream or pencil of sweet light." "That night," she wrote, "was the sweetest night I ever had in my life."[73] These narratives engage seventeenth-century Puritan models of sex in which "female" bodily weakness allowed for greater supernatural influence. They also connect "female" piety with other cultural traditions, such as James Gronniosaw's possible invocation of West African spirit possession: in a narrative dictated to "a young lady," Gronniosaw, a former slave in New York, "saw (or thought I saw) light inexpressible dart down from heaven upon me, and shone around me for the space of a minute. I continued on my knees, and joy unspeakable took possession of my soul."[74] Embodied affective performance of abjection, followed by rapturous joy and pleasure, signals their sense of God's love and their own salvation.

These converts spoke and wrote themselves into an evangelical public that offered them an ambivalent embrace. Like many nineteenth-century Native Americans, African Americans, and white women who modified the conversion narrative form to enable their own publicity, these eighteenth-century converts' frequent qualification of their visions and senses as "thought," or otherwise imagined, attempts to negotiate the greater scrutiny applied to representations and affective performances by the colonial dispossessed.

Edwards's rhetoric of self-dissolution and abjection translates the physical, embodied visions and sensory experiences described by many poorer converts into a largely internal, affective drama. This shift signals his attempt to promote greater rhetorical self-control and attention to rank. His attempt becomes clearer when we read his *Faithful Narrative* alongside his 1741 letter to Deborah Hatheway, a recent young convert in Suffield, where Edwards had briefly served as substitute pastor. Edwards begins by repeating his *Faithful Narrative*'s advice to "set up religious meetings," but rather than promote the certainty of conversion, in the manner of the licentious convert's "flash of lightning," Edwards recommends Hatheway *act* as though she was uncertain. Because gracious converts are under "infinitely greater obligations," Edwards writes, Hatheway should evince even more "strife and earnestness" or "earnest and violent" behavior than before conversion, being "always greatly abased for your remaining sin," "never think[ing] that you lie low enough for it," and performing acts "that make you the least and lowest, and most like a child." Because conversion is never truly certain, the best way to maintain a regenerate state is to act as though suspended in the moment immediately before conversion, a state of continuous becoming that never entirely resolves itself into being.

Public expressions of personal abjection, Edwards continues, are most persuasive when the speaker attends carefully to relative rank. When "speaking to your equals," Edwards advises, "let your warnings be intermixed with expressions of your sense of your own unworthiness . . . and if you can with a good conscience, say how that you in yourself are more unworthy than they."[75] Edwards takes care to avoid the silence that could stem from such a suspension of assurance, a silence associated with the suicide's melancholy and despair. Instead, Edwards's ideal speaking subject—his exemplary convert—generates careful speech out of the sense of sin and abjection that precedes assurance, not in the movement from doubt to assurance. The speaker's heightened awareness of social status allows him to carefully calibrate his religious expressions and performances for the demands of the audience, minimizing revivalists' overstepping of rank to maintain the revivals' legitimacy and fostering social circumstances in which further individual conversions could take place.

Edwards concluded his conversion narrative with a scene of extended weeping that may be his most striking and complex portrait of religious affect. Long before the age of sentiment, tears had been a symbol of repentance and sign of passionate religious experience. In the eighteenth century, tears became freighted in the context of sentimentalists' claims to moral self-government and revivalists' Antinomian or Perfectionist tendencies. A group of New York Presbyterians, for example, published a short tract calling Whitefield to task for, among other things, a sermon describing tears of repentance as themselves salvific.[76] Many lay revival conversion narratives followed Whitefield in developing what Henry Scougal's 1677 devotional manual, reprinted frequently in eighteenth-century New York, Philadelphia, and Boston, described as God's gift of "a beam of the eternal light" to the saved.[77] As Whitefield and Scougal recommend, these lay narratives used episodes of weeping as signs of a convert's movement from doubt, characterized by silence, into a sense of grace, characterized by song, announcements of joy, or other effusive descriptions of God's excellence. Frequently authored by creole European men of middling rank, these narratives stage the moment of "awakening" to God's grace as a singular, metamorphic experience of theosis in which "self"-destruction results in the emergence of an individuated gracious self. Such accounts lead more directly to the development of a modern liberal subjectivity characterized by interiority and a highly individuated psyche, or what William James described as the autonomous unification of a self previously unhappy and divided.[78]

In the wake of Gilbert Tennent's inflammatory The Danger of an Unconverted Ministry and Whitefield's typically self-satisfied description of "Dear Mr. Edwards" weeping "during the whole time" of Whitefield's second

Northampton sermon, Edwards's tears might even have been taken to endorse demands for a converted clergy.[79] Because these demands made conversion the primary qualification for authoritative public religious address,
they encouraged forms of lay evangelism that resembled preaching. Indeed,
many revival narratives by lay preachers and exhorters dramatize conversion
as a tearful movement from tortured silence into bold, "masculine" speech
characteristic of an earlier generation of Protestant martyrs. In making this
connection between conversion and evangelism, these narratives register the
influence of ministers in the evangelical public but also illustrate the evangelical public's threat to ministers' traditional monopoly on authoritative religious speech. For example, Samuel Belcher, in a self-written 1740 conversion
narrative used to gain full membership in Edwards's father's church, charts
his spiritual development by naming his attendance of various famous itinerants and echoing their publications. Referring to Edwards's sermon, Belcher
described his terror at falling "into the hands of an angry God . . . Cry[ing]
mightily . . . in the bitterness of my Soul for mercy." Then, echoing Whitefield, Belcher "felt my Load Go of and my mouth was Stopt and I Could not
utter one word for Some time and I fealt as if my heart was Changed." In his
"Joy and Comfort," Belcher's "mouth was opened and [he] Spake forth the
praises of God."[80] Though perhaps more typical of men, women also engaged
this trope, often in a more embodied manner. Lay preacher Susanna Anthony's narrative, as published by Edwards's protégée Samuel Hopkins, retains
the martyr's connection between her experience of pain and "bold" dissenting speech. Anthony insisted she had no irregular affective behaviors, but
when Satan tempted her to commit suicide, she "twisted every joint, and
strained every nerve; biting my flesh; gnashing my teeth; throwing myself on
the floor," and wringing her hand until it was numb. Her damaged hand, a
vivid symbol of many converts' mediated access to writing, was healed after
her experience of God's grace. Recalling this event, she claims, "often fill[s]
my soul with a holy boldness, and my mouth with arguments."[81] Describing a
sense of pain and joy engendered by both external torment and an internalized notion of sin and divine perfection, Anthony and other converts ground
their "bold" religious speech in the affective experience of suffering and
grace.

As these narratives' frequent invocations of Whitefield indicate, the link
between conversion and speech was authorized, in part, by engaging public
models of converted subjectivity with which Edwards was at pains to compete. If, as many suspect, Edwards wrote his conversion narrative in 1740 or

1741, he engaged in at least implicit dialogue with Whitefield's 1740 conversion narrative and the mass "outpourings of faith" sparked by Whitefield's accompanying preaching tour, whose New England leg Edwards helped arrange. In what would be one of the largest, most coordinated publishing and distribution events of the day, Whitefield's narrative was attractive and simply *available* to lay and itinerant revivalists and critics on a perhaps unprecedented scale.[82] As with revivalist practice more generally, the outlines of Whitefield's conversion were conventional, but the details were remarkably charismatic, describing a protean figure haplessly caught up in the spiritual battle between God and the devil.[83] Eschewing the rational argumentation and elevated, impersonal tone of much contemporary ministerial publication, Whitefield addressed his "dear Reader" directly, offered mildly salacious details of his sinful preconversion life, endorsed prophetic dreams and direct divine response to prayer, and compared himself to a Foxean martyr.[84] But it was his narrative's framing of evangelical speech as the result of divine inspiration that would prove most problematic for Edwards. After a period of intense self-doubt, sickness, and severe ascetic self-denial, Whitefield received a mysterious "suggestion" that his inexplicable "thirst" resembled Christ's on the cross. At that moment, he wrote, "I perceived my Load go off" and "could not avoid singing Psalms wherever I was." This inexplicable, joyful, spectacular transcendence of illness and self-doubt was reenacted in his public preaching, which dramatized what Nancy Ruttenburg describes as his overcoming of bodily limits and church or civil attempts to restrict his speech through the practice of "compulsive public utterance" and "aggressive uncontainability."[85] Whitefield's multiple public personae allowed him to qualify or revise this and other more charismatic passages while continuing to express such sentiments elsewhere.

Edwards's weeping intervenes in Whitefield's account of conversion and religious expression by addressing the connection between tears and speech. Edwards's converted subject is, like Whitefield's, generated out of the repetition of the performance of conversion, but the pleasures and public presence of Edwards's subject are generated by the "loud" performance of self-isolation, weeping, and silence. Overcome by an acutely affecting sense of God's excellence, Edwards experienced "a kind of a loud weeping" that lasted for hours, so that he was "forced to shut [himself] up" in a room "and fasten the doors." This self-isolation is the somatic experience of a previously figurative desire for self-effacement, one associated, in an earlier episode of weeping, with a sense of personal abjection and total dependence on Christ.[86] His assertion of self-control (locking himself up) at the very moment of self-dissolution enables an extended affective performance of abjection but also disrupts Whitefieldean conversion narratives' association of affective performance and speech: during his weeping, Edwards concludes, he "could not *but as it were* cry out, 'How happy are they which do that which is right in the sight of God!' "[87] By presenting his self-isolation as literal and his speech as metaphorical, Edwards reverses Whitefield's, and many lay preachers', use of abjection as the prelude to religious speech. Imagining a form of sublimity that rejects Whitefield's "compulsive public utterance[s]" and works against emerging liberal subjectivity, Edwards narrates the enclosure of his otherwise uncontrollable affective religious performance in a space of guarded isolation.

Edwards's account of tearful self-isolation here resembles seventeenth-century Puritan converts who, when their sense of personal humiliation failed to lead to a sense of divine love, found themselves lost in "shame's isolated silence," but it proposes an alternate path to religious speech.[88] Edwards describes his room as a place of emotional reflection, a private space of tearful isolation from which to better imagine public action.[89] In the language of spiritual warfare some revivalists adopted, Edwards's isolation signals not a withdrawal from the revivalist public but a strategic shift of the field of battle into the less impersonal public of the letter.

In closing his account with a scene of tearful, meditative self-isolation, Edwards also offers insight into his decision to circulate his narrative privately. By insisting that his speaking subject be grounded in the sense of abjection and uncertainty, Edwards's conversion narrative attempts to manage revivalist speech by engaging the narrative practices of the colonial dispossessed and translating them into a more entirely affective register, but he may have recognized that his narrative was likely to go awry in the evangelical public. Given the potential audience for his conversion narrative, Edwards's decision not to publish, along with his subsequent preference for analytic treatises and sermons over the more widely accessible narrative form (notwithstanding *The Life of David Brainerd*, which deserves more detailed consideration elsewhere), suggests his awareness of the capacity of the evangelical public to transform the meaning of his work and reluctance to expose himself to broad and intense scrutiny. By circulating the letter privately, Edwards could better predict and control the audience, influencing those of similar or higher rank while minimizing other interpretations and transformations of his account.

Conversion and Masochism's Philosophical Bases

Edwards's conversion narrative frustrates the genre's contribution to the development of a modern liberal subject by insisting on the uncertainty of grace and limiting the public authority granted to the gracious self. In his conversion narrative's description of his affecting sense of God's grace, Edwards describes a divine sublimity that closely resembles Kant's sublime, which Deleuze and several literary critics have identified as an important basis for the literary and philosophical development of masochism. Deleuze, whose analysis of Leopold von Sacher-Masoch's *Venus in Furs* (1869) offers the best account of masochism's philosophical bases, argues that a necessary precondition to masochistic desire was the Enlightenment transformation of the law from a Platonic/Christian model, in which the law is dependent on a higher principle, such as "the good" or God, into a Kantian/Oedipal model, in which the good is premised on the law, in which "moral law is *the law*" and in which the law is "by definition unknowable and elusive" because it must constantly disguise those things it bans.[90] This Kantian/Oedipal model, Deleuze concludes, helps create the modern subject by premising subjectivity on an acceptance of guilt.[91]

Kant's description of the law's sublimity has much in common with Edwards's Calvinistic account of God's terrible power, as both are fundamentally unrepresentable, free from human intentionality, and beyond human influence. Indeed, the shift from the Platonic/Christian model to the Kantian/Oedipal model was effected, in part, by the Calvinist logic of salvation by faith alone that Edwards champions. Kant's formulation of moral law reflects an Edwardsian understanding of predestination: those who obey the law, rather than feel righteous, are bound to feel, as Deleuze writes, "guilty in advance." Agreeing with Edwards in the fundamental unrepresentability of sublimity but attempting to liberate humanity from the strictures of religion, Kant removes that guilt from its moorings in the idea of a transcendent omnipotent God.[92] By grounding subjectivity in the "universal rational religion dwelling in every ordinary man," Kant makes irrationality the "sin" of Enlightenment.[93] Kant's attempt to translate Christian law into humanist rationalism offers a mirror image of Edwards's attempt to incorporate affect into a strict Calvinism.

The political implications of these two opposing descriptions of the sublime help explain Edwards's defense of extreme religious affect in two subsequent treatises, *Distinguishing Marks of the Work of the Spirit of God* (1741) and *Some Thoughts Concerning the Present Revival of Religion in New England* (1742), that stand as theological companion pieces to his conversion narrative. In attempting to limit the power of affect to challenge existing ecclesiastical hierarchies of speech, Edwards's sublime counterbalances evangelical speech by women, the young, the poor, and other marginal groups against the liberal humanist constructions of subjectivity that would also threaten ministerial power.

Because Kant's theory of sublimity derived from his attempt to transform Burke's political and aesthetic notion of sublimity into moral and idealistic concepts, a brief review of Burke's differences with Edwards will help clarify the way in which Edwards's political concerns contributed to his construction of sublimity. Burke and Edwards both develop Shaftesbury's account of sublimity in "A Letter Concerning Enthusiasm" (1707), which offers a limited endorsement of "divine enthusiasm" resulting from "ideas or images received [that] are too big for the narrow human vessel to contain" and used "to express whatever was sublime in human passions."[94] Sharing this common point of departure, Burke's description of sublimity, which is frequently credited with offering the earliest description of pleasurable emotional pain, agrees with Edwards's account of his painfully pleasurable sense of God's power.[95] Though rhetorically aligned in their description of sublime power, they differ in their evaluation of the source of pleasure. Burke's illustration of sublimity as the sense of "shrink[ing] into the minuteness of our own nature" and being metaphorically "annihilated before [God]" closely resembles Edwards's description of his response to God's excellence.[96] Burke's path to sublime pleasure also resembles a notion of conversion as a singular, metamorphic "new birth," or the emergence of a saintly self out of the destruction of the sinful self, in which the sense of God's terrible power is transformed into rapturous joy through God's grace. For Burke, however, this painful sense of power, which he calls terror, can delight only if its source is placed at some distance through active and strenuous exertion. Burke here follows Shaftesbury's conclusion that only "enthusiasm" guided by "reason, and sound sense . . . sedate, cool, and impartial; free of every bypassing passion, every giddy Vapor, or melancholy fume," can be judged as divine.[97] Indeed, Burke's account of sublimity may have been influenced by the political irregularity produced by affective revivalism in the 1740s: he began the treatise at Trinity College, Dublin, before 1749, and, in his later considerations of colonial self-government, was clearly skeptical of American enthusiastic religion. Edwards also follows Shaftesbury in endorsing rational judgment and encouraging converts' increased self-control in their expressions of personal abjection. Edwards moves away from Shaftesbury by emphasizing that God's power surpasses human judgment, and away from Burke by embracing the divine sublime and maintaining the accompanying sense of sublime power.

Burke, by describing sublime pleasure as the result of escape from divine power, presents a fantasy of self-creation through flight that provides an aesthetic framework for the construction of bourgeois liberal subjectivity in eighteenth-century England.[98] Edwards's sublime attempts to forestall a Burkean departure from his script by describing encounters with overwhelming divine power as pleasurable, thereby disallowing Burke's path to self-creation. This difference helps account for Edwards's refusal to reject even the most harmful performances of affect. What Burke and Shaftesbury condemn as the "horrid convulsions" of "languid and inactive . . . nerves" incapable of overcoming the source of terror, and what other anti-revivalists called "Visions, Trances, Convulsions [and] Epilepsies," Edwards describes, in *Some Thoughts*, as being "weakened by strong and vigorous exercises of love" to Christ.[99] In characterizing weakness and pain as "exercises of love," Edwards embeds sublime pleasure in the experience of divine power and defends ministerial power against a specifically liberal threat emanating from the staging of the emergence of a gracious self.

Edwards's opposition to Burke's conception of the self as defined by a flight from overwhelming power is based on Edwards's theological association of the phenomenological world with the fallen world. Edwards's faith in biblical guidance and human corruption places more severe limits on human knowledge than most Enlightenment empiricists allow. Edwards takes up the language of sensation and sympathy only to argue that the "human" experience it produces is sinful and abject, not semi-divine. In so doing, his conversion narrative presents a challenge to the genre's role in the development of modern liberal subjectivity, interrupting its development of an individuated psyche by repudiating the movement from "sinful" to "gracious" self. Edwards refutes emerging liberal descriptions of human nature as compatible with the divine by describing faith as the joyful acceptance of absolute human abjection and endorsing an affective, tearful experience of both personal abjection and God's sovereignty. In this way, Edwards's tears in his conversion narrative ambivalently refigure St. Francis's blood. Both are shed in a sacrificial manner, but while St. Francis describes his experience to all who will listen, Edwards's tears are accompanied by a retreat into meditative isolation and the more private realm of the letter. By adopting the individual affective experience of sorrow and selflessness to reestablish Calvinist uncertainty, Edwards conflates the affective realization of abjection with the joy of redemption.[100]

Edwards's relationship to masochism's Kantian foundations lies in his location of pleasure in the experience of weakness and overwhelming divine power. This relationship is complemented by his preemptive refusal to follow other Enlightenment writers, including Kant but especially Adam Smith and Francis Hutcheson, in their development of the connection between affect, sympathy, and moral virtue.[101] Edwards's conversion narrative, in endorsing an affecting sense of God's excellence and personal abjection, appears to promote a proto-masochistic pleasure in self-disruption by staging a proliferation of the desire for abjection and a loss of self-control. Edwards thereby seems to posit a religious subject whose desires are premised on the same logic that, as Marianne Noble argues, would structure the more "properly" masochistic pleasures of nineteenth-century American sentimental literature, in which the religious discourse of eroticized submission to the divine is gradually transformed into a secular discourse of transcendent erotic submission.[102] However, as Sandra Gustafson's analysis suggests, Edwards has a more immediate and more vexed relationship to this sentimental literary tradition than Noble indicates.[103] Edwards's portraits of exemplary converts in the *Faithful Narrative* draw directly on English sentimentalism in its staging of scenes of death and suffering, and his conversion narrative adopts affect as a way of frustrating the development of a modern self, separable from God, for whom such suffering might be perverse.

The pleasurable affective experience of abjection that Edwards describes was in the process of becoming perverse through Enlightenment humanism's promotion of common sense as the basis for moral action and social cohesion. Theories of common sense, as developed by Smith, Hutcheson, and others, propose that our innate sympathetic response to suffering, combined with our natural inclination toward pleasure and away from pain, will prompt us to alleviate suffering in others. Edwards, in contrast, proposes that such sympathy is dependent on divine blessing or grace. In the absence of grace, our sense of pity is determined by the discrepancy between the sufferer's actual state and what we consider his or her proper state. Pity is thus a mode of judgment rather than a sensational or physical response. For example, Edwards's discussion of "self-love" and "private affections" in his *The Nature of True Virtue* (1765) takes a middle path between Scottish Common Sense

philosophers and cynics such as Bernard Mandeville. Edwards agrees that
sympathy is a basis for society and moral virtue, but he follows Mandeville's
account of sympathy as governed by the extent to which the sufferer's interests are aligned with the observer's and that sympathetic pain may be mixed
with pleasure.[104] In following Mandeville's proposal that sympathy produces
an ambivalent reaction to others' suffering, Edwards allows for Sade's eroticization of suffering, which demands a sentimental, Richardsonian interest in
the sufferer.[105] This ambivalence, in which the sympathetic experience of suffering excites simultaneous pity and delight, would play an important role in
the sexualization of erotic suffering.[106]

Edwards perfected his strategy of invoking and then intervening in the
connection between abjection, evangelical speech, and the development of a
Lockean liberal self in his *Treatise Concerning Religious Affections* (1746). As
several scholars note, *Religious Affections* reworks Locke's *Essay on Human
Understanding* by offering a measured evaluation of the intimate, embodied
relationship between individual affect, thought, and social order.[107] *Religious
Affections* explores how the affectionate speech of a body of believers can *productively* disorder civil and religious society. Disruptions in both individuals
and communities may, if properly discerned and managed, forward the work
of grace. Key to this evaluation is Edwards's extended metaphorical comparison of the disruptions of individual bodily function caused by religious affect
to the disruptions of New England's civil and ecclesiastical body caused by
revivalists' disorderly speech. Just as each convert should use his or her affecting sense of individual abjection as a means to evaluate his or her spiritual state, so must the church body in New England use the tumult caused by
the revivals to evaluate their divine destiny as a social and spiritual
community.

In *Religious Affections,* Edwards proposes that contemporary ministers
risk repeating the seventeenth-century New England Puritan failure to form
a wholly divine community if they do not distinguish spiritual corruption
from divine influence.[108] He evaluates the revivals' effect on New England as a
discrete community of believers, explicitly revisiting and partially sentimen-
talizing the seventeenth-century New England Puritan association of feminine weakness, wifely subjection, and maternal suffering with submission to
patriarchal government. Compressing the most vivid and literal descriptions
of physical suffering from Lamentations 1 into a single sentence, Edwards
asks his readers to imagine the daughter of Zion as she "lies on the ground, in
such piteous circumstances . . . with her garments rent, her face disfigured,

her nakedness exposed, her limbs broken, and weltering the blood of her own wounds, and in no wise able to arise." Edwards sentimentalizes the image of the suffering woman by condensing Lamentations' diffused and insistently metaphorical images of suffering into an intensely physical suffering felt by a single figure. Edwards complicates the sentimental trajectory of the trope by taking special care to associate the daughter of Zion's wounds with the blood of the "menstruous woman." Zion has "none to comfort her," Edwards writes, because she is tropologically related to the "menstruous woman" whose corrupting influence caused her to be shunned.[109] Rather than entirely discarding the ritual suffering and sacrifice of Levitical law in his sentimental image of the daughter of Zion, Edwards attempts to contain her communicative potential by making her both pitiful and unclean, exemplifying the dangers of improperly managed evangelical speech.

This introduction of sympathetic suffering into the trope of Zion's daughter locates Edwards in a long Christian discourse of abjection that Julia Kristeva aligns with the origin of psychological interiority. Reading Edwards's use of figures of abjection against Kristeva is especially helpful as a means of evaluating the ways in which revival affect might complicate psychoanalytic categories as transhistorical truths.[110] Edwards's use of a sentimentalized figure of abjection to delimit the boundaries of evangelical speech resembles what Kristeva, following Freud, calls the incorporation of Christian speech into a masochistic economy. Kristeva writes that early Christian writings introject the abject into the clean or pure Levitical self to create "a wholly different speaking subject," internally divided between the clean and the unclean.[111] Recalling that the root of "cadaver" is "*cadere*, to fall," Kristeva notes that this abject subject lives on a tenuous "border," mired in the substances that mark Edwards's daughter of Zion: a "wound with blood and pus . . . body fluids . . . defilement."[112] Speech, for this abject subject, becomes a means by which abjection can be ejected but maintained. The abject subject's perpetual irruption into speech is accompanied by a sense of pleasure at encountering or accessing the infinite through speech, because at the moment of speaking sin, the sinful self realizes and, to some degree, resolves its own sin.[113] At the same time, the passage also illustrates the anachronism of locating Edwards within a masochistic economy, as Edwards collapses the antithetical relationship Kristeva establishes between the masochist's use of *jouissance* for the benefit of symbolic or institutional power and the martyr's use of displaced *jouissance* to create a discourse that "resorb[s]" the subject into a religious community or divine Other.

The impossibility of locating Edwards's use of figures of abjection within either Oedipal or Kristevan categories, despite Edwards's sustained engagement with the philosophical and tropological concepts that would become central to the literary and psychological development of masochism, helps shed new light on accounts of the political or structural valence of masochistic practice.[114] Freud's masochist, for example, is never wholly or even mostly geared for the benefit of symbolic or institutional power but rather uses the structures of power to produce an inappropriate pleasure. He subverts institutional morality by demanding the infraction of a moral code as the prerequisite for the pleasure of punishment. Kristeva, accepting Freud's description of a masochistic economy but denying its capacity to subvert institutional morality, supposes that the masochist's apparent subversion actually works to maintain the structures of power that allow for masochistic pleasure. As a result, her proposition that the martyr's discourse of *jouissance* could in some way participate in a masochistic economy without, in some way, supporting institutional power sets an incredibly high bar.

In contrast to Kristeva's separation of the martyr's subversion from the masochist's support of those structures, Judith Butler and Leo Bersani propose that masochistic attachments to symbolic or institutional power can simultaneously reinforce and undermine that power.[115] Butler argues that the "regulatory regime[s]" that produce desire are themselves "produced by the cultivation of a certain attachment to the rule of subjection" and can therefore be resisted intrapsychically and through performance.[116] For Bersani, masochism's spectacular dramatization of the erotics of suffering encourages "an antifascist rethinking of power structures" that may ironically result in its own "self-immolating" destruction.[117] Bersani's notion of sexuality itself as fundamentally masochistic and marked by self-shattering (*ébranlement*) offers a productive movement away from masochism as a drive toward a broader notion of a masochistic antirelational refusal of sociality. This refusal cannot be valorized politically but does serve to break up psychic formations or specific ideological superstructures. Bersani follows Laplanche's return to the notion of primary masochism in his account of the infant's receipt of painfully inscrutable messages, or "enigmatic signifiers," from a sexual other (e.g., a parent) and translation of those messages into an interpersonal, social context. If we accept this broader notion of masochism's ability to make the psychic pleasures of pain explicit and public, we can hear an echo of Edwards's negotiation of revivalist sympathetic public discourse.[118]

Although the discontinuities between Edwards's models of mind and

heart and modern psychoanalytic models of subjectivity and subject formation are too great to allow for analogy, it may be worth considering how Bersani and Laplanche's notion of masochism recapitulates the drama of
conversion. The speech of Edwards's ideal convert, issuing from a place of
suspended certitude about salvation, resembles Bersani's masochist's public
self-shattering, inasmuch as they both figure moments of intense emotional
self-abasement and self-erasure as necessarily forgotten or moved away from
and yet also necessarily remembered and repeated. Edwards's uncontrollable
weeping describes a moment of ideal self-dissolution. Conversion entails internal, affective, psychic struggle but is primarily a relational experience between the self and the divine. The convert's most important "existence," in
other words, lies in the relationship between the soul and a transcendent
God, the ultimate "Other" for whom all works are meaningless for salvation.
Nevertheless, it is in their evangelism, properly managed by editorial discre-
tion and bodily self-control, that converts become significant by entering
into a millennial Christian narrative.

Inasmuch as Edwards's use of the evangelical discourse of abjection pre-
figures what Bersani and Butler identify as the "self-immolating" or resistant
quality of attachment to subjection, its potential to disrupt existing hierarchies of speech is necessarily entangled with its attempt to maintain those
hierarchies, as its promotion of abjection worked in and through its management of lay preaching and publication. Whether in his *Faithful Narrative*, his
own conversion narrative, or his later treatises on conversion and revivalism,
the difficulty with evaluating Edwards's use of a discourse of abjection as entirely in favor of or opposed to the maintenance of institutional power derives from Edwards's navigation of a revival discourse in which the form of
subjectivity invoked through that discourse was itself unstable and contested,
helping establish a white male revolutionary liberal subject as well as African
and Native subjects and communities. The radical promise of affective revival
was tied up with its incorporation into public ministerial practice. Edwards's
attempt to contain the communicative potential of an affective performance
of abjection participated in the revivals' eventual contribution to the rearetic-
ulation of power along new liberal republican lines but also provided Native
and African Americans theological principles and public models for stabiliz-
ing and managing affective religious communities in the face of increased
skepticism and hostility.[119]

Subsequent chapters follow two generations of Christian social reformers
as they moved away from church-based social reform and toward

nonsectarian radical evangelical organizing in the public sphere.[120] Many of these reformers read Edwards's work; even those who did not would have been influenced by his epistemology of conversion. In particular, the cultural reverberations of eighteenth-century notions of conversion, suffering, and publicity resound in nineteenth-century developments of race, including racializations of religious abjection, speech, and publication.

CHAPTER 2

_____

Indian Abjection in the Public Sphere

In January 1836, William Apess, a Pequot, adopted Mashpee, and former Methodist preacher, twice delivered his "Eulogy on King Philip" at the Odeon, a luxurious Boston lecture hall that was a short distance from the Brattle Street Congregational Church where Jonathan Edwards gave his first recorded revival. The "Eulogy," as part of its celebration of Indian martial and moral virtue and denunciation of English creole violence, took issue with an emerging racial conception of Indian drunkenness or what Edwards and his disciple, David Brainerd, had called Indians' "drunken and Pagan howlings." Apess's long missionary career helped him recognize a new wrinkle in the Euro-American view of Indian drunkenness. Drunkenness had long denoted Indian abjection in the absence of European missionary sympathy and connoted human abjection in the absence of God's grace. In the late eighteenth and early nineteenth centuries, however, the denotative and connotative value of drunkenness grew apart. Drunkenness and paganism, wedded together in the animalistic practice of inarticulate "howlings," became more closely linked to an intrinsic racial identity rather than to faith or religious practice.

As the "Eulogy" demonstrates, Apess was already in the process of crafting an Indian public subject through temperate ascetic self-control. By using reformist Methodist rhetoric and organizing to create an Indian subject capable of full participation in the Early Republic's urban and print public spheres, he modified the tactics of eighteenth-century Indian Christian writing and anticipated the more militant nineteenth-century rhetoric of Indian resistance. Moreover, Apess's use of abjection developed within medico-scientific discourse and humanitarian reform discourse to construct an oppositional Indian Christian male identity in the public sphere.

By the time he took the stage at the Odeon, Apess was a veteran of the

sectarian and political public spheres in New York and New England. He had
entered the world of print through *A Son of the Forest* (1829, 1831), a hybrid
conversion narrative and political tract that draws on reformist Methodist
temperance discourse, revivalist accounts of affective conversion, and public
proposals for education, military and Indian reform. Appearing regularly in
Connecticut and Massachusetts, Apess had, since 1833, focused his efforts on
Mashpee sovereignty, publishing two books, delivering several lectures, and
organizing nonsectarian, multiracial camp meetings where he spoke and
preached as the founder and leader of the "Free and United Church." In these
later pursuits, Apess was "much caressed" by Frederick Douglass, William
Garrison, and other prominent reformers whose inclination to support Native American political organizing had been frustrated by Cherokee slave-
holding. Like Douglass, Garrison, and the Grimké sisters, who would mount
the Odeon's stage two years later, Apess's participation in public-sphere political reform was an outgrowth of his earlier participation in sectarian preaching, publication, and organizing.[1] But reformist Methodism did not simply
provide a training ground for Apess's later Mashpee organizing. It enabled
him to challenge national sectarian and political organizations' movement
away from ecumenical and egalitarian principles.

In the 1820s and 1830s, the prominence of divisions within Methodism
led Apess's contemporaries to carefully distinguish him from his more mainstream brethren. As the *American Monthly Review* noted in 1832, Apess was
not simply a Methodist but "a Methodist of the independent order"; that
same year, Samuel Drake made much the same distinction in his *Indian Biography*, writing that "[t]he Rev. Wm. Apes, of the Independent Methodist
order . . . is preaching occasionally among us."[2] The distinction was even
more important for Apess himself, as his account of the nexus between labor,
property, race, and religion in the Early Republic engaged key reformist
Methodist concerns. Apess's first publication, the 1829 edition of his *A Son of
the Forest*, was particularly marked by a strain of reformist Methodist temperance rhetoric.

This temperance rhetoric engages with the concept of abjection in the
model of conversion narrative put forth by Jonathan Edwards, playing with
its central tension between silence and speech. As Chapter 1 describes, Edwards faced critics who suggested that the problems of revival lay in religious
emotions themselves or in the characters of religious converts. Edwards
countered that limitations on circulation could allow for salvific and dramatic performances of emotion, a proposal dramatized by his letter

describing his weeping while "shut up" in a room. Apess takes up the notion of Indian abjection to resist limitations on circulation that were grounded in emerging notions of racial difference, rather than rank. *A Son of the Forest* was one of a series of politically active, religiously dissenting evangelical conversion narratives by people of color, including Samson Occom, Olaudah Equiano, John Marrant, and Jarena Lee, that sprang from "Awakening" revivalism.[3] Like many of his fellow evangelicals of color, Apess engages in providentialist tropes such as bodily dispossession, strange illness, and recovery that marked eighteenth-century revival conversion narrative. Evangelicals of color were often more directly influenced by Whitefield's model of "compulsive" expression and circulation than by Edwards's recommendation for more limited circulation, but their public expressions were, as Occom puts it, "Constrained" by conditions not of their own choosing. They thereby effectively labored under the expectation of limited circulation similar to that which Edwards recommended.[4] Apess negotiated this constraint by adopting a type of reformist temperance rhetoric that defines the material practice of the convert as ascetic and links conversion to anticolonial resistance. "Intemperance" becomes the master trope for the white destruction of Indian communities, while "temperate" Indian public subjects control their bodily drives, emotions, and, most important, their labor, including the labor of publicity itself.

The mouth, from which speech issues and drink enters, embodies what Apess calls his "great trial" as a preacher. Apess's service as "mouth for God" becomes a crucial metaphor for his writing and publishing as an Indian Christian.[5] Characterizing himself as God's embodied vocal instrument, Apess announces the triumph of divine word over corrupt flesh. Reformist Methodist temperance writing helped shape Apess's presentation of his public speech and writing. A broadly conceived model of temperance shaped reformist Methodist print publicity and economic critique, and Apess used this model of temperance to challenge the racialization of intemperance in earlier sectarian and popular nineteenth-century evangelical temperance narratives. This reformist discourse may have been a remnant of Federalist-era readings of the individual body as a microcosm of the body politic, but Apess used it in a new way by rejecting its paternalism and insisting on reciprocal responsibilities for laborer and employer alike. Apess's revisions of his temperance prose for his 1831 edition of *A Son of the Forest* obscure his connections to reformist Methodism and place more weight on his innovative use of sentiment. These changes reflect transformations in reformist

Methodism as well as his own development as an author and orator in the broader evangelical public.[6]

The Temperate Style of Reformist Methodism

Historians and literary critics have acclaimed Apess's speeches as almost unparalleled triumphs of Native oration in the U.S. public sphere. But, some six years earlier, Apess gave at least one other, heretofore unremarked oration whose circumstances suggest a more regular appearance of Indian speakers in religious contexts. That oration, on a Sunday in late June 1830, featured Apess as the third and final preacher at a daylong fundraiser for the newly organized reformist Associate Methodist Church in Manhattan, just east of City Hall. By his own account, Apess was already an experienced and well-traveled Methodist preacher, but he had received his preaching license from New York's Methodist Society (a more established reformist Methodist church) only one year before. Apess entered the world of print at approximately the same time, shepherding his first publication, the autobiographical *A Son of the Forest*, through a New York print shop in July 1829.

If he had been living in the city, Apess may have joined in the public acts of piety, including mass prayer meetings and swelling church attendance, that followed the severe winter of 1828. Heralded as a season of revival in the evangelical press, the meetings helped lay the groundwork for a season of radical labor organizing: the spring, summer, and fall of 1829 would see the development of the Working Men's movement, Francis "Fanny" Wright's and Robert Dale Owen's lectures, and a flurry of publications from associated labor and Freethinking presses. The Associate Methodist Church was itself a radical milieu. Apess's fellow preachers that Sunday, William Summersides and an unnamed colleague, were missionaries from the Primitive Methodist Connexion, an English sect whose history helped ground Eric Hobsbawm's interpretation of working-class evangelism as a public strategy for resisting state classification and dispossession. Summersides and his companion had recently arrived in the country to build the Connexion's North American membership and, like Apess, had good reason to hope for a warm welcome among New York's reformists. Primitive Methodism's founders were originally inspired by the brief English sojourn of extravagantly uncouth American revivalist Lorenzo Dow, who was, in the 1820s, a senior elder in the Methodist Society. The Primitive Methodists' appearance at the Associate

Methodist Church suggests a loose transatlantic association of sectarians organized in opposition to the increasingly bourgeois accoutrements and interests of formerly dissenting or disestablished religious societies.[7]

Apess funded his work and supported his family by peddling religious
books, a common Methodist itinerant practice he would continue throughout his public life. In the lean season of 1829, he distributed and sold *A Son of
the Forest* after his preaching and speaking engagements. Reformist Methodist events helped Apess reach a receptive audience. This was especially important because, at fifty cents, his small volume, with its limited print run,
cost four times as much as the far grander books churned out in stereotype
by the Methodist Episcopal Church's (MEC) Book Concern.[8] Apess wove reformist Methodist rhetoric into his work. His lengthy account of his departure from the MEC, in particular, could have been pulled from the pages of
reformist periodicals. That account decried the MEC's foundation on "*monarchial* principles" while applauding the Methodist Society's "found[ing] on
republican" principles and recommended that all Methodists "contend" for
"*mutual rights*," a phrase that, in its service as the title of the most explicitly
political reformist Methodist periodical, was synonymous with the reform
movement. If George Whitefield's preaching tour provided a material and
ideological basis for the U.S. Revolutionary War by linking the colonies
through print and prayer, it sometimes seems like Methodist dissidents returned the favor by navigating reform in the language of revolution. For
many disenfranchised and otherwise abjected Americans, the emotional im-
pact of revolutionary rhetoric was intensified by the revolution's vexed legacy,
as the new degrees of freedom for some fell short of the revolution's most
radical promises. This was certainly true for Apess, who linked "mutual
rights" and Indian rights by using this quintessentially reformist description
of his dispute with the MEC to cap his chronicle of the wrongs that the
wealthy committed against "unoffending" Indians. He described social, legal,
and economic oppression of Indians as the result of unchecked power and
self-interest, adapting reformist Methodist arguments against the MEC's "tyrannical" government to build public support for Indian rights under an implicitly tyrannical U.S. government.[9]

The reformist Methodist public has a vestibulary relationship to both the
MEC and subsequent nineteenth-century political reform movements such
as abolitionism. As Sandra Gustafson writes of the nineteenth-century public
sphere more generally, it is difficult to differentiate "between a dominant
'public' and a resistant 'counterpublic'" among early nineteenth-century

Methodists. While there may have been sporadic resolutions into a dominant MEC public and a reformist Methodist counterpublic, the highly mobile character of public religious activity prevents any simple description of the reformist Methodist public as a counterpublic. One complication derives from the MEC's marginalization of traditional Methodist forms of worship and behavior. In the eighteenth century, the Methodist style that evolved in England's North American colonies helped define Methodism's contribution to the development of the public sphere as a disruption of aristocratic hierarchies of oral performance and textual authority. Early Methodism was, as Apess has it, notoriously "*noisy*," a phrase epitomized by eighteenth-century camp revivals, in which participants were marked by bodily habits of dress, prayer, singing, and reading. Early Methodism was also remarkably plural. Depending on participants, Methodist worship combined elements from English, African, Indian, and other folk or vernacular customs. Though grounded in oratory, Methodism developed mutually reinforcing relationships between oral performance and print. It contributed to the development of the print public through its innovations in publicity (most famously surrounding Whitefield's field meetings) and explosion of lay conversion narratives, journals, prophetic tales, and other accounts that circulated widely in print and manuscript. Early Methodist print culture was ephemeral, promotional, fractious, declamatory, and contentious.[10]

Recent critics agree that Apess was attracted to Methodism because of its incorporation of such popular, vernacular, and prophetic traditions. Apess's critique of the civil, ecclesiastical, and economic control exerted by a white plutocracy, they suggest, was grounded in his early experience with Methodism's use of ecumenical practice and rhetoric to challenge New England's Congregationalist and Presbyterian establishment, amplified by his use of Native and African American spiritual traditions. Methodism in New England had several appeals to the poor, people of color, and others among the colonial dispossessed: the glamour and fame of Methodist leadership, the sect's relative openness to Indian and African spiritual practices, and dissenters' opposition to established churches all aligned Methodists with the lived experience of social and economic marginalization. This argument is especially useful for understanding Apess's historical relationship to Methodist worship as a youth in Massachusetts, which was, from 1818 to 1833, the sole remaining state with an effectively established church. In this period, Methodists in Massachusetts likely preserved a traditional style that offered Apess a firmer position from which to challenge a Congregational mainstream.

Other states began disestablishing their churches earlier. In those states, Methodists and other formerly dissenting sects began to compete directly for converts in the new religious marketplace. To attract wealthier members, Methodists promoted humanitarian rhetoric over accounts of persecution and increasingly restricted authoritative preaching and writing to those who endured travel and self-willed, ascetic exertion in support of the faith, rather than persecution or marginalization per se. Eventually, with the rise of settled Methodist pastorates, even this ascetic rhetoric tapered off. In the "disestablished" states Apess worked and preached in as an adult, and in Massachusetts after 1833, the MEC's status as one church among many allowed market forces to guide changes in Methodist discourse. This ushered in a period of experimentation that temporarily increased the heterogeneity of Methodist rhetorical and aesthetic styles. Ultimately, growing racism within the church and changes in state religious law precipitated Apess's departure from Methodist organizing. However, during this period of experimentation, the several varieties of reformist Methodism served as reservoirs of dissent, allowing Apess and other members of the colonial dispossessed a foothold in the public sphere.

Working in this unsettled religious and political atmosphere, Apess engaged a reformist Methodist temperance discourse valorizing ascetic labor to develop a stable oppositional Indian male public subject. Writing a generation after the U.S. Revolution, Apess posited this ascetic, temperate subject as the heir to revolutionary idealism. Contrasting the debauched state of the army during his service in the War of 1812 with a rhetoric of marshal sacrifice, Apess imagines ascetic self-control as enabling two linked ideals: temperate Indian resistance and public recognitions of the civic equality of the poor. Apess's endorsement of bodily self-control would have been relatively familiar to Awakening revivalists such as Edwards, as would his negotiation of the difficulties of print circulation, but the role of ascetic discourse in mediating Apess's opportunities for publication and circulation was not. It was by narrating self-control that Apess could transform a putatively "Indian" experience of suffering and abjection into the basis for public-sphere speech and organizing. Operating in a manner that would resound in the nineteenth-century rhetoric of Indian resistance, Apess's early work reverses the polarities of savagery and civilization in reformist temperance discourse. Apess's narrative of ascetic labor thereby allows him to enter a reformist Methodist public while ambivalently embracing a notion of Indian abjection, which he locates in a ruined, feminized private sphere.

Apess's early prose evinces the reformist Methodist public's "third way" as an evanescent vestibular public. Stylistically, reformist Methodism rested somewhere between an eighteenth-century traditional Methodist public style and the emerging liberal-rational polite evangelical style that would dominate nineteenth-century Methodist publishing and prose. Methodism, notoriously fractious, saw the origins of its "reform" movement in late 1784, when the MEC organized alongside other new national political and religious institutions as a centralized, hierarchical national body. Critics accused the new national MEC of abetting or acceding to pent-up demands, among some local congregations, for a movement away from the principle of spiritual equality. The MEC accommodated slavery, segregated worship, and otherwise institutionalized legal and public-sphere restrictions on the participation of women and African Americans. This shift participated in the more general disintegration of intensely ecumenical New Light evangelism in favor of an exclusionary sectarianism, conformity, and centralization aligned with the demands of the state and market, exemplifying Habermas's model of the collapse of radical public-sphere organizing in the hands of politically accomodationist leadership.[11]

Sustained reformist Methodist organizing in opposition to the MEC first developed in urban African American communities from Baltimore to Boston, where, as part of the formation of independent African Methodist churches and publishing houses, it helped create an African American identity. The New York reformist Methodist community began when black congregants of the John Street MEC "mother church" began organizing separate meetings and eventually the Zion church, still within the MEC. In 1819, Zion trustees made the politic decision to call as their preacher William Stilwell, a white MEC itinerant and nephew of a prominent John Street trustee. One year later, simmering discontent with MEC centralization, segregation, and bourgeois aesthetics caused new schisms. When the John Street church underwent a "lavish refurbishing," including curtains, a carpeted altar, and expensive decorations, some congregants took umbrage at what they saw as a material expression of the MEC's movement away from its "primitive" principles. Led by Stilwell, about 300 members separated and formed the Methodist Society, which Apess would later join. After Stilwell announced his intent to leave the MEC, James Varick and other Zion deacons, worried about their own autonomy within the MEC, decided to separate independently. They published a Zion discipline and welcomed other African Methodist congregations into their fold, retaining Stilwell until they could find a suitable replacement. In 1822, Stilwell and other Society elders ordained Varick and

Abraham Thompson as the first elders of New York's African Methodist Episcopal (AME) church.

Although the Methodist Society was intimately associated with the Zion church, neither the *Friendly Visitor* nor Stilwell's history of the church discussed the connection. This was due in part to the strength and independence of New York's African Methodist community but also to the difficulty of recognizing such connections when the MEC was instituting new ideological norms of authoritative religious experience. In the late eighteenth century, some urban Methodists moved away from their traditional public style by refraining from ecstatic bodily performances and discounting their divine origins. In the early nineteenth century, the MEC adopted a liberal public style that helped feminize ecstatic bodily performance by associating authoritative religious expression with bodily self-management and a tightly controlled, professional prose governed by what Susan Juster calls "the rationalism and empiricism" of "enlightened discourse."[12] The MEC also moved away from the "intimate self-disclosure and emotionalism" favored by artisanal Methodists and racialized the African spiritual practices that had contributed to the development of the traditional Methodist style, much to the chagrin of African Methodist elders, who were attempting to transform AME practice along the same lines.[13] The traditional Methodist style thus could mark even white reformist Methodists and exclude them from the "privilege of abstraction" sometimes granted to propertied white men in the liberal public sphere. Although MEC leaders rejected the public performance of ecstatic spiritual practice and other forms of somatic piety by subjecting them to rational analysis, they created the MEC hierarchy as a white fraternal community within which sentiment could flow freely. By limiting participation in the MEC hierarchy to itinerant preachers, they privileged ascetic suffering and a willed endurance of travel more accessible to white men. Itinerancy, figured as an alternative to a feminizing domestic life, encouraged Methodist travels into "the wilderness" that extended and racialized national domestic space. Itinerancy and oppositional politics could coincide, as it did in local Methodist resistance to Cherokee removal, but even then they underlined public restrictions on the movement of men of color.[14]

In the 1820s and 1830s, religious publishing houses such as the Methodist Book Concern and American Tract Society developed mass-media publication and distribution techniques that propagated the new evangelical public style, with Methodist Book Concern director Nathan Bangs most responsible for instituting it. Beginning with his exclusion of "curious tales, wonderful narratives, and miraculous phenomena" from the new *Methodist Magazine* (1818–30), the Book Concern's periodicals and newspapers promoted "reason," gentility, and cultivation in an attempt to showcase what Bangs called the MEC's solidarity with "the cause of literature and science." The MEC responded to reformist organizing, along with similar agitation in Baltimore and Philadelphia, by closing their presses to advocates of reform. In response, reformers developed separate public institutions, including itinerant lecturing, corresponding societies, pamphlets, and the three periodicals that, prior to the *AME Magazine* and *Christian Recorder*, made up the bulk of reformist Methodist publishing: Philadelphia's *Wesleyan Repository* (1822–24), Baltimore's *Mutual Rights* (1824–30), and New York's *Friendly Visitor* (1825). Some, such as reformist Baltimore Methodist minister Alexander M'Kaine's *History and Mystery of the Methodist Episcopacy* (1827), echoed the sensationalism of the era's populist exposés of large institutions such as the Roman Catholic Church and Bank of England.[15] However, because Nathan Bangs and the MEC press readily marginalized these works as "strange" or "anomalous production[s]," most reformist prose took another tack.[16] Reformist periodicals, for example, combined an uncontroversial selection of surprising tales, incidental literature, and spiritual guidance common to sectarian magazines of the day with reformist denunciations of luxury, unjust labor practices, and tyranny.[17] Bangs's position as a leading anti-reformer meant that reformist Methodists could not entirely embrace the MEC's new liberal-rational style if they hoped to distinguish themselves from the MEC. However, because the Book Concern successfully expanded the evangelical reading public, albeit unevenly and irregularly, the MEC's success demanded they selectively adopt its principles if they hoped to reach a broader reading public.[18]

A notice for Apess's appearance at the Associate Methodist Church, printed in the *New York Evangelist*, illustrates this paradox at the heart of the reformist Methodist public. Apess's association with New York's reformist Methodist community aligned him with the most progressive, economically radical elements of Methodist reform, but their exclusion from the Book Concern pushed them toward the Charybdis of a business-minded but nonsectarian evangelical print culture, epitomized by the *Evangelist*. These nonsectarian evangelical publications, committed to Finneyite revivalism and the promotion of a paternalistic Christian and republican ideal of disinterested benevolence through commercially oriented participation in the public sphere, have often been understood as accommodating radical utopianism to

THE

𝔉𝔯𝔦𝔢𝔫𝔡𝔩𝔶 𝔙𝔦𝔰𝔦𝔱𝔬𝔯,

BEING A COLLECTION OF

SELECT AND ORIGINAL PIECES,

INSTRUCTIVE AND ENTERTAINING,

SUITABLE TO BE READ IN ALL FAMILIES

NEW-YORK:

PRINTED FOR, AND SOLD BY, WILLIAM M. STILWELL, NO. 108 CHRISTIE-STREET.

J. C. Totten, Printer.

1825.

Figure 1. Title page, Stilwell, *Friendly Visitor*, 1825. General Research Division, The New York Public Library, Astor, Lenox, and Tilden Foundations.

capitalist ideology. Apess, like other reformers, had to use the commercial public sphere to achieve publicity while relying on gaps in MEC relationships with the print trade for production and consumption. Stilwell, for example, used MEC printer John Totten to publish and distribute the *Friendly Visitor*. Apess used Methodist portraitist John Paradise, whose portraiture had appeared on several MEC frontispieces and in Bangs's *Methodist Magazine*, to paint and engrave the frontispiece of the elegant second edition of *A Son of the Forest* (1831). To print that edition, as well as his pamphlet *The Increase of the Kingdom of Christ: A Sermon* (1831), Apess selected George F. Bunce, a nonsectarian and not exclusively religious printer who had recently worked for, among others, the Zion congregation and the newfound Baptist Missionary Society.[19]

The *Evangelist*'s description of Apess as "of the Pequod tribe of Indians" helps establish the terms of Apess's participation in the reformist Methodist public. While Apess would continue to promote himself as a "missionary *to* the Pequot tribe" for at least the next few years—he advertised his 1832 lecture "On the Principles of Civilization" in Boston's Boylston Hall under those auspices—Apess's appeal as a reformist Methodist in New York hinged on his even closer self-identification with a Native identity that was something of a double-edged sword.[20] It tapped into a deep reservoir of public fascination with Native Americans in general, and especially Pequots, in and around their tribal homeland and among Native audiences.[21] At the same time, it limited Apess to the traditional missionary roles of fundraising for itinerancy and church building, frustrating his engagement with other issues. His temperance narrative allowed him to address a broader spectrum of concerns, including questions of colonization, by redefining the relationship between Indian identity and publicity.[22]

Temperance writing was a vital site for developing the concept of race and racial identity. Midcentury Washingtonian temperance discourse helped transform the concept of race by describing it as an internal, emotional, and intellectual trait, and temperance organizing helped define African American community in the early and mid-1800s. African American temperance organizers offered Apess an important model by using notions of "positive collective incorporation" rather than a disembodied abstraction of citizenship to expand the black public. They did this in two ways: first, by creating a "temperate" collective body that resisted public ownership and functioned independently in the public sphere and, second, by presenting white racism and African enslavement as forms of intemperance. Apess followed African

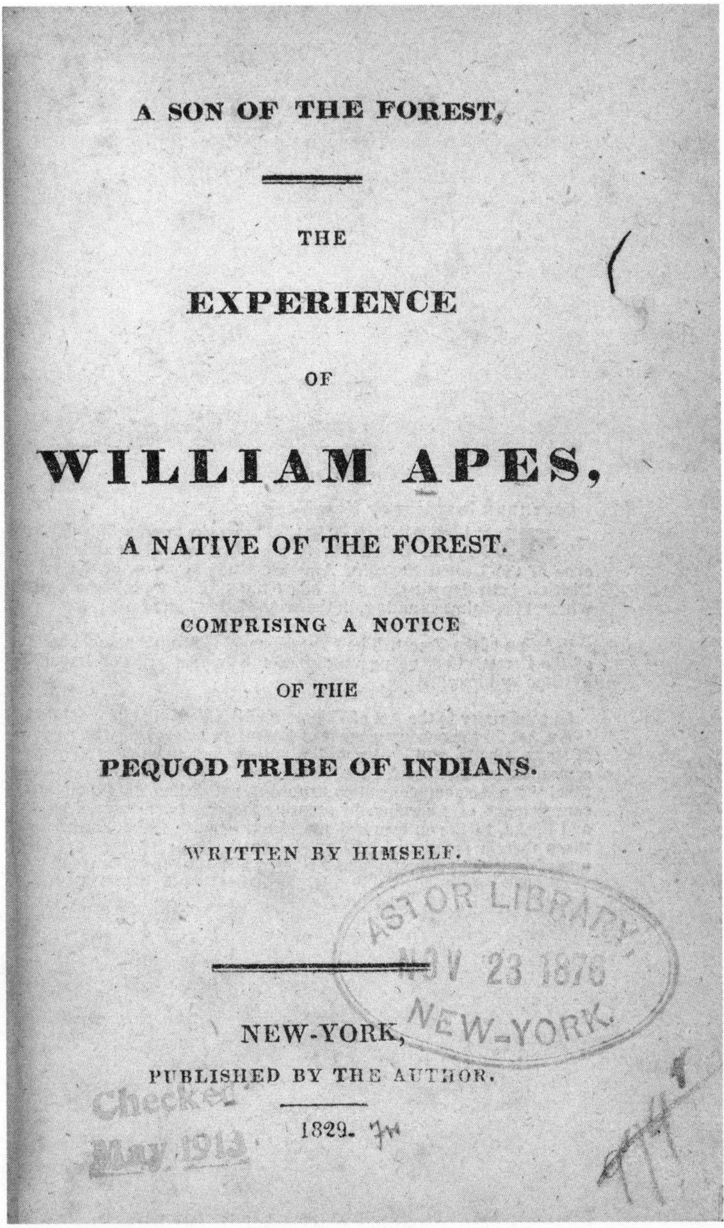

A SON OF THE FOREST,

THE

EXPERIENCE

OF

WILLIAM APES,

A NATIVE OF THE FOREST.

COMPRISING A NOTICE

OF THE

PEQUOD TRIBE OF INDIANS.

WRITTEN BY HIMSELF.

NEW-YORK,

PUBLISHED BY THE AUTHOR.

1829.

Figure 2. Title page, Apess, *A Son of the Forest*, 1829. Rare Books Division, The New York Public Library, Astor, Lenox, and Tilden Foundations.

Figure 3. Frontispiece, Apess, *A Son of the Forest*, 1831. Rare Books Division, The New York Public Library, Astor, Lenox, and Tilden Foundations.

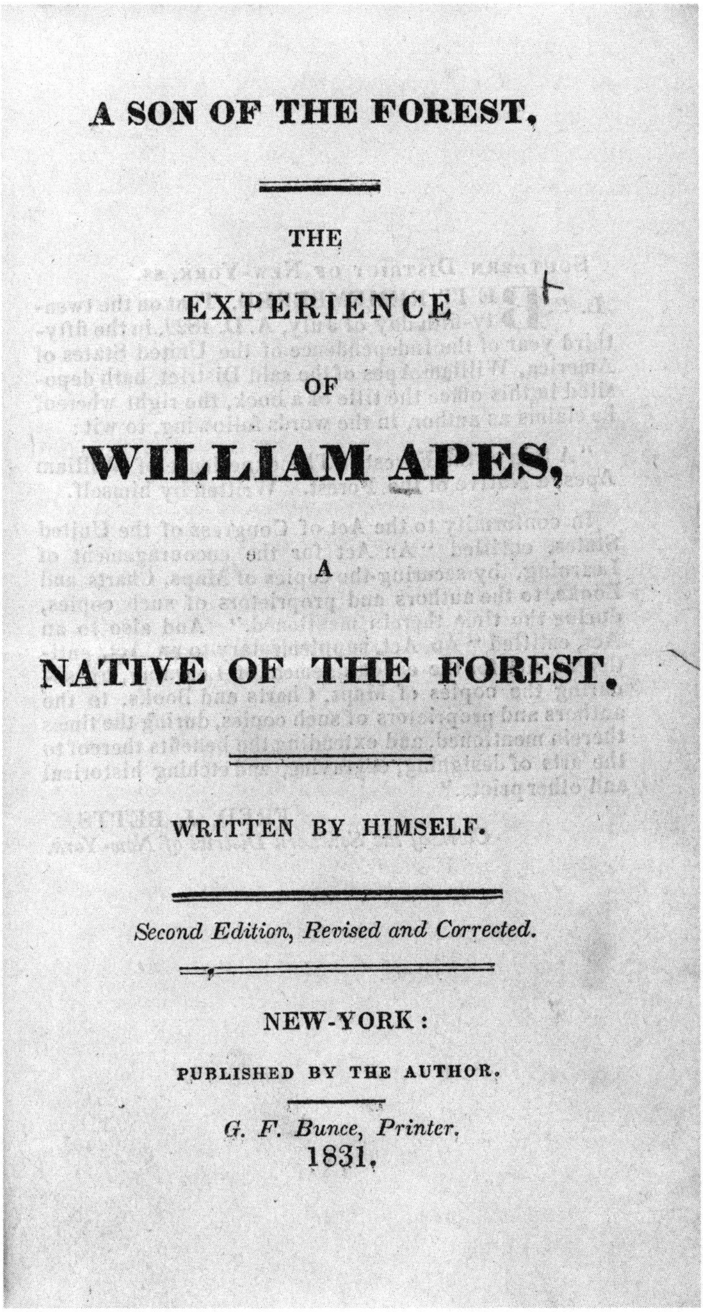

A SON OF THE FOREST,

THE

EXPERIENCE

OF

WILLIAM APES,

A

NATIVE OF THE FOREST.

WRITTEN BY HIMSELF.

Second Edition, Revised and Corrected.

NEW-YORK:

PUBLISHED BY THE AUTHOR.

G. F. Bunce, Printer.
1831.

Figure 4. Title page, Apess, *A Son of the Forest*, 1831. Rare Books Division, The New York Public Library, Astor, Lenox, and Tilden Foundations.

American precedent by reappropriating a racialized identity and redetermining its political content but found it difficult to construct a comparable collective corporate Indian identity within a religious body that, at least until his work at Mashpee, lacked a substantial Indian presence.[23]

Like his reformist African American brethren, Apess also had to overcome the racial connotations of intemperance among evangelical audiences. As several critics note, romantic Indian novels, melodramas, and historical fictions in the period caricatured the drunken Indian as brutish and abject to help romanticize the white "inheritance" of Indian land. These romances reenvisioned U.S. political and social borders by staging spectacles of Indian disappearance in the face of U.S. modernization. In Cooper's novels, for example, rum transformed Chingachgook into "a Christian beast" and destroyed the Indian "race" to serve the "cupidity" of "the white man." These genres' images of Indian drunkenness have eclipsed the development of the trope in evangelical temperance narratives, which were at least as popular in the period. Evangelical temperance tracts, like their romantic counterparts, project bodily drives onto Indian and other nonwhite figures but do so largely along religious and cultural lines. Evangelical tracts from the first four decades of the nineteenth century attributed drunkenness to a "brutish" lack of bodily control associated with religious and cultural difference, but widespread acceptance of biblical accounts of a common human ancestry prevented absolute racial division of the sort that would be seen later in the century. Images of intemperance in tracts from 1800 to 1840 speak most clearly to the anxieties of missionary organizations whose evangelizing projects accompanied U.S. and English imperial expansion. In the early 1800s, evangelical tracts coalesced around liberal denunciations of individual self-corruption and elite republican demands for social cohesion, offering sensationalist psychological explanations of intemperance as a descent into brutishness caused by "animal stimulus" or nervous "excitement." In the 1820s and 1830s, the tracts participated in broader public political organizing and moved toward an inchoate association of "brutishness" with racially inflected religious difference. One widely reprinted tract used to form the Massachusetts Society for the Suppression of Intemperance, for example, figures drunkenness through a pastiche of sensationalized biblical and Oriental religious practices. Serving as a "graven image, or . . . false god," drink is the nation's "grand Moloch," with "four thousand self-devoted human victims" "immolated every year upon its altars." This sacrifice, the tract concluded, was tantamount to the "sanguinary rights" of the "Hindoo" at

Juggernaut. The resulting "ravages" of drunken "brutes" and the associated "havoc of property" threatened the security of national political and economic structures. Defining intemperance through notions of savagery, brutishness, and heathenism, evangelical temperance tracts from the 1820s and 1830s worked to stabilize social order and class division within white communities around the exclusion of the uncivilized non-Christian from the national and religious body.[24]

Evangelical temperance tracts' preference for marking differences of cultural and religious practice and belief, rather than the romantic preference for embodied racial difference, may simply be a matter of ideological focus, but that ideological focus was especially vexed for Methodists. By associating intemperance with irrational, emotional religious practice, evangelical temperance tracts reflect a concern with the embodied forms of worship that were characteristic of a traditional Methodist style. Mirroring the movement of revivalism from the obscure to the powerful, intemperance "extend[s] its ravages [and] triumphs" from the abject ("the refuse of society") up the social "rank[s]" to the minister and lawmaker. It destabilizes the nation by destroying sympathetic bonds between men, husbands and wives, and fathers and children. This characterization of intemperance troubled reformist Methodists, in particular, whose success in the religious marketplace depended on their capacity to distinguish themselves from the MEC by invoking a traditional Methodist style while avoiding accusations of spiritual excess.

AME leader Richard Allen, in his posthumously published 1833 autobiography, treads this narrow path in much the same way as Apess. Allen historicized the development of his breakaway AME church by tracing the roots of a reformist Methodist public to a pamphlet circulated at the MEC founding conference. The pamphlet, with a sharp wit, repetition, and rhythmic scriptural wordplay characteristic of a traditional Methodist style, announced "when the Methodists were no people, then they were a people; and now they have become a people, they were no people."[25] The pamphlet defined reformist principles in its denunciation of hierarchy, wealth, and respectability as stumbling blocks. Excerpting from the pamphlet allowed Allen to integrate the pamphlet's "outsider" critique into his own temperate prose. In distinction to the pamphlet itself, Allen maintained a direct and factual tone, standard grammar, and straightforward organization that helped secure his professional status and establish the respectability of the AME church.[26]

Like Allen, Maria W. Stewart, and other black Methodist writers, Apess's measured irony, insistence on his own logic, and rhetorical sincerity connect

his prose to a "temperate" reformist Methodist public style. My description of
this style as temperate reflects Methodist reformers' selective importation of
some traditional or "primitive" Methodist practices into the well-structured,
moderate rhetoric characteristic of a liberal-rational MEC style. This style
went well beyond prose composition. In their magazines and corresponding
societies, reformist Methodists promoted a broadly conceived, ascetic notion
of temperance encompassing a range of relationships between the body and
the world. These relationships, in revivalistic fashion, enabled the self to transcend abject bodily desire and commune with the divine. As articulated in
"On Christian Temperance" from *Mutual Rights*, temperance is a spiritual
inclination rather than "a mere restraint," allowing for an ecstatic "communion with [God]" as a source of all "enjoyments" and a refusal of all "animal
gratifications." In their condemnation of bodily desires that counteracted divine communion, reformist Methodists perpetuated what Betsy Erkkila describes as eighteenth-century temperance ideology's "conceptualization of
the body as a source of agency and responsibility," combining it, for political
purposes, with even earlier notions of intemperance as a form of apostasy.[27]

In the reformist Methodist public, temperance was mediated by public
discourse in all its forms, including reading, writing, and performance. Each
of the reformist periodicals' introductory statements argue that politically ef-
ficacious public organizing requires both a temperate prose style and a temperate emotional state. For example, the *Wesleyan Repository*, edited by
humanitarian reformer William Stockton, weds humoral associations of an
intemperate "hot" style with newer emotional terms from sensationalist psychology when it warns it will refuse to publish "communications . . . dictated
by an over-heated zeal." Stockton associates public debate of church reform
with the embodied social effect of humanitarian reform more generally, insisting that "temperate discussion" will never "lead the blind into a ditch, or
turn the lame out of the way."[28]

In *A Son of the Forest*, Apess helped establish Indian respectability by
drawing on reformist periodicals' temperate style but still had to wrestle with
the way that even reformist Methodist periodicals depicted Indians as un-
suited for some forms of public-sphere engagement. *A Son of the Forest*'s
many parallels between Indians and Methodists take on reformist Methodist
periodicals' missionary tracts. These missionary tracts liken Indian and
Methodist religious practice but leave little room for Indian participation in
Indian religious or political reform, let alone Methodist reform. The longest
reformist Methodist missionary tract, "Lectures on Missions to American

Indians," links church, temperance, and missionary reform through a sensationalist psychology in which nervous excitement produces socially proscribed behaviors. Published serially in the *Wesleyan Repository*, the "Lectures" were first delivered by prominent reformer, preacher, and political activist Nicholas Snethen, who would later contribute to and edit *Mutual Rights*. Snethen associated "the peculiarities of [Indian] lives and manners" with "those of the intemperate." Both suffer from "a derangement or excess of excitement" that induces idiocy or madness and keeps them in states of physical and social abjection. Snethen's proposal engaged the emerging humanitarian understanding of racial difference as an internal quality but then credited this "excess of excitement" entirely to "habits," accepting the civilizing arguments popularized by Samuel Stanhope Smith while shying away from Smith's environmentalist claims. Though privileging a European Christian cultural norm, Snethen did not accede to scientific and romantic accounts of innate racial difference. Most important, Snethen argued that "imitation" must be a *reciprocal* practice between missionary and convert. Missionaries, Snethen wrote, should promote economically productive, "civilized" behaviors by engaging, adopting, and modifying existing Indian cultural practices. Their success depended on the correspondence of Indian habit and a traditional Methodist style: Methodist "heat," reflected in "the heart of the unprejudiced Indian," may succeed where the "formal and less fervent method" of other sects' "schools" might fail. At the same time, Snethen reveals some anxiety about the resemblance of Indian and traditional Methodist styles by subordinating both to his own humanitarian plan. Abandoning the principle of reciprocity and acceding to the norms of rational-critical public-sphere debate, Snethen concluded "Lectures on Missions" with a thoroughly scientific, systematic proposal for the reformation of Indian diet, visual arts, and music that would wean them away from that "hot" Methodist style. "Lectures on Missions" endorsed Indians' immediate but temporary participation in a "hot" reformist Methodist public as a prelude to cultural transformation whose contours would be decided upon, in advance, from within public spheres whose very "temperance" precluded Indian participation.[29]

Apess's treatment of Indian intemperance in his 1829 *A Son of the Forest* adopted Snethen's endorsement of bodily drives and a broadly conceived notion of temperate labor but rejected Snethen's preemptive limitation on Indian participation in rational-critical public debate. It did so by offering an anticolonial temperance narrative that drew on a specifically New York reformist Methodist economic reading of temperance. Apess's attribution of drunkenness to intemperate greed, as well as his prescription of temperate labor, trade, and employment practices as the cure, resembles the recommendations of Cornelius Blatchly's 1822 "Essay on Common Wealths," the first publication of the Methodist Society–affiliated New York Society for Promoting Communities. Blatchly traced the desire for status, vanity, and pride to "nervous" drives largely produced by social conditions. "Every sin," Blatchly wrote, is "an act of intemperance: and a pure abstinence is nothing but a denial of self." Private property, in which "men's interests are so opposed to each other," created such antagonism "that only a little sympathy can exist." Like Apess, Blatchly characterized intemperance as a sinful fulfillment of bodily drives shaped by the social world. Evangelical temperance narratives' pervasive projection of bodily drives onto culturally other, non-Christian subjects, however, demanded that Apess go further than Blatchly by redrawing the relationship between Indian collective identity, masculinity, bodily desire, and public speech.[30]

Apess's temperance narrative used evangelical temperance narratives' metaphors of rape, disorder, and dispossession to construct an Indian history of U.S. imperial expansion. By combining two evangelical temperance narrative forms, the cautionary tale and the positive exemplum, in a sympathetic, first-person narrative of temperate labor, Apess created a public Indian subject capable of moving between the positions of "degraded Indian" and rational critic of the missionary system. He did this, first, by engaging the rhetoric of fatherhood that dominated the New York Working Men's debates on property in the wake of the 1828 New York Constitution's increased property requirements for men of color and continuation of universal suffrage for white men. Apess argued that the white male destruction of Indian republican fatherhood produced an Indian domestic sphere as a site of seduction, abuse, and disease. He begins by engaging his readers' sympathy through a first-person narrative of his and his sister's beating by his parents and grandparents. In a sensationalistic narrative reminiscent of Benjamin Franklin's earliest temperance prose—an article describing a girl's neglect and murder by drunken parents—Apess described his and his sister's bodily pain, including starvation, nakedness, humiliation, mockery, freezing, and, finally, a clubbing that "had broken [his] arm in three different places." Apess attributed his mistreatment and his resulting indenture to his father's absence. Then, merging family history into tribal history, Apess summoned sympathy for Indians as a "race" by drawing on the language of seduction. Romantically describing Indian land as a domestic home to "the ashes of their sires," Apess accused white men of emasculating Indian men by "seduc[ing]" them from those "lawful possessions" and "into a love of" alcohol. Once-productive Indian fathers, "assiduously engaged in supplying the necessities of those depending on them," became unsteady drunks "reeling about intoxicated" and "neglecting to provide for themselves or families." The ruined individuals and domestic spheres, in turn, affected the tribal body. While previous generations engaged in regular seasonal migrations, purposefully "roam[ing] . . . over their goodly possessions," contemporary tribes were "scattered abroad" in their drunkenness. Ultimately, corrupt Indian republican masculinity allowed white men to seduce Indian women through "violence of the most revolting and basest kind," a sign and symbol of utter Indian abjection. [31] By attributing Indian drunkenness to intemperate white male greed and lust, Apess transformed the generic figures of the drunken Indian man and seduced Indian woman into moral and spiritual indictments of U.S. colonial expansion.

If sympathetic romantic descriptions and public performances of lost Indian masculine virtue helped white men establish their place in an increasingly capitalist economy and fragmented, mobile social world, *A Son of the Forest*'s condemnation of white cupidity as responsible for that lost virtue allowed Apess to establish his authorial control and retain his audience's sympathy. He did so by shifting suddenly from his sensational, sympathetic narrative of domestic and social decay into a didactic liberal-rational analysis, proposing that the "conduct" of his grandparents must be "the effect of some cause." Reiterating the ubiquitous association of intemperance with brutishness by naming it "the beastly vice," Apess directly addressed "reader[s]" who presumed Indian cruelty was grounded in immutable racial character. Because savagery is produced by "ardent spirits," Apess reasoned, logic and the historical record make "the whites" responsible for Indian savagery, as they introduced his "countrymen" to liquor with the express purpose of seducing them from their possessions. Apess's shift into a liberal-rational style heightened his temperance narrative's dramatic tension by highlighting the gap between his two personae as narrator: a sympathetic Indian child and an authoritative Indian preacher. Transferring his readers' sympathy from child to preacher, Apess called into question the distance between those two subject-positions, long established in evangelical temperance narrative, and dramatized his transcendence of suffering while retaining sympathetic appeal.

Apess's innovative combination of evangelical temperance narrative forms and subject-positions into the same first-person narrator prefigured the largely artisanal Washingtonian temperance movement's use of confessional narrative. While Washingtonian temperance tracts treated the tearful exchange between men as the final step in achieving white manhood, Apess, who was unable to achieve an artisanal identity in the cobbler's trade his father taught him, presented sympathetic recognition from his employer as a precondition to developing an artisanal identity through the habitual practice of temperate ministerial labor.[32] Ironically refashioning an allusion to the strict moralism of Connecticut's Presbyterian and Congregationalist churches, Apess characterized his growing Methodist faith as a development of "steady habits." He acquired these habits in three scenes of labor—intemperate soldiering, temperate farm labor, and the defense of Indian economic rights—that had helped establish his republican masculinity. Making conventional use of the conversion narrative genre's trajectory from early emotional and physical suffering, through a period of testing, to a sense of grace, Apess first described himself as "steady" just before his conversion at the age of nineteen. He diverged from the gender norms of the genre by linking bodily pain to his labor in a more consistent manner, one reminiscent of women's conversion narratives. Upon his religious awakening, "[t]he anguish of my soul," Apess wrote, "afflicted my body to such a degree that I was almost too weak to perform my labour." During his period of testing, Apess described his stint in the army as an entry into "hell upon earth" where "sober men" were transformed into "confirmed drunkards" by a corrupt U.S. government that even refused to pay for his service in the War of 1812. Connecting this period of trial to his earlier narrative of childhood suffering and tribal dispossession, Apess rued how intemperance had made him fight for "the white man, who had cheated my forefathers out of their land." Conversion narratives had long been a valuable means for evangelical Protestants to elicit sympathetic exchange, and Apess's introduction of temperance discourse into the conversion tale allowed him to transform the moral value of intemperance by granting his relapses a spiritual resonance.[33]

In narrating the final stage, grace, Apess shaped an embodied Indian masculine identity capable of the duties of fatherhood and rigorous itinerant labor. Apess did make use of expressions of emotional pleasure and pain, but his gracious life was marked more by work than feeling, or more by work *as* feeling. After a long period of testing, his gracious life began with his full assumption of "steady habits" during his work as an itinerant farm laborer. In a short vignette describing his work for "Mr. Hail, in Gloucester" at "harvest time," Apess explained that farmers customarily distributed liquor to help laborers work harder, but when Hail offered the day's "half-pint of spirits," Apess refused. While "[s]ome persons say, that *they* cannot do without spirituous liquors," Apess wrote, he preferred "molasses, or milk and water." By taking the radical temperance position of total abstinence from liquor, Apess claimed that he could "not only stand labor as well" but actually "perform[ed] more than those who drank the spirits." He then linked temperate labor to an amelioration of the ruined Indian domestic sphere by observing that the aptly named farmer Hail's extra payment of "three dollars and twenty-five cents" was "sufficient to buy [his] poor dear children some clothes," a socioeconomic lesson he reinforced by marking how his pay increased from intemperate work at "eight dollars a month" to temperate "labour work at twenty dollars a month."[34]

Just before Apess reached this happy conclusion, he interrupted his vignette to declare his intent to again enter the public sphere by "publish[ing] an Essay on Intemperance."[35] *A Son of the Forest*'s correlation of temperate labor with masculine identity echoes many evangelical temperance tracts of the day, and may have been especially welcome in a reformist Methodist public. Apess's narrative bears a striking resemblance to a brief anonymous temperance tract, "An Address to Master Mechanics, Whom It May Concern," that appeared in Stilwell's *Friendly Visitor* some four years before Apess published *A Son of the Forest*. The temperance techniques that "An Address" describes were widely discussed, but similarities in detail and trajectory suggest at least the possibility of direct influence. "An Address" began, much like Apess, by contradicting the "general opinion that a man needs liquor who labors hard." The habitual drinker, "An Address" proposes, actually "unmans himself" by becoming neither "a fit husband, a good parent, nor a true friend"; abstinence from "grog" in favor of "molasses and water" and a snack, the tract concludes, will produce happier men who have "their full pay to take home to their families." "An Address" recounts the substitution of a molasses drink for liquor, the exchange of liquor for extra pay during harvest, the use of that pay for supporting the family, and the importance of temperate labor for becoming a "gentleman" by acting as a good husband, parent, and friend. The author of "An Address" then offered a personal narrative of labor as "a young man" when he worked "on the farm for [his] support" and "was in the habit of drinking spirits during hay and harvest." One harvest season, he wrote, his employer made him "drink milk, or milk and water, and eat a bit of bread and butter" rather than drinking liquor, and "instead of lacking spirits," he "gained strength, every day that [he] worked."[36]

The differences between Apess's vignette and "An Address" reveal some of the ways that reformist Methodist rhetoric both enabled and frustrated Apess's development of an Indian identity. While Apess's vignette and "An Address" both endorse the reciprocal moral and economic responsibilities of master and laborer, "An Address," like most of the *Friendly Visitor*'s prescriptions for social reform, was deeply paternalistic in tone and content. It addressed the master and credited the farmer with requiring temperate labor. Apess's vignette, in contrast, addressed the laborer and emphasized his volition. Most important, while "An Address" treated farm work as the labor of youth and presented the author as distant and superior to his narrated self, Apess brought his story closer to his narrating self by making temperate farm labor central to the public recognition necessary for establishing his fatherhood, his ministry, and the very narrative the reader was engaging. Apess concluded his temperance narrative by reinforcing the connection between his capacity to preach and his temperate labor habits, marked by their regularity, consistency, reliability, and other signs of male responsibility. After Hail paid him and treated him "like a gentleman," Apess "held a prayer meeting" with the family, who were "loath to part with" him because of his "godly life." Hail and his family had benefited from Apess's preaching and embraced him in tearful worship.[37] Repeatedly referring to preaching and writing as "holy work," Apess represents them as types of temperate labor that, when recognized and reciprocated, form a genuine religious community.

While the *Friendly Visitor*'s paternalism may have enabled the Methodist Society's development as a new denomination in New York's religious marketplace, it did not address the needs of many Methodists of color, who were less able to become masters or tradesmen. *A Son of the Forest*, on the other hand, extended Apess's spiritual labor by teaching employers and employees alike to support traditional standards of economic morality. Apess's use of temperance to achieve reciprocal public recognition presaged his claim in *Indian Nullification* that the Mashpee's formation of temperance societies indicated their capacity to develop self-directing civic bodies deserving state recognition.[38]

Later in *A Son of the Forest*, Apess offers a negative example of reciprocal responsibility between employer and employee that placed his Indian subject in an uneasy middle ground between systems of free and slave labor. Apess's account of the economic discrimination, suspicion, and fraud he faced as a laborer suggests that, like other Indians, especially those who had some African ancestors, he was more susceptible than whites to economic and legal exploitation. Echoing his earlier description of indenture as establishing a proximate economic, legal, and public status for the "drunken Indian" and the "poor African," Apess writes that he was once forced to work as a cobbler to pay off a debt he "did not honestly owe." During a season of temperate farm work in "the land of steady habits," Apess's employer "undertook to treat [him] as he would a degraded African slave," driving him off with a "cart stake" when Apess asked for his pay. Having "been cheated so often," Apess fought back, "determined to have [his] rights this time, and forever after." Apess's rejection of slavery and its association with blackness worked to racialize free labor in opposition to African identity but located Indian labor in a third position that emphasized African Americans' and Indians' similar experiences of indenture and labor in New England. Just as Frederick Douglass's resistance to his overseer's beating marked his acquisition of independent masculinity, Apess's violent resistance to economic exploitation helped establish the full authority of his Indian public subject.[39]

"Objectionable Parts" and "Lasting Blessings"

Apess's 1829 attempt to adapt reformist Methodist rhetoric in support of Indian rights proved to be swimming against the tide of Methodist reform. In 1830, the reformist Associate Methodist Church became the backbone for the new Methodist Protestant Church (MPC), which would eventually take in most white-dominated reformist congregations. Despite the role of women and African Americans in establishing their parent organizations, the MPC eliminated voting rights for women and allowed local conferences to determine the rights of nonwhite men. These changes affected representation in and by the church. They were introduced in a new editorial policy at the sole surviving reformist Methodist periodical publication, Baltimore's *Mutual Rights*. To popularize the magazine, church leaders rechristened their new house organ as *Mutual Rights and Methodist Protestant* (1831–34) and recommended it eschew contentious subjects in favor of polite literature. John Harrod, a Baltimore printer, bookseller, and former editor of *Mutual Rights*, nominated Gamaliel Bailey Jr. as the new editor. Harrod reasoned that Bailey's liberal education and experience would allow *Mutual Rights and Methodist Protestant* to become a more worldly and genteel publication. Beginning with the issue of March 1831, Bailey obliged, heralding the incorporation of reformist Methodism into a broader liberal evangelical movement.[40]

Apess participated in this transformation of reformist Methodism. His second edition of *A Son of the Forest* was transformed in much the same way as *Mutual Rights and Methodist Protestant*. As a consumer good, the second edition was conspicuously fine. The body of the text, set in clearer print on larger and finer paper, was preceded by an elegant frontispiece depicting Apess in simple yet tasteful dress, with a calm and direct gaze. Apess's textual revisions complemented these material improvements. They granted his ministerial authority firmer rhetorical footing by hewing more closely to the new evangelical style, improving his argumentative consistency, and elevating his prose. Most prominently, Apess started the second chapter of his second edition with two new paragraphs of rational ministerial commentary on the function of the soul in determining the "operations" of "the Spirit of Divine Truth" on the mind. Apess's smaller deletions also moved him further away from a traditional Methodist style and toward the polite literature of the evangelical public. Apess's 1831 account of childhood suffering, for example, minimized the providentialism associated with traditional Methodist conversion narrative in favor of measured analysis. To make the narrative fit with bourgeois sexual mores, Apess also removed some salacious details from his account of a drunken frolic in New Haven, including his visit to a "dance house," a common euphemism for a brothel.

The clearest mark of Apess's participation in reformist Methodism's movement away from sectarianism was his deletion of the long closing account of his departure from the MEC and subsequent licensing by the Methodist Society. This excision, by far the lengthiest, is often read as a sign of his movement away from religious organizing altogether and toward a presumptively less Christian, "Indian" organizing. However, while the excision did unmoor his call for Indian rights from earlier, more sectarian modes of reformist Methodist publicity, it actually participated in the more general subsidence of reformist Methodism into the evangelical public. Smaller changes in style and tone also mark his embrace of reformist Methodism's move into a broader evangelical public sphere. Many changes move away from tropes associated with traditional Methodist conversion narratives. For example, Apess deleted an episode describing his providential rescue from the woods and subsequent beating by his drunken grandparents. He also excised a visceral sentence describing his sensation of choking and strangulation during an illness brought on by religious anxiety. These changes decreased the scenes' sensational power and minimized the providential quality of his recovery and subsequent preaching.

These changes were part of Apess's larger authorial strategy. As Barry O'Connell notes, Apess's 1829 edition is "more roughly written . . . often more direct, detailed, and even poignant in its awkwardness." The rhetorical power of this "roughness" was not lost on Apess, whose 1829 preface used it to authenticate his account of privation by attributing it to his "entire want of a common education." His 1831 preface, in contrast, appealed to a more sophisticated evangelical public, mentioning the book's improved organization and grammar and noting that "those parts which some persons deemed objectionable" were "stricken out." The new edition, with its elevated prose style, improved material quality, and lack of overt sectarianism, offered readers what Apess called a more "lasting blessing."[41] Whether Apess was in direct contact with publishers and editors such as Harrod and Bailey or simply following larger trends in reformist Methodist publicity, his changes allowed *A Son of the Forest* entrée into broader networks of distribution. The new 1831 edition received several public notices, including an advertisement by Harrod in the same month the new *Mutual Rights and Methodist Protestant* came off the press.

Apess's excisions of sectarian rhetoric in the 1831 edition coincided with his increased organization of identity in and through race. For example, he increased white culpability for his grandparents' drunken cruelty, attributing it "in great measure" to whites rather than "in part." He also flattened his characterization of his first indenture holders, the Furmans, by eliminating some descriptions of his emotional attachment and their love for him. At the same time, his defense of Indian rights drew less on republican fatherhood, tribal identity, and paternal inheritance and more on sentimental rhetoric. While Apess's 1829 edition began with a description of the Pequot tribe, his 1831 edition compressed that account to move quickly into his sensational, sentimental tableau of rape, dispossession, and familial disintegration. He peppered his account of his childhood suffering with new guideposts to direct his readers' emotional response and assure them of his own sensibility. Noting that the thought of childhood suffering still "makes [him] shudder," that his "very heart bled" for his starving sister, that female drunkenness promotes "unfeeling" conduct, and naming that conduct "cruel and unnatural," his revision more fully engaged the sentimental rhetoric that would help popularize later social reformers' prose.[42] Finally, a small but telling deletion suggests that the movement of the reformist Methodist public into the

evangelical public sphere led Apess to curtail his more radical economic critique. In his second edition's account of his travels after army service, he still
described white "rum!" as destroying a well-ordered Indian community but
no longer noted that the Indians he met "held all things in common." As a
whole, his anticolonial critique in the 1831 edition leaned more heavily on
sentimental racial identity and less on distinct sectarian, tribal, or rank-based
identities.

By participating in the reformist Methodist movement into the evangelical mainstream, the 1831 edition of *A Son of the Forest* achieved a more enduring place in evangelical print culture and midcentury social reform.[43] Like
other participants in the reformist Methodist public, Apess eventually followed the Methodist Episcopal Church in its adoption of a polite style that
would become typical of the new evangelical mainstream. This shift coincided with reformist Methodists' acceptance of other norms of formerly dissenting churches, including the institutionalization of racial hierarchies of
seating, speech, and rank, which may have encouraged Apess's interest in
publications that, though still clearly marked by his Methodist experience,
were primarily nonsectarian calls for "Indian reform." In his later work,
Apess rejected a strict gendering of Indian virtue: Apess's "Eulogy on King
Philip" invokes an image of vanishing Indian republican virtue that played on
the popularity of sentimental Indian melodramas and "demonstrations" of
Indian speech. Apess complicates a narrowly republican image of Indian virtue by grounding Philip's republicanism in his capacity for a distinctly Christian suffering. The subsidence of reformist Methodist rhetoric into a broader
evangelical public sphere that would alternately nurture and shun the most
radical social reformers speaks to a generative tension within midcentury
politically reformist publics. As with reformist Methodism, political reformers were caught between oppositional critique and bodily practice, on one
hand, and notions of circulation and publicity traditionally understood as
centripetal, leading toward or attempting to invoke a "public." Some of the
veterans of Methodist reform would take on important roles in these new
politically reformist publics. For example, editor Gamaliel Bailey went on to
be a distinguished abolitionist printer; his brush with an anti-abolitionist
mobbing in Cincinnati and serial publication of Harriet Beecher Stowe's
Uncle Tom's Cabin speaks to some of the deep links between Apess's publicity,
reformist Methodism, and abolition that my next two chapters trace. What
combination of rhetoric, material practices of publication and speech, and
circumstances of opposition would best meet the personal and political aims

of these political reformists? How would rhetorics, practices, and circumstances of embodied suffering give shape to those aims? Apess's dissatisfaction with sentimental representations of Indian republican virtue and Indian abjection may stem from a perennial problem within Smithian sympathy itself: the need to maintain distance between spectator and sufferer. As my next two chapters will explore, sympathetic discourse, by figuring the spectatorial self as possessing an agency not granted to the suffering other, depends on maintaining the gap between the two positions. At its worst, sentiment, by interiorizing and naturalizing the experience of suffering as proper to specific groups, works to petrify sufferers in a state of anguished supplication. Following Thomas Laqueur's foundational account of humanitarian narrative, scholars have established ways in which public discourses of sentiment helped institute gender and racial difference, whether in straightforward evocations of pity or in melodramatic and minstrel representations of nonwhite suffering.[44] Such problems with sentiment were widely recognized at the time, not as structuring elements of sentiment but rather as deficiencies in the individual spectator or sufferer. In turn, these attempts to individualize bad feeling or "perversions of sentiment" contributed to the development of perverse sexual practices and desires.

CHAPTER 3

The Martyrology of White Abolitionists

In 1845, the hand of a white ship captain, Jonathan Walker, became what might seem like an unlikely icon of abolition. Branded "SS" for "slave stealer" by a U.S. marshal in Florida, Walker's hand was daguerreotyped, engraved, woodcut, and printed on thousands of broadsides. Abolitionist newspapers and antislavery almanacs in New England and Pennsylvania ran sensational accounts of the branding, often accompanied by the hand's woodcut print. Other reform-minded papers, including the New York *Tribune* and Charles Spear's penal reform magazine *Prisoner's Friend*, ran with the story for their own ends.[1] Sophia Little composed "The Branded Hand," an allegorical poem dramatizing slaveholders' conversion to abolitionism.[2] The woodcut hand appeared on the title page of Walker's book, and Walker himself, during a speaking tour of northern and western cities, dramatically revealed his hand to the crowds.[3] The hand's popularity took even ardent abolitionists by surprise. With self-conscious humor, Boston's *Emancipator and Republican*, under the winking headline "That Hand," used the genre of the celebrity itinerary to report on the travels of the "branded hand" woodcut: "Next it goes to Woonsocket, for the Patriot. Then it is engaged at Northampton, for the Herald."[4]

The success of the "branded hand" was part of a more wide-ranging reformist political movement that drew, for its iconographic and sympathetic power, on nineteenth-century religious attempts to overcome "perverted" sympathy and recuperate it for political ends. This chapter and the next will consider such attempts, focusing on white reformers' attempts to enter the public sphere by using a rhetoric of embodied suffering. Critics often describe the association of embodied suffering with blackness and femininity as part and parcel of the public sphere's demand for disembodied abstraction.[5] White martyrology helps shed new light on the way in which the process of abstraction produces modern conceptions of race. Suffering provides white abolitionists a vehicle for the classic public sphere activity of political critique by producing their whiteness in the face of anti-abolitionist attempts to unsettle their racial identity.[6] As we saw in Chapter 1, eighteenth-century evangelical conversion discourse encouraged the public imitation of sensational experiences of pain and affective senses of abjection. Jonathan Edwards attempted to harness the sensational experiences of abjection most associated with the "enthusiastic" revival practices of the poor, women, Indians, and Africans via intensely affective written and oral performances carefully attuned to rank. In the process, Edwards and other revivalists elaborated converted subjectivity as an affective, psychological, internal condition. This notion of converted subjectivity provided a template for the subsequent mapping of modern notions of racial difference onto earlier notions of class, gender, and cultural difference. Early nineteenth-century religious writers fully engaged this mapping process. In the 1820s and 1830s, as Chapter 2 describes, religious disestablishment and the burgeoning of religious print culture helped William Apess and other sectarian reformers of color gain a toehold in the public sphere by constructing an oppositional racial identity around the principles of affective, political, and rhetorical self-control. This chapter will consider midcentury white abolitionists' elaborations of race and gender difference in the nonsectarian martyrological discourses they engaged to legitimate their publicity. It reads work by Walker himself, William Garrison, Wendell Phillips, Beriah Green, Edward Beecher, Thomas Stone, Harriet Martineau, Maria Chapman, and, finally, Harriet Beecher Stowe, whose famous martyrdom of Tom in *Uncle Tom's Cabin* (1852) parodies white martyrology in a conflicted attempt to clear space for black martyrdom.

The Branded Hand and Martyrological Imagery

Walker's branding put populist and business-minded elements of the Northern press in a difficult position. They were well practiced at rebutting accusations of physical cruelty against slaves and deriding abolitionists as emotionally unbalanced and politically "ultra." Attacking Walker himself, though, would only propel the narrative of persecution that helped sustain the "hand" phenomenon. Instead, Walker's opponents targeted the success of abolitionist publicity itself, mocking abolitionists for making hay of Walker's suffering. *Niles' National Register* archly observed that the "Branded Hand"

was "quite a hit, admirably adapted for exciting sympathy and making political capital of."[7] Philadelphia's *Public Ledger* mocked the transience of abolitionist publications by suggesting that an upstart Providence newspaper
named "The Branded Hand" would soon be renamed "The Burned Fingers,"
as subscribers would be out their money.[8] Though prejudicial, *Niles'* and the
Public Ledger captured important elements of abolitionist publicity in the
U.S. Abolitionism was a creature of the market, shaped by and eventually
shaping economic development. Abolitionists made friends and raised funds
through holiday "antislavery fairs" and "Free Produce" stores that displayed
abolitionists' transatlantic market connections in the most material terms.[9]
Abolitionist orators entertained audiences with a lively, evangelical style, one
well suited to reproduction in newspapers, almanacs, broadsheets, and other
ephemeral print that extended abolitionists' public reach.

The abolitionists who promoted Walker's "branded hand" inherited their
market approach from the new churches and reform societies that sprang up
in the wake of state disestablishment, as market forces began to guide church
development. In the new religious marketplace, progressives and radical reformers of all stripes, particularly within white-majority Methodist, Baptist,
and Quaker congregations in New York, Boston, Baltimore, and other urban
areas, were frustrated by the political moderation of church leaders who
could not afford to alienate wealthy congregants. "Come-outers" and other
reformers exploited the growing gap between white sectarian organizing and
what they saw as Christian moral imperative by moving into black churches,
other egalitarian churches, temperance societies, and other nonsectarian reform groups. Black congregants, pushed to the margins of churches they
helped build, were especially motivated to establish separate "African" institutions. The development of racial identity in these corporate bodies was, in
part, an early effect of market-based church organizing within transatlantic
and transnational public spheres, and the uneasy alliances between white and
black abolitionists continued this history.[10]

Despite their insights into abolitionists' techniques of publicity, *Niles'*
and the *Public Ledger* cynically occlude their support for the forms of state
and public violence that helped shape abolitionist techniques. Abolitionists
in the early and mid-nineteenth century faced sustained campaigns of individual, mob, and state violence designed to disrupt their public organizing.
Anti-abolitionists attempted to criminalize abolition by suing abolitionist
publishers and lobbying legislatures to restrict abolitionist publication in
Maryland, Maine, New Hampshire, and Connecticut. The public, legal, and

judicial hostility to abolition encouraged mobs in New England and New York to destroy abolitionists' presses and homes, pelt abolitionist orators with rocks and eggs, tar and feather them, and burn the buildings in which they met. While white abolitionists usually faced only fines, imprisonment, assault, and destruction of property, these acts frequently accompanied more severe violence against black abolitionists and free blacks generally. In 1835, for example, a mob wrecked Lewis Tappan's house before destroying three churches, a school, and many homes in a black neighborhood of New York City.[11]

Race was no less a factor in Walker's case. The branded hand's whiteness was crucial to its popularity. Abolitionists on both sides of the Atlantic had long generated sympathy for black suffering in humanitarian sensational accounts designed to turn public opinion against slavery and the slave trade. Beginning in the 1830s, white abolitionists made different connections between suffering and publicity by re-framing their own suffering as a type of martyrdom. The continuum of violence between Walker's branding, the far more intense violence against free blacks, and the systemic violence of slavery was very real, but martyrological rhetoric attempted to distance white men's experience of suffering from that of the black slave. Most basically, abolitionist martyrology made Walker's hand "a hit" by transforming the state's mark of criminality into a badge of honor.[12] Walker's willingness to suffer "stripes and bruisings, and branding irons" signaled, as the Worcester *Christian Citizen* announced, a divine "new order of knighthood in this heroic age of philanthropy" in which white male suffering confirmed the justice of abolitionists' public defiance of the law.[13]

John Greenleaf Whittier's didactic early poem "The Branded Hand," widely reprinted next to the woodcut of "That Hand" in abolitionist newspapers, offers a delicate example of this racial martyrology. Imagining Walker's public lecturing as an extension of Walker's work as a ship captain, Whittier writes,

> Then lift that manly right hand, bold ploughman of the wave!
> Its branded palm shall prophesy, "Salvation to the Slave!"
> Hold up its fire-wrought language, that whoso reads may feel
> His heart swell strong within him, his sinews change to steel.
>
> Hold it up before our sunshine, up against our Northern air—
> Ho! men of Massachusetts, for the love of God look there!

Take it henceforth for your standard—like the Bruce's heart of yore,
In the dark strife closing round ye, let that hand be seen before![14]

Whittier begins by asserting abolitionists' collective ability to control the
meaning of Walker's suffering body through the public resignification of his
brand's "fire-wrought" letters. Understood as sacred text, Walker's branded
body can communicate emotional fortitude to the "swell[ing]" hearts of the
"men of Massachusetts." Like the *Christian Citizen*'s muscular philanthropy,
Whittier's celebration of "manly" emotion introduces white male spectators
and readers into a sacred cycle of sin and redemption. Placing the white
American man alongside Robert "the Bruce," this cycle could secure "Salvation" for the Christic "living presence in the bound and bleeding slave" within
a historical cycle of sacred violence.[15] The resulting fraternity of liberty, associated with Scottish rebellion against England and Rome, is implicitly anti-
imperial and dissenting. It is also explicitly formed in Christian Europe's
battle against "Paynim" (pagan) Africa: in romantic legend, Robert's em-
balmed heart served as a "standard" for Scottish Crusaders in Granada.[16] The
metaphor is an intricate one, associating the strong "heart" of white abolitionists with Robert's "heart," proslavery forces with heathen Africans, and
black slaves with "conquered" Spain. Whittier's martyrology thereby likens
abolitionists to Scottish Crusaders, proslavery whites to African Muslims,
and black slaves to conquered territory in need of liberation. Like Walker's
branded white hand shining forth amid "dark strife," the martyr's eloquent,
willed suffering stands out in Manichean contrast to both the slaveholder's
infidel heart and the inarticulate, abject agony of the black slave.

The three cuts in Walker's own book, the *Trial and Imprisonment of Jonathan Walker* (1845), offer a more direct schematization of the racial politics of
abjection and publicity in white abolitionist martyrology. They use visual
tropes of affective gazing, entrapment, and physical deformation to justify
Walker's publicity by first entangling and then disentangling him in slave abjection, a move Saidiya Hartman terms "supplant[ing] the black captive."[17] The
first cut in Walker's book, "Common mode of whipping with the paddle," illustrates a generic sensational account of torture in the service of a plantation
elite.[18] The cut appears, somewhat incongruously, in Walker's narrative of his
own suffering while in prison. It reminds readers of the evils Walker fought
against and in some way substitutes for an illustration of his own prison suffering. In the cut's center, a dark-skinned woman is staked sideways to the
ground, her face contorted in a scream. She is straddled by a bearded white

Common mode of whipping with the paddle.

Figure 5. "Common mode of whipping with the paddle." Walker, *Trial and Imprisonment of Jonathan Walker*, 1845. Library of Congress.

man poised to strike with an upraised paddle. These figures cast a dispropor-
tionately large shadow onto a dark-skinned child on the left. The child averts
his or her gaze from the scene and turns to face a fence, evincing appropriate
emotional horror at the suffering he witnesses. The fence, with its strong vertical lines, emphasizes the woman's and child's isolation from Florida's domestic pleasures and exotic natural beauty, elements signified, respectively, by a
house and palm trees behind the fence. This juxtaposition of torture with domesticity and exoticism recalls the obscenity of the plantation Gothic genre,
which often showcases the way in which sympathy has been perverted or
"hardened" by witnessing, or engaging in, torture. Such affective perversion is
embodied by the pair of planters in fine suits and broad-brimmed hats who
voyeuristically gaze at the torture from the right. One planter is the torturer's
visual double. He shares the torturer's wide-legged stance and has a cane between his legs that echoes the stake between the torturer's legs. This uncanny

The author confined in the pillory.

Figure 6. "The author confined in the pillory." Walker, *Trial and Imprisonment of Jonathan Walker*, 1845. Library of Congress.

mirroring of the torturer's body literalizes the planter's perversion of sympathetic response: rather than feeling the sufferer's pain, the planter replicates the experience of torturing, with a smile indicating his perverse pleasure at the sensation. The other planter seems less affectively perverse but more responsible, as his upraised hand and pointed finger appear to direct the torturer. Some moral reprieve is granted to the torturer himself. Like the child, with whom he is linked by the odd shadow, the torturer faces down and to the right, away from the viewer, perhaps indicating his own shame and entrapment in the planters' service. Readers, as viewers of the scene, are aligned with the planters, suggesting our own imperiled affective position.

The second cut, "The author confined in the pillory," appears some ten pages after the first. It engages the same visual tropes—isolating vertical lines, bodily deformation and pollution, perverse spectatorship—to illustrate Walker's experience of abjection as akin to the tortures of slavery.[19] Walker appears, like the tortured woman, in the center of the scene, his body similarly deformed and immobilized. He is yoked in a pillory affixed between two Doric columns, the strong vertical lines of which recall the fence in the first cut. Walker, again like the tortured woman, is surrounded by finely dressed gentlemen, this time in more formal top hats. One gentleman pelts Walker's downcast head with eggs, which ooze down Walker's face and distort his features, much as the woman's face was distorted by a scream. Even as the cut correlates Walker's abjection with the woman's, the cut's title frames his abjection as redemptive by connecting it to his subsequent participation in the public sphere as an "author."

Indeed, *Trial and Imprisonment* does not leave Walker in his abject state for long. Four pages later, the third and final cut, "United States Marshal branding the author," dramatizes Walker's redemption from abjection by reorganizing the first two images' visual tropes.[20] While the vertical lines in the

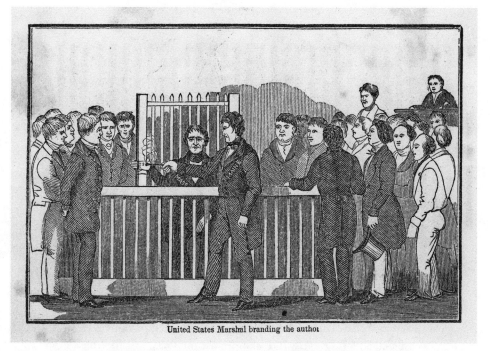

United States Marshal branding the author

Figure 7. "United States Marshal branding the author." Walker, *Trial and Imprisonment of Jonathan Walker*, 1845. Library of Congress.

first and second cut isolate the captive and emphasize their physical deformation, those in the third cut reinforce Walker's own liberty and echo his erect
carriage. Walker's body, now located off-center, is again framed by strong
vertical lines, this time of a sort of low iron pen. His hand is tied to railing in
a manner that recalls the woman's tying to the post and his own restraint in
the pillory, and he is again surrounded by fine gentlemen. In the third cut,
though, his hand opens freely to receive his branding and his posture is admirably erect and relaxed. Perfectly echoing the famous "Branded Hand"
woodcut, Walker displays his hand to the assembled gentlemen and the
reader. Taken as a whole, this third and final cut transforms the deformations
of abjection into badges of honor. Abjection is a trial by fire that authorizes
Walker's entry into the public sphere. Walker's technique here resembles
Frederick Douglass's more famous use of his aunt's suffering, in the 1845 *Narrative of the Life of Frederick Douglass*, to enable Douglass's own entry into the
public sphere.[21] I will return to this resemblance below, simply suggesting for
now that Walker's narrative and Douglass's, published in the same year and
by the same office, point to a shared abolitionist strategy for authorizing publicity by instantiating racial and gender difference.

The illustrations in *Trial and Imprisonment* do not offer a similar redemption for slaves, who remain utterly abject. They do, however, promise redemption for readers: the third cut makes Walker's honor metonymically accessible
to his readers and New Englanders in particular. In the manner of a political
cartoon, Walker's coat is inscribed with "MASS," for Walker's home state of
Massachusetts, while the coat of the U.S. marshal holding the brand is inscribed with "MAINE," for his home state. With these letters on their cloth-
ing echoing the "SS" of the brand, the inscriptions suggest that public political
debate among New Englanders has the potential to give new meaning to the
brand and, potentially, to other forms of state violence. Properly engaging in
that debate will free readers from the perversion that the first cut attributes to
spectators of plantation violence.

These three cuts' relatively straightforward use of abjection in the service
of white abolitionist martyrology opens onto a deeper and more complex
world of suffering that helped define race in the mid-nineteenth century.
Much valuable criticism has described the parasitic relationship between embodied black suffering and white abolitionist publicity, but the role of embodied white suffering in establishing white abolitionist publicity (even
before John Brown) has received less attention.[22] White abolitionist martyrology participated in the broader premising of the antebellum public sphere,

popular culture, and law on black pained embodiment, but it did so in a unique way. White abolitionist martyrology developed notions of racial difference in concert with sympathetic and parodic representations of black suffering. Sensational descriptions of slave suffering in abolitionist poetry and prose, along with comic descriptions of slave suffering in minstrelsy and other "entertainments," helped create race as an internal, affective state—one wrinkle in the larger post-Enlightenment premising of Western subjectivity on affect.[23] Sympathy and satire helped clear ground for white publicity by "locking" African Americans into the position of exemplary sufferers.

In white abolitionist martyrology, the function (or malfunction) of the public sphere transforms the abjection caused by physical suffering into an apotheosis of glory. Unlike sympathy and parody, white martyrology presents distinct but interdependent cycles of black suffering, white suffering, and white speech. These produce race as both affective and embodied, on the skin and in the voice. White abolitionist martyrology redefined and entrenched white masculinity by reessentializing voluntary self-sacrifice as a white male trait different from and superior to the slave's involuntary subjection. As white men, they choose their suffering. This choice makes their suffering superior to the black suffering it attempts to prevent. Martyrological suffering was a willed opening of the white male body to states of abjection that, in other white abolitionist accounts, defined slave subjectivity. Martyrological accounts of embodied white suffering and abolitionist sensational representations of black suffering both rely on sensation and sympathy to elicit readers' affective response and disparage slave societies as ideologically stagnant. However, sensational representations of slave torture evoke sympathy to help ameliorate physical suffering, while martyrology evokes sympathy for physical, emotional, or ideological suffering to promote the imitation of that suffering. Martyrology thereby distinguishes between black suffering as worthy of pity and white male suffering as worthy of admiration and imitation. Rather than turning white abolitionists "black," martyrology grounds and fixes their whiteness by insisting on the distinct and self-determined nature of white suffering, distancing them from notions of blackness defined by involuntary pained embodiment. Martyrology enabled white abolitionist public dissent by redefining and reentrenching their whiteness. Operating in a manner that recalls the early modern English distinction between martyrdom and Indian suffering, martyrological discourse locates white male suffering within a redemptive spiritual narrative while offering blacks only the most limited space to "witness." Black abjection was prerequisite for the development of an abolitionist public that could then register violations of norms of publicity as disruptions to whiteness. The suffering white male body becomes a text enabling an enviable, willful dispersal of the white self into the public sphere. Embodied black suffering, in contrast, destroys the black voice, which appears in public only when produced by white abolitionists themselves.

Critics of Jürgen Habermas's notion of rational, disembodied public-sphere actors show how the ostensibly featureless public self is both embodied in performance and constructed against black, female, and other forms of embodiment.[24] White abolitionist martyrology suggests that Habermas's notion may be honored in the breach. Because white abolitionist martyrology highlights the failure of abstraction that, at least nominally, enabled white male publicity, it was a risky and polarizing rhetoric.[25] For white male abolitionists, the martyr's suffering is a material sign of the nonexistence or fantasy of that rational, disembodied ideal. When abolitionists draw the boundaries of the white male martyr's body, they map the distortions of the public sphere in an attempt to shift their place within it. Martyrology, by making pained, embodied white masculinity crucial to the first stages of publicity, offers an uncanny rehearsal of public-sphere "disembodiment," dramatizing the achievement of publicity through embodied suffering and speech.

As part of a broader reformist attempt to use radical, often nonsectarian, evangelical speech and publication to make the public sphere a sacred space, white abolitionist martyrology celebrates the white male will to suffer in the service of social development, philanthropy, and humanity.[26] In moving white abolitionists away from a criminal identity and constructing white suffering in opposition to black suffering, martyrdom contributed indirectly to humanitarian constructions of the poor, criminals, and blacks as requiring similar public controls. Like humanitarian reformist discourse, white abolitionist martyrology failed to affect its most radical ends because it premised white male publicity on the continuation of this difference. Unlike most other reformist discourses, however, martyrology makes white men's embodied suffering central to white publicity, with black suffering serving as its foil.

The Origins of White Abolitionist Martyrology

How did martyrology, which had largely disappeared from evangelical public discourse, become so popular among abolitionists? Martyrdom retained some of its original power to license dissent within communities of faith that exerted a strong influence on abolitionist organizing. The Quaker influence was especially significant: Quakers in England and the American colonies were among the earliest and most prominent abolitionists; Quakers used martyrology to justify their separation and dissent; and mystical, ecstatic suffering still helped define faith and legitimate leadership.[27] In the eighteenth century, Quakers participated in the larger sectarian trend away from mystical suffering and toward ascetic practice, and the notion of faith as "living martyrdom" became disconnected from political dissent. At the same time, many remained at odds with the "worldly asceticism" of other Protestants, taking to heart the lessons of Joseph Besse's martyrological *Sufferings of the People Called Quakers* (1753). John Woolman, for example, used a broadly conceived notion of asceticism to construct a self that partially resisted America's emerging, slave-dependent capitalism.[28] In the nineteenth century, separating Hicksite and Progressive Quakers revived the connection between martyrdom and dissent in their embrace of radical abolition. Fully one-third of the attendees at the founding meeting of the American Anti-Slavery Society (AASS) were Hicksite, Progressive, or other Quakers, as were many prominent abolitionists, including Whittier, Lucretia Mott, and the Grimké sisters.[29]

One watershed event in the history of abolitionist martyrology occurred during William Garrison's brief term as editor of Quaker Benjamin Lundy's pioneering abolitionist newspaper, *The Genius of Universal Emancipation*. While Lundy was away, Garrison revived Lundy's defunct "Black List" column, which compiled specific, sensational accounts of slavery and slave trading from readers' letters, other papers, and firsthand narratives. Garrison's "Black List" picked up where Lundy left off or felt he could not go, offering a sensational procession of "HORRIBLE NEWS" describing "the barbarities of slavery—kidnappings, whippings, murders" and naming the merchants, authorities, and others involved to shame them in their New England homes.[30] Quaker abolitionists had circulated sensational representations of slave suffering within the community to "perfect" their religious body, but Lundy and Garrison used them to "enlighten," as one correspondent wrote, "the public mind."[31] Most important for the history of abolitionist martyrology, Garrison's publication led to his prosecution and imprisonment for libel.[32] Garrison's 1834 jailhouse pamphlet describes his experience in a high martyrological dudgeon, announcing his "willing[ness] to be persecuted, imprisoned and bound" for the cause and naming himself one of the "white victims" to slavery who "must be sacrificed to open the eyes of this nation."[33] As a willing victim to a system that would otherwise leave him unmolested, Garrison constructs white abolitionist subjectivity around a racial logic of redemptive white sacrifice for black suffering.

Martyrology allowed Garrison to amplify his public presence but drowned out the voices of those he would save. Garrison's later claim that English abolitionist Thomas Buxton thought he "must be black" because "no white American" could so effectively "plead for those in bondage" suggests that Garrison's speech and writing may have marked his voice as "black," especially in the relatively disembodied transatlantic abolitionist print public.[34] Less charitably, we might say that Garrison, worried about his place at a time when black abolitionists were entering the public stage, used martyrological discourse to establish his right to wield the authenticating value of the black voice. Indeed, the humor of Garrison's anecdote comes from Buxton's long hesitation to identify Garrison as white: expecting a black man, Buxton did not shake Garrison's hand until he "scrutinized [Garrison] from head to foot" to determine his race. This scene of confusion, bodily scrutiny, and interrupted mutual recognition between ostensibly white men speaks to the anxieties of white abolitionist martyrology in its attempt to establish white male public authority through heroic white suffering, materially embodied in the written and spoken word.[35]

Republican and Christian Strains

Three years after Garrison's account of his imprisonment, Elijah Lovejoy's murder by an anti-abolitionist mob in Alton, Illinois, occasioned abolitionists' first widespread use of martyrological oration and publication. These texts helped establish martyrology as a rhetorical pillar of abolitionist organizing and offer a cross section of white male abolitionist martyrology in the period. Taken together, they reveal three dominant, overlapping rhetorical strains—mystical, republican, and Christian—that help tease out the relationship between black suffering, white suffering, and white speech.[36]

Jonathan Blanchard's description of the martyr's blood diffusing and distributing Lovejoy's voice through Alton's public and private spaces illustrates
abolitionist martyrology's resemblance to other forms of mysticism that became popular among a broader liberal public at midcentury:

> *I'm the voice of blood!* And I wail along
>   As the winds sweep sullenly by; . . .
> In street, lane, and alley, in parlor and hall,
>   That sepulcher voice is there
> Crying—" 'Hear, hear the martyr's imploring call!
> O God! see the blood!—how it follows the ball,
>   As he sinks like the song of despair;
> But I come—the precursor of sorrow, I come
> In church-aisle and dwelling, in cellar and dome,
>   To cry with the tongue of the air;' "[37]

The martyr's ability to move across space and time, his suffering and weakness, his bodily openness to divine presence, and his ability to speak the truth
of reform from beyond the grave, for example, resemble spiritualist practices
such as possession and spirit-rapping. Martyrological mysticism thereby anticipates what several critics have noted as the affinity between spiritualist
subjectivity and the notion of free association prized by Garrison and Gerrit
Smith and dramatized in Henry "Box" Brown's public performances.[38] Mysticism had the potential to "render bodies completely unreadable" in terms of
race and gender, but more often served to reassert the white male body's ability to exceed normal expressive limits by entering into the public sphere.[39]
With a body as text and text as body, the white martyr is a speaking subject of
pure "blood." Blanchard's trope of the "voice of blood" engages, in a mystical
register, emerging scientific notions of racial difference derived from notions
of family descent and consanguinity ("Saxon blood") and shows how they
were understood or constructed alongside notions of publicity grounded in
norms of bodily display and coherence (whose blood should appear, and
when). The visibility of the white martyr's blood—his disrupted embodiment
and violent self-abstraction—allows him to enter a corrupted public sphere,
mark it as such, and potentially correct it by his presence.

Abolitionist martyrology finds a generative tension in the gap between
the embodied and disembodied public subject. The mystical, republican, and
Christian strains variously oscillate between displaying the martyr's suffering

body and showing the martyr's transformation into a type of self-abstracted public figure, absent but omnipresent. This tension is especially strong in republican martyrology, which first developed around U.S. Revolutionary figures such as Nathan Hale. The most famous abolitionist republican martyrology is Wendell Phillips's "The Murder of Lovejoy," an extemporaneous 1837 Faneuil Hall oration that brought the young lawyer's punchy style to the public eye. Rising to rebut Massachusetts Attorney General James Austin, who praised Lovejoy's mobbing as a second Tea Party, Phillips compares Lovejoy to "the first martyrs in the cause of American liberty." Phillips recruits the very portraits lining Faneuil Hall to support his argument. Imagine, he says, the "pictured lips" of those Revolutionary martyrs "broken into voice to rebuke" his opponent, Austin, as a "recreant American—the slanderer of the dead." Phillips's uncanny vision of speaking portraits eschews sensational representations of white male suffering in favor of mystical, nostalgic revivifications of the noble dead, materially present in the space of the hall itself. Many printed versions of Phillips's oration use the moment of Phillips's uncanny vision to grapple with the interaction between oral and print performances. Embedding Phillips's written text in his original embodied performance and reception, some print editions, for example, interrupt Phillips's oration to note, parenthetically, that Phillips was "pointing to the portraits in the hall" and received "applause and counter applause."[40] Overall, republican martyrology's alignment of abolitionist fighters with Revolutionary heroes participates in what Dana Nelson describes as a hierarchical ordering of male sociability through the reorganization of masculine aggression "under the banner of whiteness."[41] Phillips, who later supported Garrisonian "disunion," here criticizes both Austin's reactionary conservatism and Garrison's pacifism by describing fighting abolitionists as the true heirs to the nation's early martyrs. Abolitionist republican martyrology maintained the martyred body's mystical communicative power but rejected sensational representations of embodied white suffering in favor of linking the martyr to the Revolutionary dead.

The martyr's whiteness becomes more explicit in republican martyrology's recurring, almost reflexive description of Lovejoy—a Presbyterian minister and printer—as "a martyr to the great and inestimable rights of the freedom of the press."[42] Abolitionists attempted to broaden Lovejoy's popular appeal by attributing his suffering to a defense of white male public sphere "rights" rather than abolition per se. If properly described and discussed, they suggest, the martyr's death might correct the distortions of the public sphere caused by anti-abolitionist violence. Their persistent invocation of Lovejoy's "rights" also indicates the broader appeal of Garrison's intentionally anachronistic Revolutionary rhetoric of publicity. As Robert Fanuzzi writes, the Garrisonian public sphere includes blacks and women within the bounds of "literate discussion" but adopts the Early Republic's rhetoric of white male self-abstraction constructed against the particularity of female and nonwhite bodies. Designed to allow abolitionists to enter into a national narrative and reflect on the unfulfilled promise of the Revolution, republican martyrology reproduces this projection of embodiment onto women and people of color.[43] Unlike some Garrisonian rhetoric, though, many printed versions of Lovejoy's martyrology follow Phillips's example by highlighting their origins in embodied oratory. Few go as far as Phillips's in describing audience and atmosphere, but many are subtitled "A Discourse" or specify when and where they were "delivered." In describing the transformation of the martyr's body into a text, the printed martyrology grounds its authority in the original embodied delivery. They dramatize abolitionist martyrology's circular movement from embodied white suffering into speech and then print to encourage more suffering and publicity.

Republican martyrology subordinates Lovejoy's sympathy for slaves to his defense of his rights to such a degree that it ultimately substitutes the ideological or mental "enslavement" of white men for the legal and physical enslavement of blacks. This substitution is especially striking in Christian republican martyrologies that use restrictions on slave mobility to conceptualize limits on white male publicity. Beriah Green's *The Martyr* (1838), delivered in New York City and Utica and published by the AASS, offers an extended metaphor comparing the threats to Lovejoy's publicity with the experience of runaway slaves. Green characterizes Lovejoy's refusal to stop printing as a refusal "to be the most miserable and degraded of slaves;" he describes Lovejoy as pursued "with bloodhound eagerness" by antislavery forces in the South before being "assailed by frenzied mobs" and killed.[44] *The Martyr* epitomizes republican martyrology's use of sensational tropes of slave suffering to illustrate white mental or political enslavement. Green privileges the "runaway" Lovejoy's willed refusal of mental or political "slavery" above the suffering of actual slaves, who do not choose their suffering. Lovejoy's death outdoes that of the "dumb . . . crushed" slave because his eloquent blood will more effectively bear witness to the justice of abolition: "the voice of Lovejoy's blood," Green concludes, will make "thousands and millions of our countrymen," presumptively white, "aroused to the claims of the enslaved."[45]

Martyrology invokes sensational representations of black physical suffering to apply them, metaphorically, to restrictions on white male publicity, circuitously using suffering black embodiment to rehabilitate a white male body otherwise tarnished by the association.

This comparison of restrictions on white male publicity to slave suffering develops one of the U.S. Revolution's most significant contributions to modern racism: the troping of Americans as "slaves" to the British. A committee of black slaves in Boston petitioning for slaves' "civil and religious liberty" in 1773 noted the logical and moral gap between the attack on ideological or political slavery and the defense of actual slavery, writing that they "expect great things from men who have made such a noble stand against the designs of their *fellow-men* to enslave them."[46] Supporters of slavery, responding to these and similar English abolitionist critiques, helped develop notions of racial difference as inherent and biological to justify "African" slavery as a natural, rather than cultural, hierarchy.[47] On the one hand, the line between physical slavery and ideological slavery in abolitionist republican martyrologies is far more blurred than in the Revolutionary martyrological rhetoric on which they drew. Lovejoy's martyrologies, for example, describe his series of removals in search of a city hospitable to abolitionist publication, a search that did, in fact, end in his murder for the cause of abolition. Other white abolitionists addressed the problems caused by this distinction by focusing on black political rhetoric. The Boston *Commonwealth*, coedited by Elizur Wright, republished the petitions of the enslaved to legitimate Wright's own support for a group of black men who rescued Shadrach Minkins from a Boston courtroom in 1858 and encourage further civil disobedience against the Fugitive Slave Law. Nevertheless, republican martyrological accounts of white abolitionists' "enslavement" more often worked by distancing white political "slavery" from black physical slavery.[48]

While Phillips's "The Murder of Lovejoy" and other narrowly republican martyrologies attempt to stabilize the distinction between physical slavery and mental slavery by minimizing sensational representations of embodied white suffering, Green and other Christian republican martyrologists represent embodied suffering but distinguish it from slave suffering in two ways. First, Christian republican martyrology associates the martyr's suffering with that of crime victims, turning charges of criminality back on their opponents. Green, for example, describes Lovejoy's "dying groans" and compares his corpse to a "bleeding body of a murdered companion thrown across [other white Americans'] path."[49] Similarly, Beecher's short, psychologically

complex account of Lovejoy's death in his firsthand *Narrative of Riots at Alton*
resembles the psychological focus of popular midcentury sensational tales of
murder.[50] "[T]he eye of his murderer," Beecher writes, "was on him. The object of hatred, deep, malignant and long continued, was fully before him—
and the bloody tragedy was consummated." Sensational murder narratives
usually follow the victim's suffering with declarations of sympathy and horror, but Beecher substitutes a moment of miraculous endurance. Beecher
writes that "Five balls were lodged in [Lovejoy's] body, and he soon breathed
his last. Yet after his moral wound he had strength remaining to return to the
building and ascend one flight of stairs before he fell."[51] Beecher's innovative
perspective and temporal complexity offer a psychological and emotional
depth missing from other accounts. These new elements cement the hagiog-
raphic character of his portrait and further distance Lovejoy's suffering from
slave suffering.

Christian republican martyrology also separates white and black suffering by describing embodied white suffering in explicitly Christ-like terms
that emphasize self-sacrifice. As Green writes, Lovejoy's suffering "was of a
vicarious character," like Christ's. The spiritual logic of martyrdom makes
white suffering superior because whites "count the cost" before choosing the
martyr's path and then suffer in obedience to their "hearts."[52] In an apostro-
phe to Lovejoy as Christ, Green emphasizes Lovejoy's prevention of white
abolitionists' suffering: "Yes, brother, as we bend over thy bleeding body, we
know, and feel, and acknowledge, that the insufferable insults, 'the cruel
mockings' and dying agonies which thou hast endured, were meant for us."[53]
In other words, because abolitionist martyrs suffer for both slaves and white
male access to civic abstraction, their sacrifice helps prevent both embodied
black suffering and white civil loss.

In Beecher's Christian republican martyrologies, this white group—the
white "us"—links the martyr's suffering to an exceptionalist notion of U.S.
expansion more commonly associated with foes of abolition. Like Green,
Beecher begins by emphasizing the white will to suffer not for slaves per se
but for Christ. Beecher attributes this Christian strain to Lovejoy himself,
recounting Lovejoy's defiant testimony at a town council meeting organized
to ban his press: "You may hand me up, as the mob hung up the individuals
of Vicksburg! You may burn me at the stake, as they did McIntosh at St.
Louis: or, you may tar and feather me, or throw me into the Mississippi, as
you have often threatened to do; but you cannot disgrace me. . . . [T]he deep-
est of all disgrace would be, at a time like this, to deny my Master by

forsaking his cause."[54] Using Lovejoy's prophetic account to emphasize his deliberate acceptance of suffering, Beecher, like Green, imagines embodied white suffering as a type of Christ's suffering, sacred in its selflessness and devotion to God. Beecher describes death as multiplying Lovejoy's voice even beyond the power of the press into the discursive spread of "civilization" itself: "Ten thousand presses, had he employed them all, could never have done what the simple tale of his death will do. Up and down the mighty streams of the west his voice will go: it will penetrate the remotest corner of our land: it will be heard to the extremities of the civilized world. From henceforth no boat will pass the spot where he fell, heedless of his name, or of his sentiments, or of the cause for which he died."[55] Beecher's representation of the public repetition of this "simple tale" as a means to achieve an unparalleled disembodied transcendence attributes the mystical quality of the martyr's suffering to the public reiteration of his death. Beecher's description of the abolitionist martyr's role in helping the "civilized world" "penetrate" the "remotest corner" contributes to a developing notion of what John O'Sullivan called America's "divine" imperial expansion.[56] Here the martyr's movement from suffering into speech is not primarily nostalgic, in association with the Revolutionary dead, but imperialistic, associated with the nation's continuing expansion.

Beecher does not use racial language to describe martyrology's role in U.S. imperialism, but other Christian republican martyrologies explicitly engaged the rhetoric of Anglo-Saxonism that helped structure Jacksonian expansionism. One of the most fascinating of these, Thomas Stone's sermon *The Martyr of Freedom* (1838), uses a deterministic notion of race to attribute Lovejoy's love of liberty to his "Saxon blood."[57] In a passage redolent with fears of political degeneration through racial degeneration, Stone writes that Lovejoy's sacrifice proves that "Saxon blood has not yet flowed wholly out of the American heart."[58] This reading of the "Saxon" foundation of American political and emotional society couples a Jeffersonian understanding of emotion, character, and politics peculiarly embodied in the "Anglo-Saxon" race with amalgamationist fears promoted, in the late 1830s and 1840s, by opponents of abolition.[59] For example, Stone's account of Saxon blood concurs with that offered in the *Democratic Review*'s laudatory review of Sharon Turner's *History of the Anglo-Saxons* (1799–1805), which described U.S. expansion as the natural expression of what Turner called the "wild" Saxons' love of "liberty."[60] Stone, here implicitly repudiating widespread rumors of the "free love" principles of "abolitionist and amalgamationist" preachers,

blames slavery for the "corruption" of the national "blood" and describes abolitionist oration, in sympathy with those deprived of liberty, as a quintessentially Saxon trait. Similarly, Green, wedding racial discourse to traditional
Christian proscriptions on bodily license, describes slavery as creating "powerful temptations" and giving "unrestrained license to every species of iniq-
uity under the most revolting forms and with the worst consequences."[61]
Green published *The Martyr* during his presidency of Oneida College, which
was fully integrated under his leadership. Green's commitment to integration, invocation of the human "family," and egalitarian insistence on the "in-
alienable rights of man—for every man" evoke monogenetic racial arguments
to resist the balder determinism of Stone's Anglo-Saxonism, but Green's distinction between white mental and black physical slavery works by associating Lovejoy's martyrdom with the prevention of amalgamation.

The logic of sacrificial substitution structures Christian republican martyrdom, and Green explicitly considers martyrology's link between substitution, representation, and political action. Lovejoy, Green writes, attempted to
correct a failure of language, a gap between representation and reality, in
which "the *word slavery* altogether failed to awaken . . . the conception of
which it was a standing symbol." This gap produced a failure of sentiment, so
that "Lovejoy saw myriads of his own mother's children insulted, wronged,
outraged;—with no eye to pity and no hand to rescue."[62] Green identifies the
failure of abolitionist sensationalism as a representational problem, but
rather than describing black suffering in a new way, Green presents it as uni-
form, generic, and entirely destructive.

> The blood of "the poor innocents," which in different parts of our re-
> public has been most wantonly poured upon the ground, they have
> uncovered; striking terror into the bosoms of the guilty, and produc-
> ing thrill upon thrill of universal horror.
>
> In a thousand ways on various occasions, they have opened their
> "lips for the dumb," and plead the cause of those who were crushed by
> insufferable burdens. For this purpose they have employed the elo-
> quence of the living voice and the energies of the press. (11)

Green's description of the "crush[ing]" of the black voice describes the logic
behind sensational representations of slave suffering (and much other reformist sensationalism) as a physical, embodied drama of pained black silence and suffering white speech. The "crushed" and "dumb" black voice is

revived in the "living voice" of white "lips" and the animated "energies of the press." The white martyr's suffering dominates this chorus, as the "voice of Lovejoy's blood" speaks even louder than sympathetic white "lips for the dumb," entirely obviating the need for black publicity.

The ability of "crushed," "dumb" blackness to authorize white abolitionist martyrological speech resembles the way in which black female suffering operates in some black male abolitionist prose. As I briefly noted above in my discussion of Walker's *Trial and Imprisonment*, these forms of mute suffering resemble Frederick Douglass's description of his Aunt Hester. The "terrible spectacle" of Aunt Hester's scourging is Douglass's "blood stained gate," Douglass's "entrance to the hell of slavery," and something Douglass will never forget, but it is not a moment that enables Hester's speech or publicity.[63] Robert Reid-Pharr proposes that Douglass and other black male abolitionists create their black public subject by abjecting black women's embodied suffering and subsequently reattaching it as a "prosthetic" or "second skin" in which "blackness" adheres. Douglass can then don this prosthetic blackness to enter the public sphere as a black man.[64] Douglass's sensational description of Hester's whipping transforms the image of the pained, unruly black body, which restricted black participation in public life, into a vehicle for black participation in the public sphere. It does so by shifting abjection onto a desiring and desirous female body while claiming its emotional, affective power for Douglass himself. Hester's sensational suffering stands as the implicit point of contrast to Douglass's eventual realization of his "manhood" in his fight with Covey and subsequent attempt to transcend, in Paul Gilroy's words, the "structures of the nation state and the constraints of ethnicity and national particularity" through his work in black churches and the abolitionist public sphere.[65]

Douglass's blockbuster account, first published in May 1845 and republished many times in quick succession, may have been on the mind of white abolitionists who, that same year, touted Walker's branding in such heroic terms.[66] Both Douglass and white abolitionist men would have found it difficult to remain in the public sphere without retaining the suffering black body as a prosthetic.[67] Although Douglass's claim to the private "rights" of "manhood" was negligible in comparison to white abolitionists, the mechanisms by which white abolitionists attempted to assert their public voice were comparable. Like Douglass, white abolitionist martyrology uses sensational representations of black suffering as a metaphor for restrictions on white abolitionist publicity while also distinguishing between their own self-willed suffering and the slave's necessary pained embodiment. They also attempt to evoke some of the dread of Douglass's assertion that, after Hester, he would "be next." In white male martyrology, white abolitionists invoke the suffering black body only to outdo it in their own public celebration of self-willed sacrifice. This sacrifice then allows white men to ventriloquize a suffering black voice.

All abolitionist republican martyrology attempted to harness black suffering for white publicity by emphasizing white male rights and silencing the black voice. Some republican martyrology that explicitly engaged racial language to distance white suffering from black suffering went even further, asserting the public rights of white men without clouding the issue by considering slavery or blackness in any great detail. These tend to draw more heavily on domestic sentiment and emphasize, rather than downplay, the tension between the martyr's embodied suffering and his disembodied speech after death. For example, Stone's racial determinism dovetails with his use of domestic sympathy to enable white male publicity. He juxtaposes Lovejoy's suffering with feminized white domestic suffering and, later, embodied black suffering, moderating some of the "obscene" power of white male suffering by integrating that suffering into a complex, extended sentimental scene. Lovejoy's family, Stone writes, was once sheltered in "the quiet valley of the Kennebec" but is now in tatters, with his father "passed from the earth" and his mother "left in an age of widowhood to mourn the son of her pride."[68] Rather than mourn his passing, Stone suggests that we should "exult that God has given [Lovejoy] to fight such a fight" and describes Lovejoy's blood as "the seed of a glorious harvest" for the abolitionist cause. Evoking the trope of the martyr's crown, Stone presents Lovejoy's death as the final, defining moment of a life devoted to ascetic self-control, as his "manly bearing" and his "heroic and Christian constancy" in the face of "toils" and "trials" were "crowned by such a death."[69] Embracing sensationalism, Stone invokes the republican personification of liberty as a suffering woman by describing the "sacred bosom" of "freedom" as "torn, scarred, exposed in its humiliation" by slavery. Stone's use of embodied female suffering to excite an explicitly "Saxon" love of liberty underscores the similarity between abolitionists' sensational tropes of black suffering and Revolutionary sensational tropes of suffering Liberty, as both blacks and women serve as symbols of a republican virtue they were themselves denied.[70]

Stone then pivots away from sensationalism, claiming that the "tears" the children of Liberty "wept when they saw her thus disfigured and disgraced" are unlike tears shed for the martyr. The tears for a martyr "may be shed for a moment," but they will be the angry tears of a warrior, "such as Achilles wept over his lost Patroclus, nursing the inly burning strength."[71] While suffering women provoke tears, suffering men provoke action. Stone's turn from sensation to the classical trope of the warrior-lover embeds abolitionist suffering in what Julie Ellison has called "Cato's tears": the privileged emotional relationship between men whose ascetic self-control allows them to move from intense feeling to decisive action.[72] Stone's final image of intimate heroic love, affectingly invoking his personal relationship with Lovejoy, combines the sympathy for suffering with the Revolutionary promise of fraternal devotion (as in the Declaration of Independence's "pledge to each other our lives, our fortunes, and our sacred honor"). Stone critiques sensation in order to transform and revive it for the abolitionist cause.

White Women's Publicity and the "Real Presence" of Emotional Distress

The desire for a martyr's suffering was not limited to white men, nor was abolitionist martyrology an exclusively white male genre. Harriet Martineau's *The Martyr Age of the United States* (1838) is not only the most prominent female-authored abolitionist martyrology, but it is the most sustained and elaborate martyrology of the period, if not the century. *The Martyr Age* was the first transatlantic collaboration between Martineau, an established English writer of social criticism who circulated in Boston's elite abolitionist circles, and Maria Weston Chapman, a leading figure in those circles. First published in the *Westminster Review*, *The Martyr Age* began as an appraisal of Chapman's *Right and Wrong in Boston*, a series of annual reports of the Boston Female Anti-Slavery Society, 1835–37, and includes extensive excerpts from that work.[73] Abolitionist organizations on both sides of the Atlantic then excerpted and republished *The Martyr Age* several times from 1839 to 1840, offering less expensive editions to reach larger audiences and raise funds for the AASS and Ohio's Oberlin Institute. Despite the greater number of abolitionist martyrologies authored by white American men, *The Martyr Age* reminds us that abolitionist martyrology was transatlantic in its origins and development, offered white women a useful tool for engaging the public on both sides of the Atlantic, and was well connected to other Anglo-American humanitarian reform movements, including the reform of English imperial practice.[74]

Martineau and Chapman use martyrology to address different problems of publicity than their white male counterparts and consequently make different connections between embodiment, suffering, and publicity. *The Martyr Age* uses martyrology to justify many forms of female publicity, including moral suasion, legislative petition, society organizing, writing, and, most controversially, authoritative public speech, or "teaching," in the service of abolition. Most important, Chapman insists that without enfranchisement, "open and direct" public-sphere political speech and petition are a white woman's *only* means "of manifesting her civil existence."[75] Chapman asserts that those who call women's speech and petition "unladylike" enforce "domestic tyranny." This pun evokes the dual meaning of "domestic" as both home and nation, connecting ostensibly personal or private restrictions on female publicity with political restrictions on abolitionist speech. It positions the public sphere as a lynchpin connecting the two techniques of exclusion. Martineau may have especially appreciated the pun as she had received just such criticism in the *American Quarterly Review*: its 1837 account of her visit to America described Martineau as "so notoriously conspicuous by that unwomanly act of hers—the delivery of a speech at an abolition meeting—[that it] prevented many of the best people of Boston from showing her civility." Further associating gendered norms of public speech with embodied sexual difference, the *Review* insinuated that Martineau was a "half-and-half-woman-man," insisted that no "American women" would "get up at a public meeting" as she had done, and derided her earlier writing as "interesting *story books*" of "romance and thrilling incidents." Chapman herself recognized, and perhaps even welcomed, the destabilizing effect of publicity on her gender presentation, describing herself as "unsexed" by her work.[76] In the face of the double bind on abolitionist and female speech, Martineau and Chapman present white women's emotional suffering in sympathy with white and black male martyrs as enabling white female participation in the public sphere.

In *The Martyr Age*, mobbing becomes the crucial test for white female abolitionists. Martineau moves from Chapman's endorsement of female public speech to Martineau's own account of Helen Benson Garrison's reaction to the news that William Garrison, her husband, was dragged off by a mob to be tarred during a Boston Female Anti-Slavery Society meeting. Martineau casts the mobbing as a disruption of a sentimental abolitionist family by attributing William Garrison's presence at the meeting to his desire to escort Helen Garrison, who was "near her confinement." Martineau confronts the notion of "confinement" as a naturalized sign of female domesticity by simultaneously drawing on the sentimental appeal of pregnancy and connecting pregnancy to publicity. In a sensational scene, the pregnant Helen Garrison, "in the fearful excitement of the moment, stepped out of the window upon a shed" to see events unfold. What Helen Garrison hopes to see, Martineau makes clear, is not her husband's safe release but his tarring itself, as a result of *his will to suffer* for his principles. The "only words which escaped" her lips, Martineau writes, were " 'I think my husband will not deny his principles: I am sure my husband will never deny his principles.' " The passage emphasizes not only William Garrison's will to suffer physically, as in most white male martyrologies, but also Helen Garrison's will to suffer emotionally in support of abolitionist convictions. Martineau treats their suffering quite differently. She does not represent William Garrison's suffering in sensational terms, only gesturing at his experience by mentioning his assault by "brick-bats" as he was dragged to "the tar-kettle." In contrast, she accentuates Helen Garrison's sensational, physiological experience of emotional suffering by noting her "white lips" and "excite[d]" movement. After confirming that William Garrison never "in the least flinched from the consequences of his principles," Martineau repeats this entire drama a few paragraphs later by excerpting Angelina Grimké's letter to William Garrison. Grimké describes her own "fear" that Garrison might "compromise" and relief that he was "determined to suffer and to die, rather than yield one inch" in the face of the mob.[77] This "high" sentimental tableau of emotional suffering emphasizes Helen Garrison's devotion not to her husband but to abolition.

For her own part, Chapman rejected any connection between martyrdom and willed suffering. When a friend described her as a martyr for the cause, Chapman replied, "I can't say I have made any sacrifices. I have had my choice."[78] Standing in sharp contrast to many white male abolitionists of lesser stature, Chapman's demurral from martyrdom, like her demurral from public oration, testifies to martyrology's association of masculinity and a certain type of public performance. Rather than abandoning female martyrdom altogether, Chapman and Martineau separate it from will by attributing it to an *involuntary* female sympathetic experience of suffering. Chapman describes sympathy as "womanly devotedness," a "sympathy for the oppressed implanted by the Spirit of God in the heart of the mother . . . the wife . . . and the daughter."[79] The divinely created sympathetic female body necessarily preempts customary and legislative bans on female publicity. In place of white male abolitionist martyrology's association of publicity with "Saxon" liberty and the Revolutionary dead, Martineau figures white women's publicity as the result of gender difference. Interweaving Martineau's narrative of female emotional response to white male suffering into Chapman's arguments in favor of female publicity, *The Martyr Age* suggests that white women's abolitionist publicity fulfills a female obligation to resist "domestic tyranny."[80] By describing their emotional suffering as involuntary, Martineau and Chapman align their experience with that of slaves, imagining different, though still problematic, alliances between free white women and the enslaved.

The difference between white men's and white women's martyrology is clearest in white female accounts of the murder of Francis McIntosh, a mulatto man captured, chained to a tree, and burned by a mob in St. Louis a few months before Lovejoy's murder.[81] White men uniformly describe McIntosh's burning as a significant prelude to Lovejoy's death, invoking the familiar dyad of inarticulate black sufferer and articulate white martyr. A memorial to Lovejoy in Rochester, New York, for example, described the "groans of the dying McIntosh" as "ringing in [Lovejoy's] ears" and inspiring Lovejoy's eloquent "plead[ing] against injustice."[82] The memorial makes the emotional resonance of McIntosh's suffering available to Lovejoy while leaving his white body relatively unsullied by violence and free to speak. White female abolitionists, in contrast, begin to make McIntosh into a martyr himself. Some of Martineau's descriptions of black suffering include sensational detail, but her brief account of McIntosh's burning notes only that it occurred "under circumstances of deep atrocity," without detailing his torture. Martineau also grants him a pious death by describing his prayerful suffering but then immediately shies away by noting that "[b]ecause he was heard to pray as his limbs were slowly consuming, he was pronounced by the magistrates to be in league with the abolitionists." Deflecting some of the drama and danger of the black martyr, Martineau makes McIntosh's piety instrumental as a sign of abolitionist piety.[83] Again taking a different turn from her white male contemporaries, Martineau uses the white female abolitionist will to suffer emotionally, in sympathy with black and white male suffering, to defend white female participation in the public sphere. Her description of female emotional suffering as enabling white female publicity participated in the development of a "high" sentimental sympathy around embodied racial and gender differences. Martineau and Chapman follow white men in describing black male suffering in sensational terms, but they also describe their own embodied sympathetic suffering as sensational and involuntary. They describe their suffering as almost exclusively sympathetic and emotional, decline to portray themselves as martyrs, and come close to describing black men's suffering in martyrological terms.

Martineau and Chapman's use of black martyrdom to support white female publicity is an important precursor to one of the most popular, most despised, and most unusual examples of abolitionist martyrdom, Harriet Beecher Stowe's account of Tom's death in *Uncle Tom's Cabin*. Stowe, as an American novelist distant from Boston's abolitionist elite, had a more vexed relationship to white male abolitionist martyrology than Martineau.[84] Nonetheless, while Stowe's early rejection of female public speech and organizing in favor of domestic "influence" put her in conflict with Martineau and Chapman, Stowe follows them in grounding women's publicity on innate female sympathy. Before turning to the novel itself, we should first consider Stowe's *Key to Uncle Tom's Cabin* (1853); because the *Key*, like *The Martyr Age*, was a compilation, Stowe's departures from both *The Martyr Age* and her own white male sources are easier to discern. The most direct point of comparison is Stowe's account of McIntosh and Lovejoy in "Martyrdom," a brief chapter in the *Key*. "Martyrdom" draws from her brother Edward Beecher's account and includes several excerpts from his narrative. Stowe distinguishes between heroic white female resistance and sensational black suffering, contrasting Lovejoy's wife's valiant domestic struggle to that of the passive "victim" McIntosh, whose sensational "shrieks . . . for a more merciful death were disregarded" in a "scene of protracted torture."[85] By emphasizing McIntosh's uncontrolled bodily response to pain, Stowe refuses McIntosh the pious death granted by Martineau. Instead, she uses McIntosh's embodied suffering to further underline Lovejoy's will to suffer: after describing McIntosh's "shrieks," Stowe repeats Beecher's description of Lovejoy's "tranquil and composed . . . state of mind" and his public declaration of his will to be "burn[ed] at the stake, as they did McIntosh at St. Louis." Her brief paraphrase of Beecher's account of Lovejoy's death eliminates Beecher's gruesome commentary, psychological complexity, and attention to bodily detail.[86] Finally, Stowe reprints Beecher's biblical description of Lovejoy's death as allowing for his transcendent speech: "Though dead he still speaketh; and a united world can never silence his voice."[87] Here Stowe, to an even greater degree than Beecher, invokes sensational black suffering only to attach its emotional resonance to the white martyr's speech.

Stowe's most substantial departures from Beecher come in her framing of Beecher's narrative. She begins "Martyrdom" with a sensational description of Lovejoy's wife "struggling with men armed with bludgeons and bowie-knives" who attacked her house, granting white women access to the external assaults of martyrdom in defense of domestic tranquility. She ends with another sentimental domestic scene, not of sensational suffering but of emotional suffering. Describing Lovejoy's mother's emotional fortitude, Stowe writes that she greeted news of his death stoically, saying only, "It is well. I had rather he would die so than forsake his principles." Stowe sanctifies Lovejoy's mother's will to suffer emotional loss by comparing her to the Virgin Mary, "who saw her dearest crucified" and will be "blessed above all women." Stowe suggests that the maternal will to suffer emotional loss may even promise greater political benefit than male martyrdom. Only Lovejoy's mother's sacrifice proves that "all is not over with America."[88] Taken together, Stowe's editorial work imagines the white female will to suffer as superior to white male martyrdom because it is more entirely "vicarious," inasmuch as women suffer for the actions of men. Though she does not connect emotional suffering to white female publicity within the narrative, female emotional suffering in support of white male martyrdom and domestic security justifies Stowe's participation in the abolitionist public.

The value of martyrology and white female emotional suffering for white female publicity becomes clearer in the context of *Uncle Tom's Cabin*'s engagement of republican martyrology. If the *Key* offers a relatively straightforward use of martyrology to support white female publicity, *Uncle Tom's Cabin* contains multiple, contradictory uses of martyrdom that complicate what several critics discuss as the novel's reliance on the "real presence" of emotional distress, a topic Chapter 4 will explore in greater detail. Perhaps the most famous illustration of Stowe's use of "high" sentimental "real presence" is Stowe's narration, in *Uncle Tom's Cabin*, of Senator Bird's spiritual-political conversion. Bird's memory of his own lost child and tearful witnessing of "the real presence of distress" in the form of Eliza's "helpless agony" changed him from a supporter of the Fugitive Slave Act to an abettor in the escape of a fugitive slave. Stowe's "real presence," like white male martyrology, attempts to overcome the moral and ethical challenges to humanitarian sensational representations of embodied black suffering. White abolitionist martyrology, in moving abolitionist sentiment away from humanitarian sensationalism and toward sympathetic, psychologically complex family love relationships, may have contributed to Stowe's depiction of emotional distress. At the same time, Stowe's juxtaposition of humanitarian sensationalism, minstrelsy, and black martyrology departs from white male abolitionist martyrology and questions the moral and political efficacy of republican martyrology in particular.

Uncle Tom's Cabin most clearly differs from white male martyrology, as well as Stowe's own account of McIntosh in the *Key*, by granting Tom a martyr's self-willed determination to suffer. Tom's recurring prayer that Jesus not "let [him] give out" in the face of Legree's tortures (including the threat of being "tied to a tree" and burned) effectively combines, in one character, the martyrological tropes that Martineau and white male abolitionists parcel out to McIntosh, Helen Garrison and Grimké, and William Garrison.[89] Unlike Douglass or white male martyrs, Tom is no defender of his rights. Stowe and her supporters, facing accusations that *Uncle Tom's Cabin* supported slave rebellion, pointed out that Tom "is the most faithful of servants," who only "chose to die, with the courage and resolution of a Christian martyr, [rather] than save his life by a guilty compliance" with "unlawful commands."[90] As I discuss below, Stowe's racial logic works to limit the consequences of black martyrdom, but Tom still offers a significant challenge to white male abolitionists' exclusion of black men from the martyrological tradition.

Stowe's departures from white male abolitionist martyrology serve to make Tom a paragon of martyrdom and preserve that singularity. Stowe condemns female abuses of martyrology to by ironically using the term to describe "nervous" illnesses (by Marie St. Clare, who speaks with "the voice of a suffering martyr") and the "self-sacrifice" of "benevolent" educators (by Ophelia St. Clare, who declines housework "to condemn herself to the martyrdom of instructing Topsy"). Stowe clears the greatest space for Tom's martyrdom by satirizing republican martyrology's moral and political claims in two scenes of "Black Sam's" minstrel "speechifying." The chapter "Eliza's Escape" is a comic interlude set between a harrowing description of Eliza's crossing of the Ohio River and a "high" sentimental invocation of the "real presence" of emotional distress. As a counterpoint to these emotionally freighted scenes, comic minstrelsy disciplines and stabilizes sentiment by serving as a tonic to readers overtaxed by pathos. It also allows Stowe to make less straightforward critiques. As one contemporary reviewer commented, Sam's minstrelsy "discreetly reliev[ed]" her "reader's feelings" and allowed her to voice "sly" criticism of political speech.[91] Sam's minstrelsy highlights Stowe's complex relationship to abolitionist martyrology and public-sphere abolitionist organizing more generally.

Stowe uses Sam's minstrelsy to address public-sphere exchanges between sentimental authors and their readers and between political speakers and their audiences. She engages multiple registers and audiences to mock both U.S. taste in fiction and U.S. political speech. In the first scene of minstrel

speech, Sam curries favor with his masters, the Shelbys, by offering an exag-
geratedly pious account of Eliza's crossing.[92] Working in a comic register,
Stowe patrols the boundaries of abolitionist sentiment by mocking "dilet-
tanti" authors who, like Sam, make "great *capital* of scriptural figures and
images" and foolish readers who, like Mrs. Shelby, have a "breathless, and almost faint" reaction to sensational tales of suffering and escape.[93] Stowe then
uses minstrelsy to attack the misuse of martyrology in political speech. Sam's
second speech addresses his fellow slaves in the kitchen "dominions of Aunt
Chloe," a Rabelaisian space of riot and revelry. From the moment Sam begins
his oration, uttering " 'Yer see, fellow-countrymen' " while "elevating a turkey's leg," to his final rising, "full of supper and glory, for a closing effort,"
Stowe's humor derives from collapsing the supposedly disinterested, disembodied classical republican oratory into self-interested, gross embodiment,
here marked as black.

Earlier in the novel, Stowe introduced Sam as a prevaricating and canny
man with "a comprehensiveness of vision and a strict lookout to his own personal well-being, that would have done credit to any white patriot in Washington," and she extends this satire here.[94] Sam's speech is an actual "political"
speech (in the "low" world of black "domestic politics") designed to entertain
his audience long enough for him to eat. As Sam announces in his perora-
tion: "Yes, my feller-citizens and ladies of de other sex in general, I has
principles,—I'm proud to 'oon 'em,—they's perquisite to dese yer times, and
ter *all* times. I has principles, and I sticks to 'em like forty,—jest anything that
I thinks is principle, I goes in to 't;—I wouldn't mind if dey burnt me 'live,—
I'd walk right up to de stake, I would, and say, here I comes to shed my last
blood fur my principles, fur my country, fur de gen'l interests of society."[95]
Stowe here uses minstrel malapropisms and pratfalls to target the hypocrisy
of New England politicians who make use of martyrological rhetoric while
neglecting the plight of actual slaves, particularly in their enforcement of the
Fugitive Slave Law. Sam's claim to "stand up for yer rights" "and "fend [slave-
catchers] to the last breath!" is deflated by his friend Andy's recollection that
Sam "telled [him], only this mornin', that [he would] help this yer Mas'r to
cotch Lizy." More generally, Sam's speech critiques the white male use of republican martyrology to claim a moral authority derived from forms of suffering that were, far more often, the slave's lot. Sam "volunteers" to be burned
at the stake, but ultimately he has no say in the disposition of his body, a
point Stowe underlines with the sale of Harry and Tom. Sam's exaggerated
martyrology, particularly his literal rendering of the metaphor of walking

"right up to" the stake to defend an ever-changing "principle," skewers white abolitionists' claims of willing affliction. It reveals the posturing of white male martyrology's focus on voluntary pain, ridicules its distinction between embodied black slavery and ideological white "slavery," and suggests that republican martyrology is no more than a parody of slave suffering. In contrast to Sam's political buffoonery, Stowe aligns herself with "poor, simple, virtuous" Aunt Chloe, the household cook, who provides the moral of the story. Silencing Sam by announcing that "one o' yer principles will have to be to get to bed some time tonight, and not be a keepin' everybody up till mornin'," Chloe shows how political speech necessarily yields to practical domestic authority.[96] Stowe, playing both politics and domesticity in a minstrel key, pulls the rug out from under the notion of "disinterested" political claims to suffer for "principle" and suggests such rhetoric is bound to fall short of domestic practicality.

There is a tantalizing ambivalence in Stowe's use of minstrel speech. On the one hand, Sam's speeches do not reappropriate minstrelsy in the manner of William Wells Brown's Cato or Charles Chesnutt's Uncle Julius.[97] Sam's minstrel "speechifying" mocks white political discourse but does so by holding black republican speech itself up for ridicule. Stowe reserves the "subversive" character of Sam's mimicry for her own attack on republican martyrology. The success of Stowe's critique therefore reinforces minstrelsy's location of pained embodiment at the heart of black subjectivity. On the other hand, in addition to using minstrelsy to critique political speech herself, Stowe describes Sam's usual orations as "burlesques and imitations" of political speeches, delivered to groups of slaves and whites gathered at the outer edges of political meetings.[98] This seems to raise the possibility that parody and mimicry might help construct oppositional subjectivity, as Douglass does when he compares the officious speech of "slaves of the out-farm" to that of "slaves of the political parties."[99]

Perhaps despite itself, then, Sam's speech offers something more. If the imperfect alignment between minstrel, sensational, and sentimental constructions of pained black subjectivity allows them to mutually support one another, it also allows the gaps and contradictions between them to come to the fore. The humorous context of Sam's reference to being "burnt . . . 'live" may allow for some "sly" reflection on the limits of both white abolitionist martyrology and Stowe's own insistence that Tom's martyrdom results from religious ideals unconnected to national political claims.[100] Sam's comment is one of a unsettling series of references to slave burning: Classy sensationally warns that Emmeline consider the "black, blasted tree, and the ground all covered with black ashes" before she attempts to run away, and Legree threatens to tie Tom "to a tree, and have a slow fire lit up around." These references foreshadow Tom's eventual martyrdom, but also offer something more.[101] There is poignancy in Sam's parodic willingness to die at the stake for "his country" and the "interests of society" that is missing from Tom's "high" sentimental martyrdom. Invoking Foxe's martyrs and McIntosh's burning alike, Sam describes a punishment that, in the novel and the historical record, was readily used to terrorize blacks who attempted to employ or influence public political speech. Though Stowe only represents black political martyrology in a comic register, Sam's buffoonery may critique the inadequacy of Tom's "purely" religious martyrdom to prevent black torture.

In this way, Sam's minstrel rendering of republican martyrology may also serve as a sort of internal critique of the novel's attempt to distance Tom's death from black political organizing and slave revolt. Stowe's denial of a black desire for national abstraction imagines a new form of domestic martyrdom, substituting cabin for cross, but it also denies Tom entry into emerging black and egalitarian martyrological traditions growing out of black and integrated churches, Latin American anti-imperial movements, and abolitionist labor publics. Beginning in the mid-1850s, these traditions maintained the centrality of self-willed suffering but denied its relationship to whiteness: John S. Rock, Charles Lenox Raimond, Frances Harper, and other black abolitionists organized an 1858 Faneuil Hall commemoration of Crispus Attucks and other Revolutionary black martyrs. The Cuban novella "El negro mártir" (1854) insisted that diasporic African antislavery organizing could produce full republicanism in the Americas. Henry Bleby's 1868 account of Jamaica's "Morant War" described Paul Bogle and George William Gordon as martyrs. Henry Garnet and Martin Delany offered martyrological treatments of Cuban poet and revolutionary "Plácido" Gabriel de la Concepción Valdés.[102]

These black and egalitarian traditions challenged and transformed white martyrology's already unstable connection between race and suffering, particularly in martyrologies of John Brown. Some martyrologies by Garrison, by Brown himself, and in U.S. wartime propaganda extended the white abolitionist martyrological tradition to make Brown a model for Northern white militarism. Brown's whiteness became increasingly important in Reconstruction and Gilded Age martyrologies characterizing his "valor," "religion," and "sense" as a "Saxon" racial "inherit[ance]" from his "long line of English, Dutch, and American ancestors."[103] Other texts integrated Brown into the developing black and egalitarian martyrological traditions. Most famously, James Redpath's *Echoes of Harper's Ferry* offered a toast to "slave insurrection" and denounced Henry Ward Beecher for "'snuffing out' of his account the five colored men" who were also martyred in the raid. Redpath's comments echo a larger body of martyrologies, delivered in many forms of print and in front of diverse black and labor audiences, encouraging integrated political organizing. Several sectarian publications polarized their readership in editorials praising Brown's raid as igniting "the Spirit of God," implicitly associating slave revolt with divine will. Unitarian minister Moncure Daniel Conway, speaking to a mixed crowd of German unionists and black abolitionists in Cincinnati, described Brown as "the last apostle and martyr" of Thomas Paine. Jacob Manning, pastor of Boston's Old South Congregational Church, delivered a speech introducing Brown into the black martyrological tradition by describing him as a white Crispus Attucks.[104] These martyrologies would insist on the connection between black suffering, white abolitionist suffering, and black publicity in the late nineteenth century.

The vexed nature of black political speech comes to a head in Stowe's treatment of colonization and may point to her unsettled opinion on both.[105] As part of *Uncle Tom's Cabin*'s colonizationist solution to the problem of black spiritual and moral degradation, Tom's martyrdom confirms a black presence at the heart of the Christian "fellowship of man" but describes the U.S. civic body, including the public sphere, as fundamentally white. Stowe does not represent black suffering as a means to allow for black political speech or black participation in the public sphere except in George Harris's defense of colonization. Even then, it is Harris's divided racial status as a "mulatto," in contrast to Tom's "truly African features," that allows him to speak with authority on both black feeling and white nationality. Harris gives voice to both a finely tuned racial determinism as well as an elective notion of racial identity defined by sympathy. He attributes his commitment to blackness, particularly his unwillingness to pass, to his "sympathies" for the suffering of his black mother and sister, whose sale, whipping, and beating he earlier described in sensational terms. Conversely, Harris credits his ambition to create an "African *nationality*" in Liberia to his paternal racial inheritance, as "full half the blood in my veins is the hot and hasty Saxon."[106] Harris's description of the distinct "missions" and "eras" of the Anglo-Saxon and the African races works with Tom's martyrdom to define black subjectivity around a desire for religious transcendence that leads to further black Christianization (of Sambo and Quimbo, at Tom's deathbed, and of Africans in

Liberia).[107] Stowe thereby rejects Garrison's creation of "black" interiority around the desire for national abstraction (participation in the political body of the nation), proposing instead a desire for spiritual abstraction achievable by blacks and white women. Nevertheless, Harris's sketch of a post-Saxon "era" links Liberia to the midcentury republican revolutionary struggles "that now convulse the nations" and positions Liberia as a corrective to the unfinished republican revolution in the United States.[108] In the figure of the mulatto, Stowe imagines the black desire for spiritual abstraction as working alongside a fundamentally "Saxon" African nationalism to create a new sort of sympathetic nationalism.

The racial and gendered logic of suffering in Stowe's *Key* and other domestic sentimental fiction of the period thereby dovetails with the development of racial difference in white male abolitionist martyrology but offers a different emphasis. White male abolitionist accounts of martyrdom use the "obscenity" of embodied white suffering to establish the moral bankruptcy of slave law while dramatizing the scene of embodied white male suffering as a means of achieving white male publicity. Sentimental fiction represents white men's suffering as obscene and degrading but allows for a Romantic glorification of briefly described punishments meted out in response to male rebellion. In contrast, sentimental and sensational fiction situates white women's and blacks' experience of suffering, powerlessness, and abjection to enable what Nancy Bentley calls "transcendent grace or enriched dignity and identity."[109] While white abolitionist martyrology refuted state and public connections between the black body and the criminal abolitionist body, sentimental fiction aligns the "natural" sympathy of black and female bodies.[110] As I discuss in my next chapter, Stowe's difference from white abolitionist martyrology has significant implications for the development of masochism. Some forms of masochism eroticize racial difference by temporarily reversing or suspending racial hierarchy in elaborately structured scenes of mastery and submission. Other masochisms, as I will show, follow *Uncle Tom's Cabin* and its other cultural manifestations in offering more complex sets of associations between race, religion, desirable suffering, and republican revolution.

CHAPTER 4

Masochism, Minstrelsy, and Liberal Revolution

Why did nineteenth-century masochists name *Uncle Tom's Cabin* as a point of departure for their fantasy? Germinal accounts of masochism in the exchanges between sexologist Richard von Krafft-Ebing and his patient-correspondents offer a potent image of solitary childhood novel reading.[1] Freud located *Uncle Tom's Cabin* on his masochistic patients' childhood bookshelves, and other sexological, psychoanalytic, and popular accounts mention *Uncle Tom's Cabin*, alongside Christian martyrologies and boarding school novels, as fueling the narratives, desires, fantasies, and performances developed under the name of masochism.[2] Historians and literary critics have, therefore, often regarded *Uncle Tom's Cabin* as an almost singular lynchpin connecting masochism and antebellum American literature. Some of this regard is well deserved. Stowe's novel was the single most important attempt to redefine humanitarian abolition in the nineteenth century. It developed an intersubjective "real presence" of emotional distress that distinguished *Uncle Tom's Cabin* from the more conventional humanitarian sensationalism with which it engaged.[3] However, the naming of *Uncle Tom's Cabin* may promise a false interpretive stability.[4] For mid-nineteenth-century readers, the novel was difficult to separate from its service as a touchstone for a larger public-sphere movement that included an exceptional array of written and illustrated texts, commercial products, and performances. The masochists' citation of *Uncle Tom's Cabin* points to the novel's service as a common ground or meeting place in the mid- and late nineteenth-century public sphere as it was transitioning from an elite to a more popular, middle-class public. In naming and discussing *Uncle Tom's Cabin*, abolitionists, scientists, politicians, critics, and everyday readers, writers, and speakers entered this meeting place to offer competing accounts of religion, race, and power. As both a series of texts and a public-sphere meeting place, *Uncle Tom's Cabin* was intensely polyglot, multilingual, multitemporal, and otherwise full of conflicting claims.

This chapter will reconsider early masochists' accounts of "reading 'Uncle Tom's Cabin'" on the basis of two shifts from "primary" to "secondary" objects of study—from the novel *Uncle Tom's Cabin* to the wider public-sphere meeting place of "Uncle Tom's Cabin" and from psychoanalytic masochism to early masochisms as they circulated in an elite medical and literary public.[5] It will do so with an eye to the complexities of masochism for men of color. With one important exception, considerations of masculinity, race, and masochism in the nineteenth century have been relatively unaddressed, and masochism has often been read as pathologically replicating, in an erotic register, positions of abjection contested in political, economic, and aesthetic discourse. But its deep history deserves further examination.[6]

The novel *Uncle Tom's Cabin* was remarkably heterogeneous, mobile, social, and plural in even its printed forms. The novel was transformed, variously domesticated, and reinvigorated by "traveling" from one geographic and social locale to another.[7] Stowe's original serial publication in Washington's *National Era* and U.S. and English editions of the novel (offering a slightly different final chapter composed simultaneously with the final serial installment) were rapidly followed by competing translations. These appeared in dozens of languages, shorter children's editions, and other excerpted editions. In addition to circulating through public acts of reading, loaning, gifting, and other sorts of exchange, the novel also proliferated to an unprecedented extent as a commodity. This profusion and Stowe's own interest in tracing her novel's influence made the textual proliferation of *Uncle Tom's Cabin* an immediate object of bibliographic study. The bibliography was, in turn, integrated into later U.S. editions of the novel and incorporated into the novel's publicity, even making an appearance in a Stowe exhibit at the 1893 Chicago World's Fair.[8] Material transformations of Stowe's novel worked in concert with the ideological changes (e.g., to the meaning of slavery) that her writing helped effect.

The various print editions of *Uncle Tom's Cabin* serve as a focal point for an even wider set of texts and performances that in many ways took on a life of their own. In Henry James's evocative phrase, *Uncle Tom's Cabin* was "much less a book than a state of vision, of feeling and of consciousness." This state was materialized in letters, illustrations, and newspaper reviews; minstrel, melodramatic, and other stage adaptations; satires and anti-Tom novels; public readings, recitations, and conversations; and board games, handkerchiefs, bronze casts, wallpaper, German needlework patterns, French lithographs, Limoges vases, and all of the other elements evoked by coinages like "Tom-Mania" and "*Onkel Tommerei.*"[9] For German readers in Europe and the United States, the novel was also closely associated with a vogue for African American writings translated into German and published in the wake of Stowe's novel, including Douglass's *Slavery and Freedom*, Webb's *Garies and their Friends*, and Josiah Henson's *Life*.[10] If the novel *Uncle Tom's Cabin* entered a world saturated with motifs of slavery, propagating in every-thing from humanitarian abolitionist writing to consumer goods, then the wider public-sphere meeting place that was "Uncle Tom's Cabin" engaged, entailed, and eclipsed them all.[11]

Krafft-Ebing's "primal scene" of private erotic novel reading serves as a useful shorthand for the series of public encounters with "Uncle Tom's Cabin." The variety, abundance, and availability of "Uncle Tom's Cabin," along with Stowe's moral reputation, informed readings of the novel and eased its passage into the libraries of the young bourgeoisie and aristocrats whose case histories, letters, and interpretations would form the substrate of sexological and psychological masochism.[12] These "Uncle Tom's Cabins" offer alternative sites for the production of various masochisms, fantasies, identities, and reading practices. When Krafft-Ebing's correspondent imagines himself as a slave, in other words, he takes up a history of German and German Ameri-can engagements with *Uncle Tom's Cabin* and "Uncle Tom's Cabin."

The long debate, in American studies, about the place of European revo-lutions (and the desires they helped engender) in U.S. writing reveals an ex-tended dialogue between European and U.S. accounts of slavery's literal and metaphorical meaning.[13] Masochistic readings draw on the resonance of this dialogue, focusing on U.S. abolition, German "slavery," and the place of race in that equation. Like white abolitionist martyrology's insistence that white suffering should enable greater white abolitionist access to the public sphere, the nineteenth-century analogy of black slave and European republican helped shape deterministic notions of racial difference while also, in other ways, resisting proslavery racial claims about the inherently greater senti-mental and political importance of white suffering. Slavery serves as a focal point for two sources of German bourgeois anxiety: German republicanism after the failed revolutions of 1848 and German immigrant experience in the United States.[14] These issues appear most vividly in material more or less di-rectly penumbral to the novel, including German critical responses to and unauthorized editions of *Uncle Tom's Cabin*, as well as Stowe's authorized

European prefaces, which emphasize her millennialist association of abolition and European republicanism in the wake of the revolutions of 1848. This penumbral material highlights Stowe's attempts to engage European republicanism, as well as German and German American immigrant representations of themselves as "slaves" to the state. Many of these representations hinge on a racialized troping of white "enslavement" and mixed-race heroism. These tropes reject the increasingly bifurcated, exclusive delineations of racial identity offered by slavery's defenders, even as they remain within and sometimes develop a deterministic logic of race. The masochist's desire for enslavement was primed, as it were, by an analogy between the U.S. slave and the oppressed European that was developed as part of *Uncle Tom's Cabin's* European publicity and circulation.

In marked contrast to Southern denunciations of *Uncle Tom's Cabin* as "pornographic"—part of a larger pathologization of progressive social movements as forms of disease—masochistic readings of the novel depended on the imagination of slavery itself as a perversion of humanitarian norms of self-possession. As we saw in Chapter 3, abolitionists, in their development of these norms through the notion of sympathetic responsibility, elaborated racial difference by racializing various forms of pained embodiment. Stowe's construction of the "real presence" distanced her work from sensational humanitarian representation but also leaned on parody and minstrelsy to prevent "perversions" of sentiment. This leavening of sentiment with entertaining parodic and minstrel treatments of slave suffering and political speech was vital to the novel, to say nothing of its stage adaptations, illustrations, and the other commercial products of "Tom-Mania" and *"Onkel Tommerei."* Masochistic reading attended both to "high" sentiment and the "perversions" that developed alongside it.[15] Masochism was a way of addressing the phenomenon of "Uncle Tom's Cabin" that refused to separate sympathetic moral intent from erotic potential.

The "General Relation" of Slave to Master

One difficulty in evaluating *Uncle Tom's Cabin's* place in the history of masochism arises from an inattention to the early fluidity of the concept of masochism itself. Without slighting the diversity of contemporary psychoanalytic approaches to masochism that remain in many ways foundational to my own study, it is nevertheless the case that, when Krafft-Ebing's patient-correspondent invoked "masochism," the term was even more contested and unstable. Indeed, the dialogic quality of *Psychopathia Sexualis* reflected and promoted multiple perspectives on the meaning of gender, race, sentiment, and sensation for masochistic practice. Krafft-Ebing's correspondent actively participates in the creation of an analytical discourse that could give public expression to his erotic life. Elsewhere in his letter the correspondent describes himself as part of a broad commercial erotic subculture. "Almost all prostitutes agree," he writes, "that there are many men who like to play 'slave'—i.e., like to be so called, and have themselves scolded and trod upon and beaten." Like many of these men, the masochist writes, "my masochistic tendencies have nothing feminine or effeminizing about them (?)."[16] This final parenthetical question mark, added by Krafft-Ebing himself, signals the sexologist's hesitation to separate suffering from femininity as well as his commitment to reproducing a record of their disagreement. While Krafft-Ebing asserts that masochistic play reverses gendered norms of behavior, his correspondent insists that gender is the wrong axis along which to orient the masochist's desire. The correspondent elaborates: "To be sure, in these, the inclination to be sought and desired by the woman is dominant; the general relation desired with her is not that in which a woman stands to a man, but that of the slave to the master, the domestic animal to its owner. . . . Both are owned by masters and punished by them, and the masters are responsible to no one. Just this unlimited power of life and death . . . is the aim and end of all masochistic ideas."[17]

As with many of the letters excerpted in *Psychopathia Sexualis*, this correspondent describes, in a nutshell, several concepts that Freud, Gilles Deleuze, and Jean Laplanche would later elaborate in their theories of sexuality and subject formation. These include the shift from a more mobile eroticization of the experiences of punishment to a specific attachment to certain relative positions, the preeminence of fantasy, and the paradoxical wielding of authority to enact, in play, the disavowal of authority. This disavowal takes place not only within the commercial sphere of prostitution but also within the letter itself, where the correspondent's rejection of Krafft-Ebing's analogy between woman and slave begins to develop a masochism of a slightly different color. His rejection of the "femininity" of masochism denies the pervasive scientific analogy between racial and sexual difference by distancing the slave from the woman or wife, refocusing on the fetish itself rather than the "fetish as substitute."[18]

The larger political and rhetorical question in the correspondent's claim is that of analogy or proportion. Much valuable work has been written on the pervasive nineteenth-century analogy of (implicitly white) worker to (implicitly black) slave, and the questions here are not dissimilar. In what ways and to what degrees does the masochistic correspondent desire the "general relation" of the slave to the master or of the "domestic animal" to the owner? Tabling, until the Epilogue, the question of the "domestic animal," how does the concept of the "general relation" work to ensure the masochist's distance from slavery? Can we find in this "general relation" any politically, ethically, or materially substantial bridges connecting the correspondent and the experience of slavery in the United States?[19] Out of what materials was the correspondent's notion of the "general relation" of slave to master constructed?

The distance between literary and scientific authority offered one place in which the masochistic correspondent could dissent from sexological claims. This distance is visible in Krafft-Ebing's public defense of his decision to name the "perversion" after Leopold von Sacher-Masoch, a respected journalist and writer in whose fiction Krafft-Ebing saw an elaboration of the "affliction." Sacher-Masoch's novella *Venus in Furs* (1870) has, in recent years, surpassed *Psychopathia Sexualis* as a touchstone for psychoanalytic and literary-critical approaches to masochism. As Robert Reid-Pharr writes in his assessment of masochism and race in mid-nineteenth-century fiction, *Venus* offers a profoundly conservative rendering of anti-sentimental domesticity. Sacher-Masoch uses erotic violence, Reid-Pharr concludes, to effectively warn against the "more profound violence" that will inevitably result from the "dissolution" of embodied boundaries between races and classes in the pursuit of modern subjectivity.[20] Within the narrative, *Venus* does indeed work to imagine a more encompassing normative discourse of sexuality in which femininity, blackness, and servitude disable publicity. As a piece of narrative fiction circulating in a public sphere, though, the perversions celebrated in *Venus* defy Krafft-Ebing's masculinist scientific and aesthetic position, allowing for slippage between different forms of print authority. Krafft-Ebing acknowledges the gap between sexological and literary masochism in his defense of his decision to use Sacher-Masoch's name to identify a sexual disorder. "[F]or so long and whenever [Sacher-Masoch] eliminated his perversion from his literary efforts," Krafft-Ebing argued, "he was a gifted writer, and as such would have achieved real greatness had he been actuated by [normal] sexual feelings."[21] For Krafft-Ebing, public representation is an index of desire. Put another way, the name "masochism" establishes the legitimacy of scientific discourse by asserting its dominance over the aesthetic.

The distance between *Venus* and *Psychopathia Sexualis* offers a gap from which to critique both literary and scientific authority.

If we locate the correspondent's letter in this gap between *Venus* and *Psychopathia Sexualis*, we uncover an element of temporality that both bolsters and complicates Reid-Pharr's claim. Perhaps obscure, from our contemporary remove, is the way in which the correspondent's account of slavery was nostalgic, even as it reflected a new moral and legal common sense. Brazil's abolition of slavery in its 1888 *Lei Aurea* stood at the end of a remarkable shift, in almost every country of the Americas, Europe, and Russia, away from slavery and serfdom as legally, morally, and theologically sound and toward a liberal constitutional republicanism in which other inherited distinctions such as family and race became even more important. Over the course of the eighteenth and nineteenth centuries, many things worked to make slavery revolting and repugnant, rather than natural and sensible.[22] The correspondent's particular notion of slavery—the master's absolute ownership and incontrovertible authority, the slave's physical punishment, correction, and humiliation—had been popularized by humanitarian abolitionist compilations, relations, novels, almanacs, pamphlets, icons, illustrations, and songs. Working in concert with humanitarian naval, prison, and education reform movements, humanitarian accounts of slavery had largely won the day over both the moderate Enlightenment view of slavery as a necessary evil that contravened the rights of man and divine will and the nineteenth-century U.S. defense of slavery as a patriarchy in which benevolence was guaranteed by financial self-interest and networks of social obligation.[23] When slavery would reemerge, it would be as an exception.

The origins of the correspondent's notion of "slavery" in humanitarian abolition entails an erotic engagement with abolitionist metaphors of "slavery" that both stabilize racial difference and call into question the capacity of race to mediate publicity. More specifically, the phrase "*ein Mensch den andern besitzen . . . könne*," "one man can own another," linked U.S. slavery with obsolete imperial forms of government (often "Spanish") founded on racial caste and encouraging racial mixture. For example, Michel Chevalier's widely translated 1836 account of the United States warns that slavery threatened to sink the United States "to the level of ancient communities, which were founded on personal slavery."[24] This notion of slavery's "ancient" political and social status offers a historical grounding for what Deleuze describes as the masochistic scene's fetishistic, "frozen" quality, as though in a "*tableau vivant*."[25] Like Crevecoeur's quintessentially humanitarian depiction of an enslaved man, trapped in a cage, whose suffering is observed by a sensitive visitor powerless to intercede, the masochistic scene suspends participants in these "ancient" acts of violence. At the same time, the correspondent's nostalgic investment in these "frozen," "ancient communities" invites us to consider his description as a staged historical construction rather than a representation of inherently biological or natural qualities. In the manner of Bertolt Brecht's flamboyantly anti-sentimental "alienation-effect," the correspondent's fantasy breaks through the "fourth wall" of scientific objectivity to comment on and historicize the language of desire.[26]

Hungarian Americans and the "Mixed Race"

The popularity of *Uncle Tom's Cabin* and its incredible proliferation into different forms seemed to justify U.S. abolitionists' embrace of a public-sphere, commercial approach to abolition decoupled from church or state. The "Christian" character of this commercial transatlantic public was central to the novel's development and early success. Stowe composed almost all of the chapters that would eventually constitute the first edition of *Uncle Tom's Cabin* for their serial publication in orthodox evangelical Lewis Tappan's *National Era*, an erstwhile Liberal Party organ edited by Cincinnati abolitionist refugee and physiologist Gamaliel Bailey Jr.[27] As Chapter 2 describes, Bailey's service as editor of Baltimore's revised *Methodist Protestant* made him an important figure in the subsumption of the reformist Methodist public into a more genteel, commercially minded evangelical public sphere. Despite Bailey's increasingly radical abolitionism, the *National Era* reflected his and Tappan's commitment to broad circulation in the relatively conservative climate of Washington, D.C. The commercial Christian public also encouraged John Jewett, in his subsequent promotion of the novel, to begin his first and second editions with a preface by famous London Congregationalist Rev. James Sherman (who would then host Stowe during her 1852 English promotional tour) and include lavish illustrations by Hammatt Billings. Jewett's second "Christmas gift" edition even featured a gilt cover illustration designed to resemble that of a costly Bible.[28]

Supportive critics in the United States and United Kingdom described the novel's public circulation in terms usually reserved for God's work, suggesting that the book's publication and circulation took up a divine mission. The nonconformist London literary quarterly *Eclectic Review*, for instance, describes the novel's publication as "a *marvellous* work," emphasizing the spiritual implication of their description by noting "we use the term advisedly." Though of divine origin, the scope and extent of circulation was also cause for concern. The *Eclectic Review*, in an extended account of the novel's saturation of all forms of public and private discourse, claims that *Uncle Tom's Cabin*

> is everywhere, and on every person's lips,—on the steamboat, and in the railway carriage, in the drawing room, the nursery, and the kitchen; the library of the studious, and the waiting room of the physician. It has found its way to the extremes of society, and its effect is everywhere the same. In the palace, the mansion, and the cottage, it has riveted attention. The sons of toil as well as the children of opulence have wept over its pages. It has invaded the hours of rest, has chained thousands to its perusal, regardless of fatigue and health— has broken up the monotony of human feeling, and given birth to emotions more deep and powerful than the heart of man often encounters . . . the fact is notorious that men of all classes, persons of every conceivable grade, the mechanic and the manufacturer, peers and rustics, literary men and children, lawyers, physicians, and divines, members of both sexes, of every age, and of all conceivable varieties of disposition, have perused its touching narrative with moistened eye and with agonized hearts. It has acted like a charm on the old and the young, and its impression remains in a thousand cases with the permanence and force of a master passion.[29]

This account thematizes *Uncle Tom's Cabin*'s ability to penetrate and expand the public sphere as a form of obsession or other psychological disease, as the novel could "rivet," "invade," "charm," and "master" the body, speech, and passion.

Part of the anxiety surrounding the novel's proliferation may reflect fears that the phenomenon of "Uncle Tom's Cabin" would eclipse the novel's Christian political message and thereby allow for misreadings. The possibility of misreading, including erotic misreading, was magnified by the proliferation of the novel in multiple forms with different, competing claims and priorities. Commercialization encouraged this proliferation. Following on from Jewett's use of Sherman, many publishers used prefatory material, including prefaces and subtitles, to distinguish their editions and shape their readership through different appeals. Some European editions emphasized the novel's literary character and the political resonance of its circulation. These editions featured notes, biographies, or introductions and editorial oversight by George Sand and other luminaries. An authorized 1853 French translation, organized by Maria Weston Chapman, began with a unique preface by Stowe thanking the French for freeing their slaves in the colonies and enlisting their help in the cause of U.S. abolition.[30] Other editions were more sensational and frankly sexual. John Cassell's 1852 London edition of the novel added illustrations by George Cruikshank that conspicuously eroticized white men flogging black female slaves, inflecting Stowe's representations of race, sexuality, and violence as an erotic drama of white domination and black suffering. Cruikshank's racialized conventions of representation included the use of strongly contrasting skin colors, facial features, and hair shape to produce markers of distinct racial difference.[31] Other illustrated editions offered an eroticism less determined by race. An 1853 Paris edition by Baudry's European Library, which specialized in the immediate republication of notable English writing, offered three illustrations in the sensational style of Weld's *American Slavery*. One, entitled "George's Sister," was a frankly erotic, voyeuristic flogging scene apparently borrowed from an illustration of the same scene in the 1852 *Pictures of Slavery in the United States*. However, in keeping with Stowe's account of the physiognomy of mixed-race characters, none of the figures in Baudry's edition of "George's Sister" appear distinctly "marked" as either white or black in their physical appearance, having similar skin, hair, and facial features.[32] Baudry's edition thereby fluidly adapted a range of abolitionist representations of race in a manner that privileged easy borrowing and economy rather than eroticizing racial differences in power.

Other literary or political appeals, though less obviously connected to masochistic readings, are just as important to Krafft-Ebing's correspondent's imagination of himself as a slave. German editions of the novel, which were likely important for Krafft-Ebing's patient-correspondents, are even more varied than U.K. or French editions. There were over forty-one German translations appearing in seventy-five different editions, some with copies of Cruikshank's or U.S. illustrations and others with new stereotype illustrations; there were also eleven abridgements for children, one play, and one illustrated volume, as well as several editions for school use. These German editions would circulate widely in Germany and New England and likely in Philadelphia, New York, and other German-language centers.[33]

The variety of German editions was a consequence of Germany's political fragmentation and decentralized publishing culture. In this and other ways, the European revolutionary context helped shape the novel's publication and reception in German; that, in turn, had important repercussions for U.S. abolition. In Germany and among German Americans, "Uncle Tom's Cabin" was not narrowly connected to abolitionist political organizing and was perhaps therefore more available as a space for reflection on German problems and issues. Some German editions encouraged a particularly colonizing reading of blackness, particularly black suffering, as entertainment. One inexpensive 1852 Berlin edition conspicuously moved Stowe's novel into the *Roman* tradition by subtitling it *"Eine Negergeschichte."* This term was promiscuously applied to a range of imaginative fictions about Africa, Africans, and colonial slavery; many constructed "blackness" as the horrifying sensational experience of physical violence, but some, including mid-nineteenth-century reprintings of short late eighteenth-century U.S. romances designed to promote a measured public response to the Haitian Revolution, also featured noble, heroic slaves in revolt.[34] Whether original works or translations from earlier English or U.S. abolitionist fiction, *Negergeschichte* generally promoted a humanitarian sensational abolitionism that Stowe herself negotiated carefully. Other German editions of *Uncle Tom's Cabin* made more substantive connections by linking Germans' 1848 republican revolts with both slave struggles and U.S. attempts to preserve national union.[35] These more substantive associations were encouraged by subtitles emphasizing Tom's Christianity in a manner that connected him to German readers by playing on the religious pathos of a "Christian slave" or emphasizing the political complexity of the United States by highlighting the irony of slavery in *"dem Lande der Freiheit."*

As was the case in white abolitionist martyrology, the analogy between black slave and European republican could easily subsume the former into the latter. If the relationship between American slave and European republican was conceptualized as simply or "merely" analogic, it would reprise late eighteenth-century U.S. revolutionaries' attempts to analogize British colonial rule to slavery by distinguishing British ideological or mental slavery from physical slavery as practiced in the colonies. Such a reprise was not idle speculation. The proslavery *New York Herald* went so far as to deny that *Uncle Tom's Cabin*'s popularity in Europe owed anything to abolitionist sentiment, crediting it solely to European republicans' recognition of themselves in the novel's black characters. A Brooklyn pamphlet, excerpting and recirculating the *Herald*'s claims, imagined that, when a European man reads the novel, the negro disguise does not delude him for an instant. Those rights which Mrs. Stowe claims in such powerful language for the negroes, he has been vainly struggling for a century or more to conquer for himself. Every noble impulse which she implants in the hearts of her impossible model black men, has long since taken firm root in his own. Each stifled threat that escapes from the lips of a George, has been audibly murmured time after time by himself.—Englishmen's hearts burn with fury when the sufferings of their own seamstresses are vividly delineated in the characters of Cassy and Eliza.—Many a Frenchman has felt, with George, that he was born to better things than serfdom. Germans, Hungarians, Italians, know, that whatever be the condition of the American negroes, they are themselves but slaves, and that on God's earth they are entitled to be free.[36]

The *Herald*'s attribution of Stowe's European popularity to European republicanism illustrates the unpredictable courses of sympathy between the European republican and American slave. Like white Americans' "playing Indian," the *Herald* characterizes abolition as a "negro disguise" that allowed European republicans to avoid censorship and reprisal.[37] The sympathetic power of these Europeans in blackface outstrips those of their original referents, black slaves in the United States, because white emotional interiority ("noble impulse[s]," feelings, "hearts") grants Europeans greater claim to those rights.

The *Herald*'s account of race as an internal, emotional difference mostly agrees with Stowe's own account of race, but Stowe's inclusion of mixed-race characters makes her portrait of slavery work differently in a European republican revolutionary context. To maximize the novel's appeal, Stowe's novel allows for multiple readings: the *Herald*'s revolutionaries in blackface, a white abolitionist reading emphasizing slaves' fundamental "blackness," and also a religious reading emphasizing the common soul that transcends the particularity of black or white racial identity. For the *Herald*, the "noble" sentiments of freedom are proper to the European revolutionary but "impossible" in "black men"; for Stowe, those characteristics are possible in some black men, though often, as with George Harris, in direct proportion to those "black" men's "white" blood.

Stowe's modern racial ideologies—her notion of race as a set of internal, intellectual, and affective traits creditable to blood inheritance—dovetail with and reinforce her Christian millennialism—her belief in a dawning Christian age that will precede the coming of Christ. Millennialism helped

Stowe reach audiences for whom abolition was less pressing as a political concern.[38] In marketing the novel to European audiences, millennialism works to position both abolition and republican revolution as subsidiary to a divine plan of redemption. This did not flatten out the differences between blacks and Europeans or even among Europeans themselves. Although U.S. abolition and European republican revolutions both help effect millennial change, German revolutions may have been particularly important for completing a stage of the premillennial plan that she understood Martin Luther to have begun.[39]

Stowe's authorized prefaces describe *Uncle Tom's Cabin*'s capacity to promote millennial events as in some way dependent on her status as a professional author. The prefaces uniformly figure her novel as participating in premillennial events by using what her London preface, following Daniel Webster, repeatedly calls "public sentiments" to shape an understanding of "common humanity." As part of her larger attempt to protect her profits and establish international copyright, Stowe described publicity and self-promotion, at least in this form, as containing a sacred dimension. By extending, into the commercial realm, the early role of peritextual material in shaping reader response to bibles and other sacred texts, Stowe's prefaces' assertion of her moral standing and authorial rights circle back around to ensure that the properly pious reader would contribute to a millennial end.[40]

One of the ways Stowe's professional authorship would help enable premillennial events is by allowing her to shape her novel's political value for different audiences. The meaning of race was central to her millennial calculus. In her first U.S. preface, Stowe focused her premillennialist claim on encouraging whites to see the "negro race" as naturally kind, meek, and submissive. The black race, shepherded by Anglo-Saxon Christian sympathy, could herald the beginning of the era of peace preceding Christ's return. Stowe's London preface proposed a very different relationship between race, writing, reading, and the millennium by offering different moral and economic arguments against slavery. While the U.S. preface emphasized the distance between the objects and subjects of benevolence, reiterating the popular sensational humanitarian trope of the "bound and bleeding" slave supplicating "at the foot of civilized and Christian humanity," the English preface aligns slaves with English workers. Defending her portrait of honorable Christian black men, the English preface rejects attempts to counterpose the interests of slaves and those of the English working class, a technique she would later expand in her *Key*. In other words, while white Americans should reach down to raise the pitiful black slave, English workers should join hands with honorable black Christians to rise together.

In distinction to both her U.S. and her London prefaces, Stowe's European prefaces relied more heavily on explicit millennialist rhetoric. Her European prefaces echoed the novel's role in influencing "public sentiments" and also used a series of evangelical and political appeals to give special emphasis to the role of publicity in effecting millennial change.[41] Stowe pared away most of her moral and economic claims in favor of a political-evangelical focus on abolitionist and revolutionary action as a "union of God with man." Stowe's authorized German preface, first published in an 1852 Leipzig English edition and quickly translated into German, took her London edition's equation of slaves and workers even farther by encouraging sympathy for the slave as a way to promote European immigration to the United States and direct political action by European immigrants. Connecting German republican revolution, the worldwide rise of Christian sentiment, and the rise of the black race, Stowe attempted to shape European views of U.S. abolition by encouraging her readers to elaborate the analogy between republican revolutionaries and U.S. slaves.

For Stowe, abolition and republican revolution were sympathetic movements in a divine history. Like waves meeting at sea, they could amplify one another or cancel themselves out. To help harmonize abolition and revolution for German readers, Stowe's Leipzig preface evoked a sense of common "Christianized humanity" by analogizing U.S. slavery to European economic and political "oppress[ion]." She expresses this most concretely by closing her preface with a quotation from exiled Hungarian republican Lajos Kossuth:

If therefore the oppressed of other nations desire to find in America an asylum of permanent freedom let them come prepared heart, hand, and vote, against the institution of slavery, for they who enslave others cannot long themselves remain free.

True are the great and living words, "NO NATION CAN REMAIN FREE WITH WHOM FREEDOM IS A PRIVILEGE AND NOT A PRINCIPLE."[42]

Describing the United States as "fast filling up from Europe" with immigrants, Stowe contrasts European oppression to the freedoms (and "almost immediate" franchise) that European immigrants receive in the United States. Encouraging German readers to reflexively think of U.S. abolition and republican revolution as twin struggles, she invokes suffrage as a political ideal for immigrants' home countries and a lure for immigrants to the United States and links immigrants' freedoms with their antislavery votes. The novel's revolutionary implications were apparently marketable: unauthorized German translations based on the Leipzig edition either kept her preface intact or pared down to focus almost exclusively on political and evangelical claims.[43]

Stowe's invocation of Kossuth builds upon English and U.S. abolitionist uses of European republicanism to leverage U.S. popular sympathy for European revolutions into support for abolition. U.S. abolitionists first developed the analogy between European republican revolution and abolition in the hope of translating U.S. citizens' passion for the former into support for the latter. The abolitionist press, as part of their coverage of Kossuth's triumphal arrival in New York and extensive travels and lecturing in England and the United States to promote Hungarian independence, repeatedly analogized Hungarians to slaves: Channing called Kossuth a "flying slave"; a headline in *Frederick Douglass' Paper* asked readers to "Help the American Kossuths" and described fugitives as "American Hungarians." Free blacks in Philadelphia offered a resolution that went further, describing "Austrian tyranny [as] mercy" compared to the Fugitive Slave Act.[44] Abolitionists also had to convince Kossuth himself. Prior to his arrival in New York, English abolitionists fortified Kossuth with copies of the Fugitive Slave Law and Weld's sensational *American Slavery*. Soon after his arrival, Kossuth received a delegation of African Americans who petitioned him to support abolition in the "common cause of crushed, outraged humanity." Kossuth's refusal to endorse abolition led many abolitionists, particularly black abolitionists, to reflect on their own diasporic identities and denounce narrowly "patriotic" nationalism as frustrating the embrace of a broader humanitarian philanthropy.[45] William G. Allen, a professor of Greek and belles lettres exiled to England after marrying a white woman, demanded that Kossuth "have a heart not circumscribed by national lines, and sympathies which can grasp the entire human family."[46] Garrison, encouraged by the broad shift toward his position, ratcheted up the analogy in his February 1852 public *Letter to Louis Kossuth*, describing Kossuth as a "a fugitive from Austrian vengeance, as a rebel, and as the leader in a formidable insurrectionary movement."[47] White abolitionists also saw in Kossuth a popular cause célèbre on whom they could model themselves. When Kossuth made his much-anticipated landing in New York, escorted from Turkey by a U.S. naval steamship, "Magyar-mania" reached what George Templeton Strong called an "epidemic" stage.[48] *Uncle Tom's Cabin,* published just after Kossuth's demurral from the abolitionist cause, was poised to inherit the mantle of U.S. abolitionist celebrity Kossuth declined.

Stowe's premillennialist association of the rise of Christian sentiment, abolition, and republican revolution crystallized in her authorized German preface's description of slaves as "[to] a very wide extent a *mixed race.*" Though partly a response to Southern critics who minimized "racial mixture" in the South and attributed it to abolitionist "amalgamationism," Stowe's insistence on the "mixed" racial character of slaves takes on special significance as it dovetails with her citation of Kossuth to align German readers with her mixed-race protagonist, George Harris. Stowe's invocation of Kossuth in her preface aligns her authorial persona with the character of the "mulatto" George Harris, whose bitter "declaration of independence" contrasts the U.S. public's support for the Fugitive Slave Law with their celebration of "despairing Hungarian fugitives." Stowe's portrait of Harris, as Susan Ryan points out, casts emotion, intellect, and character as aspects of racial identity but does not essentialize them or exclude volition and context in the construction of those identities.[49] From the mid-eighteenth century, humanitarian abolition treated benevolence as the mark and responsibility of the "civilized and Christian humanity" at whose foot the "bound and bleeding" slave supplicates—the terms Stowe echoes in her U.S. preface. Harris's benevolence, like his burning desire for freedom, could well have been read as a part of his "hot and hasty Saxon" racial inheritance. While some political and critical celebrations represented *mestizaje* and racial mixture as indicative of social egalitarianism, Harris represents the benefits of "whitening" or *blanqueamiento.* This benefit was highly gendered. For women, Stowe offers the tragedy of Cassy in "The Quadroon's Story"; for men, Harris's racial mixture augments his heroism by making his blackness, to some degree, a matter of volition.[50] Even if we agree with the substantial body of criticism that reads Stowe's racial logic as intense and absolute, Harris's mixed-race character still denies that the relationship between European republican and U.S. slave could be merely analogic, a matter of "negro disguise." It was Harris's heroism and commitment to blackness in the face of proslavery forces that Stowe encouraged European readers to emulate. His "mixed-race" character and embrace of blackness was crucial for Europeans' understanding of their own "slavery." Harris's embrace of blackness echoes in the suggestive psychoanalytic description of fantasy (especially masochistic fantasies of contamination and self-disclosure) as resembling the experience of "mixed-race" or "mixed-blood" characters who fear that their race will be disclosed. But while these accounts are premised on the desire to "pass," Harris offers European readers a model for revolution by refusing to pass, embracing his subordinate social position as the first step to fighting against political "enslavement."[51]

German readers of *Uncle Tom's Cabin* offered various responses to the millennial claims in Stowe's prefaces. Some reviewers used slavery as a "mere" analogy for Austrian imperial rule (the *Herald*'s "negro disguise"), while others followed Stowe's premillennialist location of both abolition and republican revolution within a divine history of redemption. A few reviewers even framed Stowe as a religious writer whose work could reform all sorts of Christian practice, including political practice. An anonymous 1852 review from the Augsburg *Allgemeine Zeitung*, later included in Charles Stowe's *Life of Harriet Beecher Stowe*, praises the novel's evocation of slave Christianity as "a Christianity of the first centuries of the Christian community, where the 'brothers and sisters' whispered their songs of praise to the Savior. . . . It is the greatness of this novel that it breaths afresh the spirit of *this* Christianity, in the face of which the chains of the slave and the purple of the Caesars fell to the dust once already, and the Roman eagle, dealt a mortal blow, lowered his proud pinions. Reading this novel we, oppressed by the sultriness of the age, feel the breezes of a new world blow refreshingly across our brow." Stowe's Christian sympathy, the review suggests, emerged from the relationship between church and state in the United States, which allowed pious communities to revive a "primitive" Christian worship with a distinctly anti-imperial cast. Evoking Roman symbols of power lately taken up by the Austrian empire, the review sharpens Stowe's premillennialist republican argument to represent the schismatic, pietistic Christianity practiced by ancient Roman and U.S. slaves as partaking of a universal, original, anti-imperial Christian republicanism that heralds the empire's demise.

German readers' sustained interest in "racial mixing" was complemented by an interest in the "German slave." European "slavery" was a central trope for German readers and reviewers, especially German immigrants to the United States, and the novel's success encouraged the multiplication of representations of German "slaves." Like U.S. revolutionaries in 1776, Germans sometimes used the term "slavery" as a mere analogy, a metaphor for their political and economic disenfranchisement in Europe. Other Germans went further, linking this analogy to their legal and physical status in the United States. German immigrants' experience of enslavement is sometimes discussed as "white slavery," but that notion itself attempts to racialize the experience of slavery as properly "black" and paper over the ways that immigrants were treated as "mixed race" or mulatto by scientific, economic, and political authorities. This treatment depended in part on the decoherence of racial categories and hence the capacity of German immigrants to be produced as "mixed race." Many Germans and German immigrants focused on the case of Marie Miller or Salome Müller, who, in a sensational 1845 Louisiana court case, gained her freedom despite scientific testimony that her physical appearance was not indicative of whiteness. The verdict was so upsetting to supporters of slavery that the governor dissolved the state Supreme Court. Early German translators of Stowe's novel also translated Richard Hildreth's *White Slave*—itself expanded and retitled in 1852 to capitalize on Stowe's popularity—in which a slave trader recommends selling "a stray Irish or German girl," who "makes just as good a slave as if there were African blood in her veins."[52] William Wells Brown, William and Ellen Craft, and other U.S. abolitionists encouraged these readings by using Müller's kidnapping to stoke European immigrant hostility to slavery and undermine slavery's racial logic. Germans in the United States also adapted abolitionist tropes to demonstrate connections between their economic exploitation and political marginalization in Europe with their mistreatment as immigrants.[53] The notion of "mixed-race" hailing was particularly resonant within immigrant communities facing greater political and economic vulnerability, where it served as a metaphor for the range of economic exploitation and physical violence to which they were exposed.[54]

Stowe's own pragmatic attention to European republican revolutions as instrumental aids to U.S. abolition, specifically to her authorial rights and profits, ironically depended on the threat of German competition in the United States. On one hand, Stowe's familiarity with German immigrants in Cincinnati, including her hiring of a "Dutch" girl as a second servant, likely influenced her sense of immigration's potential to support abolition through household labor, freeing "native American" abolitionists to work in the public sphere.[55] However, this potential needed to be shaped and controlled to ensure that immigrant support did not turn into competition. The upheaval caused by German liberal revolution and counterrevolution encouraged immigration among those bourgeois revolutionaries who were central to the development of progressive German-language publishing in the United States. One of the most renowned early German editions of *Uncle Tom's Cabin* was published in Philadelphia by revolutionary and German

American literary magazine editor Adolf Strodtmann, first in 1853 and again in later decades.[56] This edition came on the heels of at least two German newspaper translations, one of which precipitated Stowe's unsuccessful lawsuit for copyright infringement and the subsequent transatlantic public contest over copyright.

Some German readers, like their English contemporaries, did substitute class difference for racial difference in the interest of condemning the condition of the German poor as worse than that of the U.S. slave, but even these often went beyond a "merely" analogic reading of slaves as republicans in a "negro disguise." As Heike Paul argues, some of the most incisive commentary on the meaning of Stowe's work for Germans and German immigrants came from Friedrich Wilhelm Hackländer, whose *Clara, oder Europäische Sclavenleben* (*Clara; or, Slave-Life in Europe*) was popular in Germany and among German immigrant communities in the United States.[57] *Clara*, like the anonymous anti-abolitionist *Uncle Tom's Cabin in England*, evinces hostility to Stowe's work. *Clara* condemns wealthy Europeans who weep for Uncle Tom but lack sympathy for the misery of those around them, and some characters promote white European rights over and against those of black slaves. Unlike *Uncle Tom's Cabin in England*, though, *Clara* encourages readers to connect their sympathy, whether for the European worker or U.S. slave, to transformative political action.[58] *Clara*'s dramatization of German publishers' cruelty offered a particular indictment of those who play on sympathy in the absence of political action. The 1856 translation and New York publication of *Clara*, followed by an adaptation for the stage and production in two Philadelphian German theaters, constitutes a sort of running transatlantic commentary on European poverty and U.S. slavery in which the trope of "European slavery" could help forge transatlantic alliances and alliances between blacks and German immigrant workers in the United States. At the same time, *Clara* and its stage productions played on fears of enslaved black labor that were easily transferred to free black labor, fears that would be addressed and transformed through the work of minstrelsy.

Low Sensationalism, High Sentiment, and Comic Minstrelsy

Ironically for early sexological and psychoanalytic constructions of masochism, part of the appeal of *Uncle Tom's Cabin* as a book suitable for young bourgeois readers lay in Stowe's attempt to use sentiment and minstrelsy to develop a form of humanitarian narrative that might avoid eroticizing pain. Stowe's careful handling of sympathy developed within a humanitarian-pornographic sensational context, in which overstimulation of readerly sympathy risked the "perversion" or "hardening" of sentimental response. In charged political and economic debates, abolitionist texts were repeatedly attacked for encouraging such perversion, much as modern critiques of racism or sexism are themselves attacked as racist or sexist. Stowe attempted to foreclose such critiques by promoting a notion of the "real presence" of emotional distress, which encouraged a deeper emotional connection rather than a purely sensational response, as well as by carefully leavening sentiment with "entertaining" parodic and minstrel treatments of slave suffering and political speech.

Contemporary Southern denunciations of Stowe's work as a "pornographic" text catering to the "diseased taste" of "disgusting" female readers and writers drew on the historical connection between humanitarian sensationalism and pornography.[59] Sexological masochism's eroticization of enslavement and self-dispossession drew upon both the humanitarian sensational eroticization of more straightforward, algolagnic pleasures of flagellation and pain (widely discussed in the eighteenth century as "the English vice"), as well as emotionally and psychologically complex renderings of slave suffering derived from nineteenth-century abolitionism. Humanitarian sensational accounts of slave suffering developed in tandem with and reached the height of their popularity around the same time as more elaborate flagellation pornography and painting, murder narratives, and various forms of the urban Gothic novel. Together, they helped eroticize the experience of pain, including forced and voluntary sexual pain.[60] Eighteenth- and nineteenth-century abolitionist writing helped elaborate what Thomas Laqueur calls a "humanitarian narrative," in which detailed, sensational descriptions of bodily pain attempt to evoke a sympathetic bodily response in the reader and thereby motivate them to ameliorate that suffering.[61] The humanitarian narrative rendered pain obscene and therefore available to eroticization by describing embodied pain as a harm that should be corrected.[62] While these new erotics of pain were immediately explored by Sade, who credited Samuel Richardson's sentimental narratives with inspiring his work, it would take several decades for pain to become a pornographic staple.

During those decades, abolitionist humanitarian representations of slave suffering became more integrated into a larger public descriptive economy of slave suffering and offered increasingly elaborate and generalized representations of slave suffering. Early eighteenth-century abolitionist humanitarian narratives were more traditionally "humanitarian" in their focus on particularized instances of suffering grouped together in one scene. Philadelphia physician Benjamin Rush offered this humanitarian sensational representation of three suffering slaves in his 1773 abolitionist tract: "Behold one covered with stripes, into which melted wax is poured—another tied down to a block or a stake—a third suspended in the air by his thumbs."[63] Later abolitionist humanitarian descriptions of slave suffering, in contrast, often generalized many observations into a single passage, as in this account by Horace Moulton, a Methodist minister in Georgia:

> Occasionally the whipper, especially if his victim does not beg enough to suit him, while under the lash, will fly into a passion, uttering the most horrid oaths; while the victim of his rage is crying, at every stroke, "Lord have mercy! Lord have mercy!" The scenes exhibited at the whipping post are awfully terrific and frightful to one whose heart has not turned to stone; I never could look on but a moment. While under the lash, the bleeding victim writhes in agony, convulsed with torture. Thirty-nine lashes on the bare back, which tear the skin at almost every stroke, is what the South calls a *very moderate punishment!* Many masters whip until they are tired—until the back is a gore of blood—then rest upon it: after a short cessation, get up and go at it again; and after having satiated their revenge in the blood of their victims, they sometimes *leave them tied, for hours together, bleeding at every wound.*[64]

These and other passages unify a sentimental spectatorial white "I" against a mass of generic suffering black victims.

Though both eighteenth- and nineteenth-century accounts describe the body in great detail, the multiplication and generalization of such details in the nineteenth century enabled voyeuristic, spectatorial sadism on a wider scale.[65] Moulton's account was one of hundreds in Theodore Weld's immensely popular *American Slavery as It Is* (1839), the best-selling abolitionist text prior to Stowe's novel and the most substantial compendium of abolitionist humanitarian sensational representations of slave suffering. *American Slavery*'s descriptions of generic "passionate" masters and their "bleeding victims," mainly culled from slave narratives and accounts of slavery from

Southern newspapers, was one link in an immense chain of suffering largely stripped of individual context. Multiplied several thousand times over, such humanitarian sensational descriptions of slave suffering in eighteenth- and nineteenth-century abolitionist texts helped produce what Karen Halttunen calls "a new cultural linkage of violence and sex," which established both the obscenity of pain and its erotic potential.[66]

Crucial to this work was the U.S. public sphere's historical dependence on slavery. Newspaper advertisements for the sale or capture of slaves provided many of Weld's most sensational accounts and were emblematic of Weld's attempt to turn the U.S. public sphere against itself.[67] Abolitionists were therefore understandably concerned that their own sensational use of slave suffering, itself often repurposed from public sphere accounts of slavery, could to be turned to other ends.[68] Many nineteenth-century abolitionists bemoaned what Moulton calls the heart "turned to stone," a "perversion" of the sympathetic response caused by the repeated "witnessing" of cruelty, whether in person or in print. Quaker abolitionist Angelina Grimké, for example, describes her failure to become "hardened" to slavery during her childhood in Charleston as nothing short of a miracle that might help slake God's vengeance against her people: "in deep solemnity and gratitude, I say, it was the Lord's doing, and marvelous in mine eyes."[69] This hardening became associated with lower-class reading habits and tastes, extending the long-standing association of sentiment with gentility.[70] Weld's *American Slavery*, in an important precedent for Stowe, attempted to combat perversion by imagining the public sphere as a normalizing legal venue for a higher justice, a quasi-divine space in which readers' "common sense, and conscience, and a human heart" would trump the mortal law that allowed for such outrages. Weld's text, subtitled the *Testimony of a Thousand Witnesses*, presumes the racial complexion of that public sphere, with white readers redressing black suffering. By engaging the text, each reader is "empanelled as a juror" to "listen" to the evidence of suffering black flesh. Weld's text offers hundreds of miniaturized sensational humanitarian narratives in the form of editorial vignettes. These surround descriptions of a particular slave's wounds and scars as they appear in runaway slave advertisements, letters, newspaper items, or other records of life in slave society; the vignettes were themselves set inside collections of first-person slave narratives and other descriptions of Southern life. Granting to slaves and slave bodies the original and most basic meaning of martyr as "witness," Weld's juridical rhetoric still separates the testimonial function from the prosecutorial function, refusing to allow slaves to advocate

for themselves.[71] In Weld, black slaves provide the templates that white abolitionists use to organize their narratives.

American Slavery as It Is was a vital text for Stowe, who excerpted it liberally
in her *Key*, drew on its account of a pious slave's death for her image of Tom's
suffering, and allegedly "slept with it under her pillow" while she wrote *Uncle
Tom's Cabin*, bringing herself in intimate relation with the text.[72] At the same
time, Stowe attempted to avoid perversions of sympathy by playing several
genres off one another. As the most prominent non-reformist genres featuring
sensational scenes of suffering, pornographic flogging narratives, murder narratives and Gothic novels caused particular anxiety.[73] Some abolitionist writers
distinguished their prose from sensationalist fiction by appealing to moral motive, a pose many Gothic novelists had already abandoned. Slave narratives and
other abolitionist fiction consistently described their excitation of sympathy as
a means of encouraging moral development, rather than entertainment. Abolitionists also distinguished their work by insisting on the veracity of their narrative, promising a "truth stronger and stranger than fiction."[74] As the manifest
sensationalism of this promise for "stronger and stranger" prose suggests, however, the line between abolitionist writing and other sensational fiction was pre-
dictably and intentionally blurred by authors on both sides. Nevertheless, the
distinction between "debased fiction" and "moral truth" helped locate obscenity, sexuality, degradation, and perversion on the side of popular fiction, allowing "realistic," politically engaged reformist prose a greater freedom to represent
suffering and pain.

Marianne Noble and other critics, as I mentioned in the previous chapter,
take up this "classed" language in their accounts of Stowe's avoidance of the
low excitation of the "physical presence" of suffering (e.g., describing the pain
of flogging) and promotion of a high sentimental stimulation of the memory
of an *emotional* wound to engage a more complete sympathetic feeling that
Stowe calls the "real presence." Noble, though attributing Stowe's development of more psychologically elaborate sentimentalism to another source,
argues that Stowe's sentimentalism depends on the excitation of a common
experience of suffering (such as the loss of a child) to allow white middle-
class readers "genuine" access to the "real presence" of the emotional and embodied suffering of the black slave. By evoking an emotional connection, the
"real presence of emotional distress" would thereby avoid the perversions of
voyeuristic spectatorship.[75]

Stowe attempts to develop emotional or imaginative suffering, rather
than sensational embodied suffering, as a means to stabilize readerly

sentiment by endowing her characters with psychological complexity, elaborate histories, and contradictory impulses, as well as offering interwoven, multilayered sentimental scenarios, with black and white emotional suffering overlapping and interacting. In her account of the "real presence," Stowe also attempts to recuperate some of the sensational tropes of bodily suffering by presenting them as universalized or free from particularity—"*the* imploring human eye, *the* frail, trembling human hand, *the* despairing appeal of helpless agony."[76] Stowe's elaboration of the sentimental "real presence" corresponds to what a good deal of recent scholarship has analyzed as the development of race, gender, and national identity as internal characteristics—aspects of "personality"—through the disciplinary function of sympathy. Readings of abolitionist sympathy by Christopher Castiglia and others propose that representations of black suffering in abolitionist narratives helped internalize racial difference as a function of character.[77] Stowe's "real presence" is centrally engaged in this disciplinary function by grounding sympathy in the sufferer's imagination of an internal, emotional state. Stowe's "real presence" thereby participates fully in abolitionism's replacement of Enlightenment humanism's putative universalism with a romantic emphasis on social difference, spiritual complexity, and psychological depth.[78]

This distinction between high and low sentiment disguises as much as it reveals. Humanitarian sensational representations of slave suffering were so crucial to abolitionist publicity—establishing the veracity of their accounts and exciting sympathy for slave suffering—that even abolitionists who wanted to avoid "perversions" of sympathy found it necessary to engage them in some way. Many abolitionists, including Stowe, offered detailed descriptions of sympathetic feeling and attempted to more closely connect sympathy to positive political action.[79] Stowe's authorized prefaces, as we have seen, describe the millennial potential of the "real presence" of "high" emotional suffering in the public sphere. At other times, Stowe mocks the humanitarian sensational representations of slave suffering that align her novel with urban Gothic literature and other debased forms of sensational fiction. At yet other times, she introduces and adapts Gothic, comic, and minstrel forms into her text to *avoid* perversions of sympathy. For example, Stowe connects humanitarian sensationalism and the "real presence" when she adopts Gothic motifs to describe Eliza's escape, Tom's death and threatened burning, Cassy and Emmeline's "haunting" in their "loophole of retreat," and Legree's uncanny fear of his mother's hair.[80] Excepting Tom, each of these scenes endorses black women's active resistance to slavery by invoking Gothic humanitarian

sensationalism and then leavening it with comedy or Christian redemption.[81] These moments of sensational slave suffering, though relatively infre-
quent within the novel, are buttressed by Stowe's own humanitarian
sensational compendium, the *Key to Uncle Tom's Cabin*. The *Key*, a rejoinder
to critics of her novel's veracity, is constructed out of the huge body of earlier
abolitionist sensational representations of slave suffering that serve as a sort
of "common sense" upon which Stowe can draw to build her descriptions of
the "real presence" of suffering, even as she attempts to avoid the "taint" of
that earlier work. Within her novel and the *Key*, sensational slave suffering
supplements the "real presence" of emotional distress by establishing its material truth.[82]

Considering Stowe's portrait of Tom's death as a martyrdom will help explain how the disciplinary function of Stowe's work contributes to *Uncle
Tom's Cabin*'s importance in early sexological masochism. As Chapter 3 describes, Stowe's development of "real presence" in Tom's martyrdom constitutes one of her most innovative representations of slave suffering. Despite
Stowe's relatively "flat" delineation of Tom's history and psychology, Tom's
desire for, imagination, and experience of a martyr's pain is one of the few
white abolitionist attempts to describe black suffering in martyrological
terms. As Noble argues, the "real presence" of suffering in Stowe's description
of Tom's martyrdom resonates in subsequent descriptions and uses of masochism in Freud and Laplanche.[83] Nevertheless, focusing on the difference
between "real presence" and humanitarian sensationalism may obscure the
way in which Stowe's "real presence" is less a rejection of "low" humanitarian
sensationalism than an attempt to both disavow and rely on humanitarian
sensationalism. The novel recuperates the "low" cultural appeal of minstrelsy's "entertaining" forms of discipline into a "high" sentimental response.
Uncle Tom's Cabin thereby served as a new wellspring for erotic imagination
by combining the obscene pleasures of the humanitarian sensational experience or imagination of pain with a model of black slave interiority as desirous
of spiritually redemptive suffering. In other words, masochistic readings of
Uncle Tom's Cabin do not to erase or exclude humanitarian sensational representations of suffering but rather integrate them into a new representational
scheme, a new iteration of sympathetic discipline ripe for incorporation into
an erotic economy.[84]

Just as we cannot understand *Uncle Tom's Cabin* as separate from humanitarian sensational representations of slave suffering such as Weld's *Testimony*, we cannot understand it without the minstrel texts from which Stowe

drew and into which Stowe's work was subsequently drawn. Minstrel performances of embodied black suffering work hand in hand with the law and
humanitarian sensationalism to assign African Americans to what Saidiya
Hartman calls a "condition of pained embodiment," locating this suffering as
the truth of the black self, fixing it in black bodies, and obscuring the ways in
which suffering was imposed. Cuffing, pratfalls, and sexual humiliation
worked alongside humanitarian sensationalism to lock African Americans
into the position of exemplary sufferers and legitimate white abolitionist participation in the public sphere. As several critics suggest, "low" minstrelsy
serves to heighten Stowe's "high" sentiment, putting it in greater relief.[85]

Minstrelsy's disciplinary function was not lost on performers or audiences. Within the United States, blackface minstrelsy constituted one of the
earliest and most enduring ways European immigrants transformed their
own marginalization into entertaining "black" modes of being, which encouraged imitation by whites. Outside of the United States, as Tavia Nyong'o
notes in his account of the minstrel carnivalesque, the imagined cross-racial
"mimicry" and "specifically participatory character" of minstrelsy allowed
proletarian whites a sensual, embodied performance of black rural content-
ment that resulted in the exemplification of U.S. culture as "mongrel" and
racially mixed.[86] Racial performance in blackface minstrelsy was important
to the popularity and success of Uncle Tom's Cabin among Germans and German Americans. Like other Europeans, Germans fully engaged "Uncle Tom's
Cabin" in minstrelsy and song, using minstrelsy to construct their own versions of "whiteness" through the selective performance and repudiation of
"blackness."[87] In minstrelsy, the complex relationship between European immigrants and U.S. slaves entails a range of mixed or hybrid racial, class, and
other combinations.

Uncle Tom's Cabin and its various minstrel permutations transformed the
meaning and value of minstrelsy for racial identification in Europe and
among European immigrants to the United States. Before bourgeois audiences embraced minstrelsy in the 1840s and 1850s, its sentimental paternalism helped construct notions of whiteness around black difference by giving
uprooted European immigrant laborers a nostalgic image of a stable plantation family. The inaccessibility of this family marked the immigrants' own
modernity, urbanity, and incipient whiteness. In the 1850s, minstrelsy took
on sentimental elements of plot and performance to become a more respect-
able sort of melodrama. This trend was cemented in some of the many stage
adaptations of Uncle Tom's Cabin. Stage adaptations began to appear even as

the novel was being serialized and contributed to the novel's early popularity. The onset of the Civil War decreased the popularity of stage and minstrel adaptations of the novel within the United States but gave them even greater topicality and political currency in England and Europe, where the moral reputation of Stowe's novel attached to stage and minstrel productions and cultivated a new bourgeois audience. Many European cities, including Berlin and Vienna, hosted multiple productions of "Uncle Tom's Cabin" simultaneously.

These stage productions reciprocated Stowe's own substantial engagement with minstrelsy in *Uncle Tom's Cabin* itself. Stowe consulted with the producers of a few stage productions, and while some minstrel shows mocked Stowe's representation of slave piety, her novel was not inimical to minstrelsy, integrating many approaches to embodied black suffering—sentimental, sensational, minstrel, parodic, and martyrological—to produce a more complex account of blackness than earlier humanitarian abolitionist writing. Stowe's capacity to offer these sorts of innovative descriptions of slave suffering in a moralistic humanitarian narrative was vital to the novel's popularity and that of its stage adaptations.

Comic minstrelsy, which held a broad appeal to poor and middling audiences, was particularly suited to the task of correcting perversions of sympathy. Because minstrel humor eschewed humanitarian narrative in favor of bodily grotesquerie, it could offer an alternative to humanitarian sensationalism while short-circuiting the link between suffering and erotic pleasure. Stowe's attempt to address the dangers of "perversions" of sentiment in *Uncle Tom's Cabin* is thus especially comprehensive. She offers an elaborate plot, incorporates "entertaining" representations of blacks from minstrelsy and other genres to better isolate scenes of sympathy, develops elaborate characters, and focuses on the sentimental destruction of the family. St. Clare's description of the enslaved child Topsy as altogether a "funny specimen in the Jim Crow line" contributes to the sentimental bathos in Topsy's account of her complete lack of family bonds or, really, any history whatsoever; Topsy's minstrel high jinks serve to temper or assuage the emotional distress caused by the destruction of the black family.[88] Stowe's "real presence," then, depends on a naturalization of that suffering as proper to the slave body as part of the slave's transformation into property. The radically circumscribed, almost illusory notion of choice available to such "fugitive property," which Harriet Jacobs would so valiantly attempt to explain in her account of taking a lover, recalls Hartman's admonition that there is no sharp break between

Foucauldian discipline and the earlier forms of power she calls "discipline with its clothes off."[89]

Topsy was a particularly mobile figure. Though often a caricature, her appearance managed to retain the specter of black suffering and black presence.[90] In late 1852, *Frederick Douglass' Paper* published an Episcopal clergyman's account of the novel's reception in Cambridge. Repeating some of the *Eclectic Review*'s sense of the book's divine portent, the account notes that

> *Uncle Tom's Cabin* is still selling. It is a marvelous book—a revolutionary book. It is really wonderful how it has influenced not only a tender vein in our common nature, but also art, in its various departments.—Cruikshank is now illustrating it in an admirable manner. The music shops are full of songs and melodies about and from Uncle Tom. The great run at the theatres is owing to the representation of "Uncle Tom's Cabin." The windows are full of beautiful illustrations of the various scenes in it; and, by the way, the book is full of pictures. Passing through Cheapside the other day, all of a sudden, I saw in a window, a sable face, with bright eyes, shining teeth, with a most quizzical comical expression—undersigned in large letters—"Topsy."[91]

Adding a visual, aural, and generally performative account to the *Eclectic Review*'s description of "Uncle Tom's Cabin's" saturation of English print and conversation, *Frederick Douglass' Paper* evinces even more apprehension at the book's power. The account materializes the novel's threat in the "sudden" appearance of a "quizzical" black face in a window at the commercial heart of London. The smiling slave child could appear in public places where earlier sensational humanitarian images of flogging and whipping could not. She remained linked to those sensational images, with all of their distressing erotic power, while also floating free into a public commercial realm. If, as I have suggested, republican revolution helped frame Krafft-Ebing's masochistic correspondent's analogy of "the slave to the master," what of the second analogy, "the domestic animal to its owner"? As the Epilogue will consider, Topsy's smiling face evoked another disturbing historical link between the slave and the animal: the child pet.

Child Pets, Melville's Pip, and
Oriental Blackness

While much work on abjection, race, eroticism, and suffering is centered on a scopic, visual model of sensibility and sentiment, this visual model, as Chapter 1 describes, is premised on a broader sensitization of bodies in and through suffering. Thus far, this book has considered two competing but complementary tendencies in religious or spiritual engagements with abjection: first, the way religious abjection helped to construct racial difference, and, second, the way in which it rendered racial difference incoherent, often by revealing internal contradictions. The epilogue returns to the abolitionist dynamic in which white sympathy for black abjection licenses white publicity, looking this time at a tendency toward racial decoherence produced by the slippage between racial difference and religious difference in the mid-nineteenth century. It explores the eighteenth-century phenomenon of child "pets" and U.S. Orientalist accounts of "dancing boys" to shed light on the character of Pip, Ahab's cabin boy in *Moby-Dick* (1851). Cabin boys were recognized objects of male sexual desire in nineteenth-century legal and literary discourse. The cabin boy's vulnerability to rape was often discussed alongside or in terms of other physical violations, such as cannibalism, which were themselves racialized.[1] Herman Melville's delineation of Pip registered these threats but goes beyond them by using Oriental tropes to describe Pip and Ahab's complimentary psychological and spiritual injuries. Drawing on Etienne Balibar's account of "the metaphors and metonymies of racism" and the intertwined histories of "the black" and "the Oriental," the epilogue shows Pip as a child pet whose receipt of Oriental wisdom in the face of minstrel and sympathetic suffering contests a naturalized notion of black submission.

Abolitionism provided the most affecting portraits of young black male suffering in the early nineteenth century. Though many abolitionist accounts evoked sympathy by flattening young black male experience into a sea of anonymous misery, others were more subtle and complex. One of the most intriguing portraits appeared in Lydia Maria Child's 1834 *The Oasis*, a gift-book of abolitionist miscellany intended for sale at Maria Chapman's inaugural Boston Anti-Slavery Fair. Child, in her introduction to *The Oasis*, expressed hope that her collection would give Northern white bourgeois readers a richer sense of black affective and personal life, thereby reducing prejudice against mixed-race socializing. This failure of social circulation, Child felt, was a major stumbling block for both abolitionist organizing and the legal and political recognition of black Americans.

Both Child's beliefs and her editorial approach offered important new directions for abolitionist writing and organizing. *The Oasis* marks the emergence of midcentury abolitionist sentimentalism out of an earlier abolitionist humanitarian sensationalism. Child's editorial work in *The Oasis* exemplifies this transition: she excerpted John Gabriel Steadman's 1796 *Five Years Expedition*, whose graphic illustrations and accounts of torture had contributed to the eighteenth-century humanitarian-pornographic eroticization of suffering, but entirely excluded such scenes in favor of an exclusive focus on black female virtue in the figure of "Joanna." At the same time, *The Oasis* was in many ways greater than the sum of its parts. Its avowed political aims and juxtaposition of genres and styles encouraged readers to browse through the plurality of representations of blackness and, lingering over episodes that most fascinated, forge their own sense of the connections or disconnections between them.[2]

One illustration, accompanying a French tale translated by Child herself, highlights the difficulty in disentangling sensational humanitarian-pornographic suffering from sentimental and other forms of affective connection. The cut, entitled "Little Scipio," might at first glance seem far from a scene of suffering and perhaps even less available to erotic reading than Steadman's gauzy "Joanna." "Little Scipio," set inside a narrative of the life of military leader Scipio Africanus, was unusual for depicting a scene not described in the accompanying narrative. In the cut, the young Scipio serves as a "pet" or "favorite plaything" to the Duke of Orleans. Surrounded by three corseted women in tight bodices, Scipio is mounted on the back of the duke himself, whose hair serves as a bridle while he crawls on all fours.[3] Little Scipio is only playing at mastery, as the duke's subservience is established and controlled by the duke himself. But this aristocratic playing at reversals of power, set inside a narrative of Scipio Africanus's military prowess, might

Little Scipio: a favorite plaything in the family of Egalite, Duke of Orleans. Page 139.

Figure 8. "Little Scipio: a favorite plaything in the family of Egalite, Duke of Orleans." Child, *The Oasis*, 1834. Manuscripts, Archives and Rare Books Division, Schomburg Center for Research in Black Culture, The New York Public Library, Astor, Lenox, and Tilden Foundations.

have been troubling to some of the white bourgeois Child addresses in her introduction, especially in the wake of Nat Turner's 1831 revolt.

"Little Scipio" linked the erotic dangers of aristocratic luxury with military and civic disturbance. Illustrating a literal playing with positions of power, its representation of interracial, intergenerational intimacy links slaveholders' aristocratic perversions of domestic affection to domestic and political dangers.[4] Its image of aristocratic excess would feed into later nineteenth-century U.S. abolitionist attempts to warn against an erotic South by likening white mastery to Oriental tyranny, driving home the connection between slavery and Oriental dissipation by comparing the mansion to the harem. Child pets became incorporated into denunciations of the "Southern harem" as signs of conspicuous excess. In "Little Scipio," the excesses are of several possible kinds. As Amy Kaplan notes, abolitionist reform of the "Southern harem" worked in tandem with Northern missionary transformations of the Oriental harem, which white women alone could penetrate, thereby expanding the boundaries of U.S. empire while restricting, on the basis of race, access to the domestic space within it.[5] The "Southern harem" projected the imperial dimensions of U.S. empire onto a perverse domestic sphere that could be regionalized and hence contained as a Southern threat to Northern domesticity, even as it uncannily reappeared in Northern scenes of domestic tyranny, crime, and female disenfranchisement.

While abolitionist portraits of enslaved children in the Southern harem worked to establish the slaveholder as an erotic predator, they drew on a much older tradition of representing child pets that intended quite the opposite. Among seventeenth- and eighteenth-century urban European aristocrats, child "pets" or "playthings" served as faddish accoutrement. Often elaborately dressed in Oriental or military garb, child pets shared the same social and representational space with domestic animals.[6] In portraiture, especially, child pets appeared regularly as *ficelle*, exotic minor characters who, like dogs, parrots, and monkeys, set off the prominence of the major figures through contrast.[7] Throughout the eighteenth and early nineteenth centuries, various bourgeois critics of aristocratic privilege made the practice of keeping child pets appear inhumane by providing new models for childhood. These models alternately included or excluded "African" or black boys. Some contributed to developing notions of race that proposed innate differences in sensation or feeling (e.g., as Jefferson argued, Africans' "afflictions . . . are less felt, and sooner forgotten"), while others privileged age over race and argued for the essential similarity of all children.[8]

Much literary criticism of *Moby-Dick* has treated Pip as a sort of *ficelle* to Ahab, setting off and illuminating Ahab's greater madness. Just as the child pet was transformed from a sign of luxury into a sign of excess and sexual degradation, so too has Pip been read as a peculiarly sensitive marker of the dangers of tyranny. Melville therein followed abolitionists such as Frederick Douglass who used the slaveholder's ranking of animals alongside humans as a sign of the perversity of a system where men could be property. The link between child pet and animal pet remained a salient element of Melville's account of white racial fantasy in "Benito Cereno" (1855), when Captain Delano "took to negroes, not philanthropically, but genially, just as other men took to Newfoundland dogs."[9] Melville's tragicomic eroticism in his portrait of Pip flirts with abolitionist calls for reforming the Southern "harem" but avoids his earlier novels' direct engagement with other varieties of reformist rhetoric.[10] Nevertheless, Melville substantially expanded Pip's role in the wake of the Fugitive Slave Act and the April 1851 Massachusetts Supreme Court trial of Thomas Simms, and Pip appears to bear the sole representational burden in registering the multiple threats to U.S. black masculinity.[11]

Melville's oblique engagement with reform in his later work may have encouraged critics to focus on his personality and mental state rather than the work's politics. As one reviewer wrote of *Pierre*, completed just after *Moby-Dick*, Melville seemed "[a]mbitious of the character of a reformer" but capable only of "playing away at social evils" without practical effect.[12] This socially marginalized rhetorical "play" included Melville's refusal to engage in the sorts of consistent racial troping that helped reformist discourses function in the public sphere. As we have already seen, racial difference had become a commonsense principle underlying nineteenth-century rational-political debate, and Melville's rejection of consistent racial troping in favor of exploring the deep structures of race was part of his imagination of new aesthetic and intellectual horizons for reform.

If there is one scene in *Moby-Dick* that appears especially resistant to such readings of perversity, it is Pip's hallucination, in Ahab's cabin, of entertaining ranks of captains and admirals. In an exaggerated fulfillment of Child's dream of sociability between the races, Pip welcomes his guests with a hearty "fill up, monsieurs!" and notes, "[w]hat an odd feeling, now, when a black boy's host to white men with gold lace upon their coats!" Perhaps because Pip's vision of equality is both naïve and prescient, the skeptical optimist C. L. R. James called this "one of the most strangely moving passages in the whole book."[13] It is precisely here, though, that Melville subtly advances and critiques abolitionist claims to moral publicity by offering a pastiche of the child pet, Oriental "dancing boy," and plantation Gothic troping of male sexual enslavement.

We can first bring Pip back into the "pet" tradition by emphasizing not only the scene's military pageantry, French sociability, and reversal of racial hierarchy but also, just as importantly, Melville's framing of the hallucination as Pip's response to Ahab's refusal of Pip's ecstatic offer of slave gratitude. Pip and Ahab's relationship is, like Ishmael and Queequeg's friendship, grounded in sentiment and sublimity, but it does not promise the same richness or mutual fulfillment.[14] After Ahab invites Pip into his cabin, the two mutually pledge their sentimental devotion. Ahab exclaims, Lear-like, "thou art tied to me by cords woven of my heart-strings." Pip, caressing Ahab's hand, replies that the hand is "a man-rope; something that weak souls may hold by."[15] However, as we know from Lieutenant Selvagee, a man literally named for a rope in Melville's earlier *White-Jacket*, the man-rope's promise of salvation is haunted by the violence of the erotic South. Pip's abandonment on the sea, Nantucket's "own special plantation," gives him the power to "heal" his "master" through the power of sympathy.[16] When Ahab attempts to leave his cabin, Pip stops him, protesting that the captain "ha[s] not a whole body." When Ahab again moves to leave, Pip offers himself as the cure to the captain's incompletion in a phantasmagoria of slave gratitude. Pip begs "do ye but use poor me for your one lost leg; only tread upon me, Sir; I ask no more, so I remain a part of ye." When Ahab refuses, Pip keens, "Oh good master, master, master!" and Ahab threatens to "murder" Pip if he will not stop crying while promising to console Pip with the sound of his footsteps on the deck above.[17]

In dramatizing Pip's response to Ahab's protection from the crew, *Moby-Dick* draws on the history of the trope of the "grateful slave." In the eighteenth century Anglo-Atlantic world, excessive gratitude was indicative of the social underdevelopment, immaturity, or "childishness" of other cultures but was only just becoming associated with new conceptions of racial difference. To take a paradigmatic early instance, Friday's willed submission to Crusoe, as Roxann Wheeler reminds us, invokes a class-based trope of a servant's gratitude, in which the master's kindness evokes the servant's intense, irrational, emotional performance. Friday was not so much "raced" as made into a loyal and intelligent servant, albeit one marked with signs of difference other than those that would attach to English servants. The "grateful slave" tradition served as a template for deterministic notions of racial difference.

Eighteenth-century English novels of empire increasingly identify slave gratitude as "black," as did nineteenth-century romantic racialism and plantation
fiction. Eventually, slave gratitude became associated with blackness to such a
degree that Friday could be included in what Toni Morrison calls the Afri-
canist presence at the heart of canonical U.S. literature.[18] In this racial form,
the "grateful slave" justified and moralized slavery by making slave submission a natural effect of "black" character.[19] Transforming the performance of
gratitude into proof of intrinsic racial difference did not erase the performative element of submission but naturalized it as black.

Oriental imaginary and political contexts played a crucial role in racializing slave gratitude. English captivity narratives and Barbary or Turkish captivity narratives dramatize English and white U.S. slaves' disdain for displays
of irrational gratitude.[20] Royall Tyler's two rehearsals of the scene of submission in *The Algerine Captive* were especially important to U.S. developments
of racial difference. Tyler's scenes of submission are sexually degrading legal
and medical rituals that his Northern hero, Underhill, responds to not with
gratitude but with rebellion. Tyler links but then distances white male rebellion from both African female and Oriental male passivity to produce what
Jared Gardner called "dichotomous metaphors of race."[21] Over the course of
the eighteenth and nineteenth centuries, as ecstatic gratitude and conceptions of childhood both became more racialized, the "grateful slave" grew
apart from the tradition of the child pet.

Melville's portrait of Pip dissents from a straightforward racialization of
slave gratitude, proposing instead that such gratitude was ultimately caused
by social conditions. Rather than attributing Pip's submission to his racial
character, Melville attributes it to an insanity resulting from Pip's unhappy
receipt of Oriental wisdom. While Pip's leap was inspired by Melville's ship-
mate Backus, Pip's insanity owes more to *Lear's* Fool, the book of Jonah, and
broadly Oriental notions of sacred inspiration.[22] Pip's Oriental wisdom re-
leases him from human hierarchies as he sees "God's foot" pressing not upon
him alone but, like Kant's "monstrous sublime," warping the fabric of the
world, revealing a potential utopia as, instead, a "self-annihilating terror."[23]
Profanely, Ahab characterizes Pip as "that holiness," an apotheosis of divinity,
while Starbuck, hearing the "strange sweetness of his lunacy," offers a more
scriptural interpretation of his madness as it "brings heavenly vouchers of all
our heavenly homes."[24] Ishmael, with Spenserian richness, describes Pip's insanity as "heaven's sense," a miraculous conversion occasioned by Pip's vision
of an "unwarped primal world" populated by mystical creatures and "joyous,

heartless, ever-juvenile" pagan, possibly Hindu, gods.[25] Pip's Oriental wisdom integrates him into the natural sublime. This sublimity combines Burke's reading of blackness as intrinsically sublime with Kant's competing account of blackness as possibly comic, depending on both the viewer and the "type" of blackness.

Melville's Orientalism springs from a deep well of nineteenth-century U.S. Orientalist discourse, including popular urban exotic entertainment, scientific rhetoric, and political rhetoric produced by white and black Americans, most famously Frederick Douglass.[26] In terms of race, nineteenth-century white phrenology and other scientific taxonomies distinguished "Oriental" Moors from "black" Africans but also depended on the slippage between racial typologies to smooth over contradictions. Even if Melville simply distanced "the Negro" from "the Turk" or "the Parsee," he would have participated in this larger cultural negotiation of whiteness *and* blackness through the Orient, or what C. L. R. James described as Ahab's positioning between Pip and Fedallah. But Melville did much more by weighing in on competing black and white claims to Egypt's legacy: Ishmael's alignment of his speculative philosophical standpoint with that of "the earliest standers of mast-heads . . . the old Egyptians" engages African American attempts to negotiate U.S. racial citizenship by affiliating themselves with Egypt.[27] This "Egyptian" standpoint also links Ishmael to Pip, leading to the question of why Ishmael remains sane and safe while Pip becomes mad.

One way to begin to address this question of Pip's madness is to consider how Melville's Orientalist imagery draws from or addresses Protestant missionary critiques of Oriental decadence.[28] Protestant missionary Orientalism was an especially sore point for Melville. In his South Seas novels, Melville used romantic racialism to make call for missionary reform but was taken to task for a "racy" lewdness that undercut the moral framing requisite for a serious contribution. In *Moby-Dick*, Melville moved from practical reform to theological revision, in some ways announcing the bankruptcy of the Christian moral regime.[29]

Melville's so-called paganism—his extensive use of ancient and non-European mythology and anthropology—has long been understood as attempting to "replace the 'lost' symbols of Protestant Christianity" or return them to a truer, more "original" form.[30] Like most of nineteenth-century American uses of Orientalism to propel social critique, Melville's "paganism" primarily serves (as some critics say of postcolonial critique more generally) "to return to the position of the Other as a resource for rethinking the

Western self." Melville is unusual, among these U.S. Orientalists, for his sustained and manifest interest in the Near East, especially a "fascination" with "Eastern" "racial-cultural hybridity."[31] Melville's Orientalism specifically addresses what Etienne Balibar, in a memorial for Said, called the "the metaphors and metonymies of racism."[32] In Melville studies, the earliest and most interesting example of these metaphors and metonymies appears in Carolyn Karchner's assertion that Melville's portrait of Queequeg deliberately addresses "anti-Negro prejudice" by "blurr[ing] racial lines" in, for example, Queequeg's "Islamic, and even Christian features."[33] Karchner's own blurring of the distinction between race and religion in her notion of Islamic and Christian "features" moves from racial metaphor (e.g., Ahab as a "type" of "disappearing Indian") to racial metonymy, or the way race and racism function associatively, through a range of contiguities and/or slippages.[34] In addition to slippage between racial categories, slippage also occurs between markers of difference coded as historically earlier, as in Wheeler's notion of the "sedimentation" of class and religion in racial ideology. Melville's account may go even further than Wheeler by emphasizing the way in which "sedimentation" is an active process with fractures and faults communicating surprising connections between the layers.

Melville's work is generally congenial to readings of racial slippage because it invokes a series of mutually supporting performances of power and submission that, however "superannuated" and associated with "outmoded" governments, uncannily maintain themselves and thereby stand as refutations of Enlightenment modernity, white civilization, and progress. The slippage could be endless, leading to a totalizing erasure of difference—Ishmael's "Who ain't a slave?"—but Pip, as a child pet, engages specific and sometimes contradictory historical slippages between Islam, Moors, and blackness that have recently garnered attention in attempts to think through contemporary U.S. black and Asian identities.[35]

As the compound "blackamoor" suggests, Muslim faith and blackness were separable but widely thought together in the long eighteenth century. Abolitionist discourse itself, Felicity Nussbaum writes, was an important site of separating Oriental from black through different modes of political and affective action: for the Oriental, liberation from tyranny through imperial expansion; for the black, freedom from slavery.[36] The child pet was a vexed and early site of separation. In the seventeenth century, child pets' service as *ficelle* did not depend on color contrast. Some writers described the most famous pet of the age, King George I's "wild Peter," the "wild boy of Hanover," as brown-skinned, but others remarked on his ideal Greek facial features, and painters emphasized his pale skin and rosy lips. Conversations about Peter and other wild children dovetailed with conversations about human difference in the context of European colonization of Africa and North America. Skin color might serve as a visible mark of the child pet's savagery, but that was only part of the pet's value as a figure whose difference gave writers and philosophers a position of distance upon which they could reflect on questions of innate character, *ensauvagement*, and educability. Popular and philosophical writers in England and Europe used Peter and other child pets to satirize English manners and debate the effects of education and language. Swift's *London Strow'd*, for example, used Peter and a pair of "marvelous black Arabian Ambassadors" as *ficelle* to satirize English femininity: Peter, here imagined as a lord on the make, demands that his future spouse have, among other things, "at some time or other kept a great Dog, a squaling Parrot, or a Black Boy."[37]

Pets, as aristocratic possessions, were available quite early to bourgeois critiques of aristocratic artifice and demands for cultural clarity. In 1710, for example, Steele's *Tatler* printed a satirical letter from a child pet as a postscript to a parodic "advertisement" for goods lifted by a Welsh servant. The letter is worth considering as it correlates excessive female consumption, corruptions of rank, religious conversion, and black Oriental publicity. It begins, "Sir,—I am a blackmoor boy . . . by my lady's order . . . christened by the chaplain. The good man has gone further with me, and told me a great deal of good news; as, that I am as good as my lady herself, as I am a Christian, and many other things: but for all this, the parrot, who came over with me from our country, is as much esteemed by her as I am . . . I desire also to know, whether, now I am a Christian, I am obliged to dress like a Turk, and wear a turban." The *Tatler* establishes its own position in an English masculinist public by identifying the pet's insistently plural cultural and religious identities—a Christian blackamoor, "obliged" by his female master to dress as a Turk and resisting his service by circulating a public petition like an Englishman—and calling for their clearer delineation.[38] Later in the century, abolitionists would oblige, emphasizing the pet's blackness by noting, for example, that a child pet sipped tea sweetened with sugarcane harvested by his parents.

Over the course of the eighteenth and nineteenth centuries, abolitionists and proslavery critics of abolitionist "amalgamationism" both linked child "pets" with Oriental sexual dissipation, often through the iconography of the turbaned pageboy.[39] Again, the availability of these scenes for reproduction and viewing by a broad spectrum of readers depended on their circulation within moral reading publics. Abolitionists and, in a different way, anti-abolitionists both shielded their erotic representations from accusations of sexual impropriety by highlighting their political and moral intent. The moral quality of abolitionist texts allowed them to circulate among audiences that would have shunned more purely erotic texts. For example, in contrast to the outcry that effectively prevented the public viewing of Adolph Ulric Wertmüller's "Danaë and the Shower of Gold," in which a cherubic Eros acts as a *ficelle* for Zeus's impregnating shower, abolitionist sculptor Hiram Powers's neoclassical "Greek Slave" toured prestigious museums and received sustained press coverage. Nevertheless, part of the attraction of these abolitionist texts depended on the tension between the moral and the erotic. Although Powers went to some lengths to guard against erotic readings of his sculpture, the work's power and popularity in the broader public evoked this *frission*: a letter describing the "Greek Slave" in Douglass's *North Star* began by insisting "sensualism leaves the heart at once, if it had intruded there before."[40] Representations of Powers's sculpture even entered pornographic economies. Popular English illustrations parodied the sculpture by presenting a similarly posed black woman as an object of sexual desire, and a less widely circulated 1840s U.S. daguerreotype evoked amalgamationist fears by surrounding the white statue with three leering dark-skinned men in turbans. These frankly pornographic representations alternately extended and parodied abolitionist attempts to reform the "Southern harem."

While abolitionists emphasized the tragedy of child pets and the associated sexual license of the Southern harem, the *Tatler*'s comic attempt to register and control the cultural threat posed by the child pet suggests a new reading of Pip's tambourine and early "gayness." Melville's proximate references were, of course, black music and dance and blackface minstrelsy. Yet even these were constituted, to at least some degree, by the metaphorics and metonymics of race: "the rhythms of Pip's tambourine" reflected black performers' play with what Sterling Stuckey calls "the power of black dance," and the structure of early minstrel shows encouraged the "sliding" or slotting of other racial or immigrant ethnic identities into the "place" of blackness.[41] In England and Europe, especially, minstrels sat side by side with Oriental performances and were collapsed back together in late nineteenth-century work like *The Mikado* and *Urliana*.[42]

The question of submission also links the social productions of blackness with those of Orientalism. As was the case with the "grateful slave," submission was crucial to Said's notion of Orientalist practice. For Said, Orientalism was both accepted and imposed; the Orient "*could be*—that is, submitted to being—*made* Oriental." Said's uncomfortable insistence on Oriental submission opens up onto a series of discomfiting speculations about the ways in which "consent" is produced by extending material domination into the realm of ideological production. Said illustrates the submission of the Orient via Flaubert's account of an "Egyptian courtesan," an encounter that "fairly stands for the pattern of relative strength between East and West" in which "historical facts of domination . . . allowed [Flaubert] not only to possess Kuchuk Hanem physically but to speak for her and tell his readers in what way she was 'typically Oriental.'"[43] For Said, this reciprocal practice of Orientalism reveals historical questions of consent and power as developed through erotic and ideological domination, and vice versa.

As subsequent critics note, these uncomfortable questions of ideological production also apply to Said's own gendering and sexing of the process. His account of Kuchuk Hanem's submission elides Flaubert's more intense and repeated interest in the "dancing boy." This is one of a series of Said's elisions that stabilize positions of submission and domination around a gender binary at the cost of downplaying substantial, perhaps crucial, ambivalence in early Orientalist constructions of sexuality, including claims to the universality of sexual differences and the porosity or reversibility of distinctions between Eastern and Western sexual types and practices.[44] On the one hand, Orientalizing erotic behaviors enabled Western cultural amnesia about analogous European traditions such as the "child pet." On the other hand, this willful forgetting granted Orientalist tropes and motifs the power to evoke subterranean connections between East and West. Nineteenth-century U.S. depictions of the dancing boy helped develop Anglo-American religious conceptions of sexual practice and difference in ways that reveal a more diffuse notion of sexuality than we might expect. British soldier and explorer Richard Burton's 1886 notion of the "sotadic zone," in which same-sex perversions prevail, has been a crucial node for conversations about Orientalism and sexuality in Melville and other mid-nineteenth-century U.S. writing.[45] In Burton, religion intersects with knowledge about sexuality, geography, and place in complex ways. Some recent critics, noting the nonsensicality of the "zone" from a climatological perspective, propose that Burton's geographic determinism is a front for what is in fact a *religious* distinction between Christian, marked as heterosexual, and non-Christian, marked as homosexual.⁴⁶ This analysis is vital because it recognizes the importance of locating perversion at the intersection of geography/climate and religious difference. It also grants religion an active place in the production of new forms of perverse selfhood in the nineteenth century. However, this analysis may actually simplify the complexities of sexuality, religion, and climate in Burton's account. What critics call Burton's description of "homosexuality," for example, covers over a knotty mid-nineteenth-century discourse of sexual perversion. Burton is more explicit than Melville, but the names he gives to same-sex erotic acts are remarkably plural and diverse, suggesting that the shift toward a modern understanding of sexuality as central to identity was both gradual and continually structured by religion.⁴⁷

Burton's prominence in literary and historical criticism covers over a body of nineteenth-century Orientalist uses of religious rhetoric to explain the shaping of sexual practice and personhood. One of the most intriguing engagements with Orientalist rhetoric comes from U.S. diplomat Eugene Schuyler. His 1877 Turkistan travelogue offers an account of "*batchas*, or dancing-boys" that is particularly apposite for Melville's description of Pip as a figure of entertainment with moral and metaphysical significance. Schuyler initially proposes that the *batchas*' ubiquity and popularity was the consequence of a "Mohammedan prudery" that prohibited "the public dancing of women." He follows this argument from religious determinism with a humanist claim that all men have the same basic passions. Even though Islam forbids women's dancing, Schuyler writes, "the desire of being amused and of witnessing a graceful spectacle is the same all the world over." In Turkistan, therefore, "boys and youths specially trained take the place of the dancing girls." The "moral tone of the society of Central Asia," he archly concludes, "is scarcely improved by the change."⁴⁸ His notion of boys "taking the place" of girls is grounded in a notion of gender difference and substitution, but in the lengthy and detailed account that follows, the *batcha* never stabilizes around anything like the imitation of naturalized feminine spectacle.⁴⁹ Instead, Schuyler bookends his description of the *batcha* with two analogies—a knight's squire and a duenna's cosseted charge—that alternately romanticize and domesticate the dancing boy:

> In all large towns *batchas* are very numerous, for it is as much the custom for a Bokhariot gentleman to keep one as it was in the Middle Ages for each knight to have his squire. In fact no establishment of a man of rank or position would be complete without one; and men of

A Dancing Boy of Bengal.

Figure 9. "A Dancing Boy of Bengal." Wright, *Lectures on India*, 1848. General Research Division, The New York Public Library, Astor, Lenox, and Tilden Foundations.

small means club together to keep one among them to amuse them in
their hours of rest and recreation. They usually set him up in a tea
shop, and if the boy is pretty his stall will be full of customers all day
long. Those *batchas*, however, who dance in public are fewer in number and are now to some extent under police restrictions. . . . They
live either with their parents or with the *entrepreneur* who takes care
of them and always accompanies them. He dresses them for the different dances, wraps them up when they have finished, and looks after
them as well as any duenna.[50]

Although Schuyler initially claims that *batcha* dancing (and its accompanying moral degradation) was the effect of Muslim religious error, causing
the substitution of male for female, the remainder of his account indicates
that the notion of substitution was a self-conscious effect of his own narrative. Schuyler concludes his section on dancing by admitting that, despite
his previous claims, "it is not only boys who dance in Central Asia," and
proceeding to describe a "splendid *tomasha*, or spectacle—a dance of
women." This description completely revises his account of "orthodox [Is-
lamic] horror" in favor of a far more complex picture of sectarian diversity
within Islam, cultural differences between Persians and Turks, and even
simple curiosity, as "the Mussulmans [who] in general disapprove of the
dancing of women . . . do not refuse to witness it if they get an opportu-
nity." Following on from that revision, Schuyler offers another, perhaps
even more striking revision. The *batcha*'s dancing, once described as a substitute for female dancing, becomes the standard by which readers might
evaluate girls' dancing: girls' dances, Schuyler writes, are "very similar to
those danced by boys, though less vigorous and less graceful."[51] This notion
of gender imitation serving as the basis for the "real" is, at least in theory,
familiar enough but is nevertheless striking to see played out in a
nineteenth-century U.S. text.

As a queer Orientalist structure in which public performances of feminine grace appears as an imitation of an imitation, Schuyler's framework of
the *batcha* presents a historical analogy for a final element of abjection in my
work: psychological depression, understood, in Lacanian terms, as a separation from the original, "feminine" comfort of the Imaginary. This separation
has ripples of consequence for American self-conception. By beginning with
a strong absolutist moral claim to Christian superiority and ending with a
discussion of Muslim complexity and similitude, Schuyler works in a

conflicted, contradictory, uncanny Orientalist mode, both domesticating and defamiliarizing the exotic. Schuyler's reversals offers gentle instruction to readers unaware of the complexities of life in Central Asia, but his other lessons are more obscure. While Schuyler seems to enclose the threat of religious and sexual difference, concretized in the *batcha*, within a narrative of ostensibly familiar women's dancing, the absence of a female original makes even that a dangerous terrain, leaving readers with only Schuyler's relentless flow of narrative detail to carry them forward.

Melville's combination of eroticism and comedy in his presentation of Pip's enthralled submission and Ahab's protection—although more subtle than Schuyler's account of the *batcha* or even the "racy" lewdness of Melville's earlier South Seas novels—might have been too morally challenging for most abolitionist writers in the United States, who were already marginalized in the public and political spheres. Indeed, few representations of the child pet before Melville combined tragedy and comedy in their portrait of ecstatic slave gratitude. I want to close by briefly reading one representation that did: Friedrich Klinger's 1776 tragi-comedy *Sturm und Drang*. In that play, "a young Moor" enslaved to a rough sea captain saves the captain from being consumed by vengeance. Without making any claim of Klinger's direct influence on Melville, Klinger's unusual eighteenth-century incorporation of the child pet's suffering into an erotic humanitarian economy provides a useful point of reference for Melville's refusal to allow Pip's self-abasement to redeem Ahab or even save Pip himself from destruction.[52]

Sturm und Drang, first performed in Dresden in 1777, offered an intensely topical combination of political news, Shakespeare, and popular theater shot through with Pietistic emotional intensity. Briefly, the play set the perils of Rousseauian liberal individualism in the American Revolution. Its plot focuses on war and private vendetta as they interrupt various sorts of sentimental relationships. As the play begins, Lord Berkley is trying to exact revenge for the death of his wife, which he presumes was caused by the betrayal of his former friend, Lord Bushy. Berkley's son, the romantic Captain Harry Berkley, discovers Lord Bushy and orders him set adrift at sea, resulting in a counter-vendetta on the part of the young "Wild" Carl Bushy. This knot is untied when a young Moor, Captain Berkley's good-hearted cabin boy, reveals that he and a first mate secretly kept Lord Bushy on the ship, in defiance of Captain Berkley's wishes. Lord Bushy emerges to successfully exonerate himself, the two lords resume their friendship, and Wild Bushy and Caroline Berkley resume their courtship.[53]

The young Moor played a crucial role in the plot and, in some ways, stole the show. His combination of comic antics, rude speech, moral nobility, and sentimental appeal made him a favorite of early audiences, serving as a counterpoint to the high emotional "chaos" facing the English aristocrats. The young Moor's comic service is tied to a gendered shift in representations of blackness on the German stage. In court entertainment, from which Klinger generally dissented, dark-skinned male characters increasingly became helpless, inferior others. In popular theatrical representations, dark-skinned women became Orientalized as threatening objects of bourgeois male desire, possibly serving as ciphers for German dreams of empire. This shift in stage representations of dark-skinned characters helped inform German dissent from Burke's account of black sublimity, including Hegel's description of Africans as "infantile" and Lessing's account of blackness as comic, ugly, and disgusting.[54] Klinger's young Moor is infantile but also resolves the central plot conflict through active subterfuge.

Perhaps hoping his audience might wince at their own laughter, Klinger makes the young Moor's desperate subservience and appetite for pain necessary for spectatorial pleasure. In one witty exchange between the young Moor and the captain, the Moor notes that bruises on his back should be proof of devotion, while the captain counters that bruises are better proof of affection.[55] The young Moor's desperate self-abasement and desire for punishment sets limits on the ability of slave suffering to redeem the sufferer or to resolve conflict. In particular, the triumph of sentimental male friendship (between Lord Bushy and Lord Berkley) and romantic love (between Wild Bushy and Caroline Berkley) stands in contrast to the relationship between the Moor and Captain Berkley. The young Moor's tears highlight the contrast between this relationship and the play's other relationships, which use tears in more typical sentimental fashion. Earlier, when the young Moor hints to Caroline Berkley that he kept Lord Bushy alive, she tantalizes him by promising he could become her pampered slave. In a tearful scene, both Caroline and the young Moor mourn their absent loved ones: the young Moor his noble parents and Caroline her absent lover. The young Moor becomes fully integrated into a sentimental abolitionist economy by announcing his fear that "there would be no end of . . . beating and brawling" if he helped her. The English, he concludes, "teach us blacks how to cry very early," only to laugh at their tears. Caroline Berkley promises to save him from this fate, vowing "you shall not cry . . . with me."[56] However, Caroline's promise is unfulfilled at the play's end, as the young Moor is the only character whose suffering increases and remains unresolved. When the Captain forgives the young Moor for saving Lord Bushy, the young Moor kisses the Captain's forehead and twines himself around his body. He calls himself the captain's "boy," "monkey," and "dog" and begs "skin me" and "pull my skin over my head," expressions of shock that equate violence with affection.[57] The captain pinches him and jokingly offers him a midshipman's post, dubbing his words "sugarcane from a moor boy" and asking if he wants a beating. Klinger thereby reconnects the pet's status as a fetishized private sentimental object to enslavement by pairing the Moor's excessive emotion with key abolitionist signifiers of plantation slavery—sugarcane, flogging, and disfigurement—to generate humor.

The play's final scene reprises these tears and expressions of shock to establish the young Moor's participation in an affective economy that differs from either sentimental friendship or romance. In that scene, the Captain storms off stage, denouncing the "disgraceful" example set by those "get-[ting] along so well, like womenfolk, at the end." Declaring that he will resolve his crises, in manly fashion, on the open seas, he beckons the young Moor to follow and demands that the young Moor "amuse" him. The young Moor replies, "I'll cry for joy, if that amuses you."[58] These tears of joy, which echo the young Moor's earlier expressions of self-abasement and devotion, offer incomplete salvation. They clearly represent a more palatable alternative to tears caused by English cruelty, but the Captain's questionable taste in "amusement" makes the young Moor's fate uncertain. In either case, the young Moor's tears are a source of laughter for both the captain and the audience.[59]

Moby-Dick reprises Klinger's link between sublimity, self-abasement and redemption. Melville's staging of Pip's submission to Ahab accepts Klinger's separation of American slavery from the sentimental family and romance while refusing Klinger's resolution. Both authors present slaves' heightened emotion as a product of slavery rather than naturalizing it as a black performance. Like Klinger, who poses the young Moor's performance of submission as incompatible with sentimental friendship or romance, Melville dramatizes the failure of Pip's performance of submission to fulfill its promise as a solution to the conflict between slavery and liberty. In *Moby-Dick*, slavery is incompatible with democracy, but Melville turns away from Klinger's comic, somewhat absurd resolution in favor of a tragic representation of the failure of black performances of submission to fulfill their sentimental promise of "curing" white madness. While Klinger's moor is a cunning agent, actively lying and disobeying his captain's orders to help bring about the happy ending in which he could not participate, Pip's madness results, indirectly, from his inadvertent, almost unwilling disobedience in jumping from the boat.

Pip's extreme emotional response to Ahab's kindness might be read as naturalizing gratitude as black and thereby upholding the racial logic of the grateful slave, but the larger context of the scene of abandonment suggests that Pip's performance was the effect of his social abjection as a black sailor. Pip's excessive gratitude is a productive performance, inasmuch as it allows him to ameliorate the insanity caused by his abandonment at sea.[60] Pip's abandonment, Melville reminds us, was the result of his race and his class. As a black sailor, Pip is doubly vulnerable to abandonment. Not only is he working in an enterprise where sailors' lives are worth far less than the whales they hunt, but also his race, as his white shipmates remind him, makes him liable to commodification in a way that they are not. Pip's madness can be read alongside nineteenth-century psychological accounts of slavery and madness, including Benjamin Rush's 1812 abolitionist link between insanity and the experience of chattel slavery, as well as Samuel Cartwright's proslavery account (published the same year as *Moby-Dick*) of "drapetomania."[61] If we take the ship as a metaphor for national politics, the scene offers a skeptical appraisal of the role of black suffering in some abolitionist rhetoric by invoking and then immediately foreclosing on the possibility that Ahab's sympathy for Pip's suffering could save the *Pequod* from destruction. Pip's combination of marginality and centrality offers a metaphor for African Americans in Melville's national imaginary: abjected as a cynosure of loss and weakness, Pip is bound to menace Ahab, promising both completion and dissolution.[62]

Finally, Pip's dissent from romantic racialism in his service as "The Castaway" points, hesitatingly, toward another contestatory engagement with the "grateful slave" tradition: the black Robinsoniad. Harriet Jacobs's description of herself as "rejoiced as Robinson Crusoe" upon finding a gimlet in her garret and Frederick Douglass's likening of slave song to "the singing of a man cast away upon a desolate island," for example, insist on African Americans' ability to engage literary representations of faith to participate in the public sphere.[63] Pip, finding Oriental wisdom at sea but unable to redeem himself through his suffering, forecloses on the black Robinsoniad's most radical public dimensions.[64]

Introduction

1. Theodor Reik, *Masochism in Modern Man*, trans. Margaret H. Beigel and Gertrud M. Kurth (New York: Farrar, Strauss, 1941), 351–52, 356.

2. Ibid., 352, 357.

3. "Es blühen keine frische Rosen, im besten Fall entstehen Neurosen" (Theodor Reik, *Aus Leiden Freuden* [London: Imago, 1940], 334); Reik, *Masochism in Modern Man*, 351.

4. Psychoanalytic masochism does not inherit the power or value of religious abjection. Nor are the concepts necessarily related. Rather, during and after the invention of masochism in the late eighteenth century, abjection was a component of masochism, and the concepts have since been productively thought together. This "thinking together" begins with Deleuze, whose historical account of masochism's literary and Enlightenment philosophical bases suggests that masochism's challenges to certain aspects of modern subjectivity are limited by its origin within an oppositional system of sexuality that began in the eighteenth century. Gilles Deleuze, "Coldness and Cruelty," in *Masochism: Coldness and Cruelty and Venus in Furs*, trans. Jean McNeil (New York: Zone Books, 1989), 9–138; Leo Bersani, *Homos* (Cambridge, MA: Harvard University Press, 1995), 90. This history also leaves masochism an unpleasant legacy. Masochism's construction through heteronormative, misogynistic, and imperialist categories of desire has made it difficult for many women (straight or gay), many people of color, and many gay men to express masochistic desire without appearing to reify or pathologically replicate norms of deviant behavior. Neither abjection nor masochism are consistently aligned with specific identities (e.g., female, gay male, black), but early sexology developed the concepts of homosexuality and masochism in similar ways, most importantly through an unusually heavy reliance on the insights and contributions of self-identified patient-correspondents. Early sexological concepts of homosexuality and masochism "rhyme" in ways that other sexological and psychoanalytic concepts do not. While some critics make masochistic "self-shattering" a defining feature of homosexuality (indeed all sexuality or, following Jean Laplanche, subjectivity *tout court*), I would assert only this limited historical homology between the two. I do not use homosexuality as an organizing rubric, but my project's interest

in masochism and race does speak to an occluded racial component within late eighteenth-century scientific constructions of homosexuality. As Chapter 4 describes, Robert Reid-Pharr considers another defining moment of masochism's contributions to racial discourse in *Conjugal Union: The Body, the House, and the Black American* (New York: Oxford University Press, 1999), 93–95. On the history of sexological masochism, see Harry Oosterhuis, *Stepchildren of Nature: Krafft-Ebing, Psychiatry, and the Making of Sexual Identity* (Chicago: University of Chicago Press, 2000). On masochism and subject formation, see David Savran's account of Freud's moral masochist as coterminous with the Lockean liberal humanist subject in *Taking It Like a Man: White Masculinity, Masochism, and Contemporary American Culture* (Princeton, NJ: Princeton University Press, 1998), 24. Leo Bersani has also taken Laplanche's account of masochism's constitutive role in sexuality in another productive direction by describing masochistic pleasure as a formally productive and intensely intersubjective "losing of the self and discovering it elsewhere, inaccurately replicated." See Tim Dean, Hal Foster, Kaja Silverman, and Leo Bersani, "A Conversation with Leo Bersani," *October* 82 (Autumn 1997): 6.

5. On the re-definition of race, see Colette Guillaumin, *Racism, Sexism Power, and Ideology* (London: Routledge, 1995); Winthrop D. Jordan, *White over Black: American Attitudes Toward the Negro, 1550–1812* (Baltimore: Penguin Books, 1968); John Wood Sweet, *Bodies Politic: Negotiating Race in the American North, 1730–1830* (Philadelphia: University of Pennsylvania Press, 2007).

6. Andrew S. Jacobs, *Christ Circumcised: A Study in Early Christian History and Difference* (Philadelphia: University of Pennsylvania Press, 2012), 74.

7. Ibid., 99.

8. James Donnegan, *A New Greek and English Lexicon*, 4th ed. (Boston: J. H. Wilkins & R. B. Carter and Hillard, Gray & Co., 1842), s.v. "καταβάλλω," 721.

9. Denise Ferreira da Silva, *Toward a Global Idea of Race* (Minneapolis: University of Minnesota Press, 2007).

10. Thomas Jefferson, *Notes on the State of Virginia* (Philadelphia: Prichard and Hall, 1788), 153.

11. William Apess, "An Indian's Looking Glass for the White Man," in *On Our Own Ground: The Complete Writings of William Apess, a Pequot*, ed. Barry O'Connell (Amherst: University of Massachusetts Press, 1992), 155.

12. Roxann Wheeler, *The Complexion of Race: Categories of Difference in Eighteenth Century British Culture* (Philadelphia: University of Pennsylvania Press, 2000).

13. "Article 7: Original Letters, from an American Gentleman at Calcutta, to a friend in Pennsylvania," *The Analectic Magazine* 13 (May 1819): 390, 397.

14. Thomas Scott, "For the Christian Guardian (On the Crucifixion of Christ)," *Christian Guardian and Church of England Magazine* 6.4 (June 1812): 201–2, originally "On the Punishment of Crucifixion," in *The Works of the Late Rev. Thomas Scott*, ed. John Scott (London: L. B. Seely and Son, 1825), 10:230.

15. "Article 6: The Countries, Nations, and Languages of the Oceanic Region," *The Foreign Quarterly Review* 28 (December 1834): 233.

16. "Address from the Connecticut Colonization Society, 1828," excerpted in Thomas Hodgkin, *An Inquiry into the Merits of the American Colonization Society* (London: R. Watts, 1833), 26.

17. John Dunmore Lang, *Cooksland in North-Eastern Australia; the Future Cotton Field of Great-Britain* (London: Longman, Brown, Green and Longmans, 1847), 346.

18. "Anthony Benezet," *The African Repository and Colonial Journal* 2.8 (October 1826): 253.

19. On the eighteenth-century malleability of race, see Katy L. Chiles, *Transformable Race: Surprising Metamorphoses in the Literature of Early America* (New York: Oxford University Press, 2014).

20. On the larger shift, see Colin Kidd, *The Forging of Races: Race and Scripture in the Protestant Atlantic World, 1600–2000* (Cambridge: Cambridge University Press, 2006).

21. See Karen Halttunen, "Humanitarianism and the Pornography of Pain in Anglo-American Culture," *American Historical Review* 100.2 (1995): 303–34.

22. See Susan Juster, "Mystical Pregnancy and Holy Bleeding: Visionary Experience in Early Modern Britain and America," *William and Mary Quarterly* 57.2 (2000): 249–88; Phyllis Mack, *Visionary Women: Ecstatic Prophecy in Seventeenth-Century England* (Berkeley: University of California Press, 1992); Phyllis Mack, "Giving Birth to the Truth: A Letter by the Methodist Mary Taft," *Scottish Journal of Religious Studies* 19 (1988): 19–30; Elaine Forman Crane, "'I Have Suffer'd Much Today': The Defining Force of Pain in Early America," in *Through a Glass Darkly: Reflections on Personal Identity in Early America*, ed. Ronald Hoffman, Mechal Sobel, and Fredrika J. Teute (Chapel Hill: University of North Carolina Press, 1997), 370–403.

23. See Dana D. Nelson, "'No Cold or Empty Heart': Polygenesis, Scientific Professionalization, and the Unfinished Business of Male Sentimentalism," *differences: A Journal of Feminist Cultural Studies* 11.3 (1999): 39.

24. Here I take inspiration from David Savran's "attempt to press psychoanalysis into service for a historical project." Savran, *Taking It Like a Man*, 10. On some of these differences, see John Kucich's "revisionary model of masochism" in *Imperial Masochism: British Fiction, Fantasy, and Social Class* (Princeton, NJ: Princeton University Press, 2006), 17–30, and "Melancholy Magic: Masochism, Stevenson, Anti-Imperialism," *Nineteenth-Century Literature* 56.3 (2001): 364–400.

25. Feminist approaches begin with Mary Douglas, *Purity and Danger: An Analysis of Concepts of Pollution and Taboo* (New York: Praeger, 1966), and Julia Kristeva, *Powers of Horror: An Essay on Abjection*, trans. Leon S. Roudiez (New York: Columbia University Press, 1982), as well as Georges Bataille's mystical materialism in, e.g., *The Theory of Religion* (1973; repr., New York: Zone Books, 1992). Also see Caroline Walker Bynum's account of mystical asceticism in *Holy Feast and Holy Fast: The Religious Significance of*

Food to Medieval Women (Berkeley: University of California Press, 1988); Gloria Anzaldúa's embrace of the borderlands in *Borderlands/La Frontera—The New Mestiza* (San Francisco: Spinsters/Aunt Lute, 1987); Bruno Latour's concept of purification in *We Have Never Been Modern*, trans. Catherine Porter (Cambridge, MA: Harvard University Press, 1993); and Michael Taussig's notion of defacement in *Defacement: Public Secrecy and the Labor of the Negative* (Stanford, CA: Stanford University Press, 1999).

26. Subsequent feminist, African American, and gender studies that look at historical religious constructions of sexuality, desire, and abjection in the seventeenth, eighteenth, and nineteenth centuries include Joanna Brooks, *American Lazarus: Religion and the Rise of African-American and Native American Literatures* (New York: Oxford University Press, 2003), 18; Sylvia R. Frey and Betty Wood, *Come Shouting to Zion: African American Protestantism in the American South and British Caribbean to 1830* (Chapel Hill: University of North Carolina Press, 1998); Susan Juster, *Disorderly Women: Sexual Politics and Evangelicalism in Revolutionary New England* (Ithaca, NY: Cornell University Press, 1994); Phyllis Mack, *Heart Religion in the British Enlightenment: Gender and Emotion in Early Methodism* (Cambridge: Cambridge University Press, 2008). Collectively, these and other projects have informed the many other studies on which my work leans in ways large and small, including classic works on black male, gay male, and queer subjectivity, and queer of color critique examining sexuality, race, and publicity. Early work includes Franz Fanon, "The Fact of Blackness," in *Black Skin, White Masks* (1952; repr., New York: Grove Press, 1967), 109–40; Wayne Koestenbaum, *The Queen's Throat: Opera, Homosexuality, and the Mystery of Desire* (New York: Vintage, 1993), especially 117. More recent work includes Marcellus Blount and George P. Cunningham, eds., *Representing Black Men* (New York: Routledge, 1996); Roderick A. Ferguson, *Aberrations in Black: Toward a Queer of Color Critique* (Minneapolis: University of Minnesota Press, 2003); Sarita See, *The Decolonized Eye: Filipino American Art and Performance* (Minneapolis: University of Minnesota Press, 2009); José Esteban Muñoz, *Cruising Utopia: The Then and There of Queer Futurity* (New York: New York University Press, 2009); E. Patrick Johnson and Mae G. Henderson, *Black Queer Studies: A Critical Anthology* (Durham, NC: Duke University Press, 2005), Mark Rifkin, *When Did Indians Become Straight? Kinship, the History of Sexuality, and Native Sovereignty* (New York: Oxford University Press, 2011); Qwo-Li Driskill, ed., *Queer Indigenous Studies Critical Interventions in Theory, Politics, and Literature* (Tucson: University of Arizona Press, 2011); Scott Lauria Morgensen, *Spaces Between Us: Queer Settler Colonialism and Indigenous Decolonization* (Minneapolis: University of Minnesota Press, 2011); Gayatri Gopinath, *Impossible Desires: Queer Diasporas and South Asian Public Cultures* (Durham, NC: Duke University Press, 2005); Siobhan Somerville, *Queering the Color Line: Race and the Invention of Homosexuality in American Culture* (Durham, NC: Duke University Press, 2000). The concerns of queers of color, for whom divides between religious and sexual communities can magnify economic instability, encourage queer race studies' trenchant analyses of nineteenth-, twentieth-, and twenty-first-century uses of abjection. See, e.g.,

Anne Cheng, *The Melancholy of Race: Psychoanalysis, Assimilation, and Hidden Grief* (New York: Oxford University Press, 2001), 35–75; David Marriott, *Haunted Life: Visual Culture and Black Modernity* (New Brunswick, NJ: Rutgers University Press, 2007); Robert Reid-Pharr, *Black Gay Man: Essays* (New York: New York University Press, 2001); Darieck Scott, *Extravagant Abjection: Blackness, Power, and Sexuality in the African American Literary Imagination* (New York: New York University Press, 2010); Christina Sharpe, *Monstrous Intimacies: Making Post-Slavery Subjects* (Durham, NC: Duke University Press, 2010); Karen Shimakawa, *National Abjection: The Asian American Body on Stage* (Durham, NC: Duke University Press, 2003); Kathryn Bond Stockton, *Beautiful Bottom, Beautiful Shame: Where "Black" Meets "Queer"* (Durham, NC: Duke University Press, 2006). On ethics and queer performances of shame, also see Michael Warner, *The Trouble with Normal: Sex, Politics, and the Ethics of Queer Life* (Cambridge, MA: Harvard University Press, 2000), especially 36–37.

27. E.g., Kaja Silverman, *Male Subjectivity at the Margins* (New York: Routledge, 1992); Bersani, *Homos*; Lynda Hart, *Between the Body and the Flesh: Performing Sadomasochism* (New York: Columbia University Press, 1998).

28. Kristeva, *Powers of Horror*, 26.

29. See, e.g., Sigmund Freud's 1927 "The Future of an Illusion" and Oskar Pfister's 1928 "The Illusion of a Future: A Friendly Disagreement with Prof. Sigmund Freud," *International Journal of Psychoanalysis* 74 (1993): 557–58; Ernst L. Freud and Heinrich Meng, eds., *Psychoanalysis and Faith: The Letters of Sigmund Freud and Oskar Pfister*, trans. Eric Mosbacher (New York: Basic Books, 1963).

30. On queer chronology and temporality more generally, see Elizabeth Freeman, *Time Binds: Queer Temporalities, Queer Histories* (Durham, NC: Duke University Press, 2010). As Christopher Looby argues, the "intractable difficulty" of chronology in studies of "literary sexuality" must be embraced. See Christopher Looby, "Sexuality, History, Difficulty, Pleasure," *J19: The Journal of Nineteenth-Century Americanists* 1.2 (2013): 257. Queer and early American studies' common preoccupation with questions of publics and publicity is an important linchpin between them; religion and theology have, of course, long been vital to gay, lesbian, queer, and other scholarly counternarratives. Michael Cobb, *God Hates Fags: The Rhetorics of Religious Violence* (New York: New York University Press, 2006); Mark D. Jordan, "Touching and Acting, or the Closet of Abjection," *Journal of the History of Sexuality* 10.2 (2001): 180–84; Gerard Loughlin, ed., *Queer Theology: Rethinking the Western Body* (Malden, MA: Blackwell, 2007).

31. The Christian branch of this tradition was inaugurated by the imprisoned apostles singing the praises of God; it continued to develop alongside Jewish traditions, including *qiddush ha-Shem*, martyrological poetry, and the medieval European practice of loudly singing the Shema at the stake. Daniel Boyarin, *Dying for God: Martyrdom and the Making of Christianity and Judaism* (Stanford, CA: Stanford University Press, 1999); Susan Einbinder, *Beautiful Death: Jewish Poetry and Martyrdom in Medieval France* (Princeton, NJ: Princeton University Press, 2002); Jan Willem van Henten and Friedrich

Avemarie, eds., *Martyrdom and Noble Death: Selected Texts from Graeco-Roman, Jewish and Christian Antiquity* (New York: Routledge, 2002).

32. On quiet and eloquent silence in the face of torturer's rage, see John R. Knott, *Discourses of Martyrdom in English Literature, 1563–1694* (Cambridge: Cambridge University Press, 1993), 8, 32, and 39.

33. John Foxe, *Actes and Monuments* (London: John Day, 1563), 1825.

34. Michel Foucault, *Discipline and Punish: The Birth of the Prison*, trans. Alan Sheridan (1975; repr., New York: Vintage, 1995), 60.

35. Stephen Greenblatt, *Renaissance Self-Fashioning: From More to Shakespeare* (Chicago: University of Chicago Press, 1983), 74–114; for a recent troubling of Greenblatt, see Patrick Collinson, "John Foxe and National Consciousness," in *John Foxe and His World*, ed. Christopher Highley and John N. King (Aldershot: Ashgate, 2002), 10–36.

36. This account skips over a significant history of revision; e.g., on the phrase "plaie the manne," see Susannah Brietz Monta, *Martyrdom and Literature in Early Modern England* (New York: Cambridge University Press, 2005), 211.

37. Ibid.

38. Illustrations of this and other scenes of execution helped establish the relationship between suffering and speech: of the forty-five "large narrative" woodcuts commissioned for the 1563 edition, most serve as capstones to executions. John N. King, *Foxe's Book of Martyrs and Early Modern Print Culture* (Cambridge: Cambridge University Press, 2006), 183–84.

39. On early modern England, see David Zaret, *Origins of Democratic Culture: Printing, Petitions and the Public Sphere in Early Modern England* (Princeton, NJ: Princeton University Press, 2000). On English martyrdom and publicity more narrowly, including Foxe's ambivalent engagement with Catholic martyrology, see Knott, *Discourses of Martyrdom in English Literature, 1563–1694*, especially 36–46. On the erotic element of this discourse, also see James C. W. Truman, "John Foxe and the Desires of Reformation Martyrology," *English Literary History* 70.1 (2003): 35–66.

40. Elaine Scarry, *The Body in Pain: The Making and Unmaking of the World* (New York: Oxford University Press, 1985). On religious mediation, see Birgit Meyer and Annalies Moors, *Religion, Media, and the Public Sphere* (Bloomington: Indiana University Press, 2006); Hent de Vries and Samuel Weber, *Religion and Media* (Stanford, CA: Stanford University Press, 2001); Hent de Vries and Lawrence Eugene Sullivan, *Political Theologies: Public Religions in a Post-Secular World* (New York: Fordham University Press, 2006); Friedrich Kittler, *Gramophone, Film, Typewriter*, trans. Geoffrey Winthrop-Young and Michael Wutz (Stanford, CA: Stanford University Press, 1999), 1–20.

41. On gender, subjectivity, and early modern martyrology, see King, *Foxe's Book of Martyrs and Early Modern Print Culture*; Knott, *Discourses of Martyrdom in English Literature, 1563–1694*; Megan Matchinske, *Writing, Gender and State in Early Modern*

England: Identity Formation and the Female Subject (Cambridge: Cambridge University Press, 1998).

42. See, e.g., "Life of Nicholas Ridley," in Washington, D.C.'s *Washington Theological Repertory* 1 (1819): 168–75; "Worthies of the English Church, No. 1, Nicholas Ridley" in London's *Evangelical Register* 12 (1839): 49–54; "Life of Nicholas Ridley," in New York's *Evergreen, or Church-Offering for all Seasons* (New York: George W. Mason, 1848), 5:207–11; "Life of Nicholas Ridley," in Boston's *Littell's Living Age* 28 (1851): 607–9; *Blackwood's Edinburgh Magazine* 2.69 (February 1851), 131–36.

43. Spanish Catholic martyrology, for instance, engaged postconquest Nahuatl Christian *icnocuicatl* that itself incorporated Spanish themes. Rebecca Horn, *Postconquest Coyoacán: Nahua-Spanish Relations in Central Mexico, 1519–1650* (Stanford, CA: Stanford University Press, 1997); James Lockhart, *The Nahuas After the Conquest: A Social and Cultural History of the Indians of Central Mexico, Sixteenth Through Eighteenth Centuries* (Stanford, CA: Stanford University Press, 1992); Carolyn Dean, *Inka Bodies and the Body of Christ: Corpus Christi in Colonial Cusco, Peru* (Durham, NC: Duke University Press, 1999).

44. Bartolomé de Las Casas, *Brevissima Relación de la Destruycion de las Indias* (Seville: Sebastian Trugillo, 1552–53). On the Dutch development of the Black Legend in resistance to the Hapsburg government, see Benjamin Schmidt, *Innocence Abroad: The Dutch Imagination and the New World, 1570–1670* (New York: Cambridge University Press, 2001).

45. See Foxe, 22; Bartolomé de las Casas, *The Spanish colonie, or Briefe chronicle of the acts and gestes of the Spaniardes in the West Indies*, trans. M. M. S. (London: for William Brome, 1583). Thanks to John Wade, whose *John Foxe's* The Actes and Monuments Online (www.johnfoxe.org) brought "M.M.S.'s" laudatory poem for Foxe's 1576 edition to my attention.

46. Bartolomé de Las Casas, *The Tears of the Indians: Being an Historical and True Account of the Cruel Massacres and Slaughters of Above Twenty Millions of Innocent People*, trans. and intro. John Phillips (London: J. C. for Nathaniel Brook, 1656), n.p. (ii). *Teares* was intended to justify Cromwell's "Western Design" by figuring the Spanish as illegitimate heirs to "Indian Treasures" in the "*West-Indies.*" For a valuable discussion of Phillips in the Irish colonial context, see Patricia Palmer, *Language and Conquest in Early Modern Ireland: English Renaissance Literature and Elizabethan Imperial Expansion* (Cambridge: Cambridge University Press, 2001), 38–42.

47. Las Casas, *Tears*, n.p. (xxiv). For a competing reading of martyrology, see Marcus Wood, *Blind Memory: Visual Representations of Slavery in England and America, 1780–1865* (New York: Routledge, 2000), 84–85. On sensational Indian suffering, see Christopher Hodgkins, *Reforming Empire: Protestant Colonialism and Conscience in British Literature* (Columbia, MO: University of Missouri Press, 2002), 66–67; Laura M. Stevens, *The Poor Indians: British Missionaries, Native Americans, and Colonial Sensibility* (Philadelphia: University of Pennsylvania Press, 2004), 46–47.

48. On French martyrology, see Scott Manning Stevens, "Figuring the Iroquois: Portraiture from Verelst to Catlin," in his forthcoming *Indian Collectibles: Encounters, Appropriations, and Resistance in Native North America*; Kirstin Noreen, "*Ecclesiae militantis triumphi*: Jesuit Iconography and the Counter-Reformation," *Sixteenth Century Journal* 29.3 (Autumn 1998): 689–715; Allan Greer, "Colonial Saints: Gender, Race, and Hagiography in New France," *William and Mary Quarterly* 57.2 (2000): 323–48.

49. Adrian Chastain Weimer, *Martyrs' Mirror: Persecution and Holiness in Early New England* (New York: Oxford University Press, 2011).

50. Karen Halttunen, "Cotton Mather and the Meaning of Suffering in the *Magnalia Christi Americana*," *Journal of American Studies* 12 (1978): 311–29.

51. John Winthrop, *The Journal of John Winthrop, 1630–1649* (Cambridge, MA: Harvard University Press, 1996), 150. See Adrian Chastain Weimer's account in *Martyrs' Mirror*, 76–77; Amy Schrager Lang, *Prophetic Woman: Anne Hutchinson and the Problem of Dissent in the Literature of New England* (Berkeley: University of California Press, 1987).

52. Cotton Mather to Thomas Prince, June 16, 1723, in Worthington Chauncey Ford, ed., *The Diary of Cotton Mather* (Boston: Massachusetts Historical Society, 1911–12), 7:687–88.

53. On the outsized importance of print narratives in colonial government, see Jonathan Beecher Field, *Errands into the Metropolis: New England Dissidents in Revolutionary London* (Hanover, NH: Dartmouth University Press, 2009), 90–115.

54. Julie Peakman, *Mighty Lewd Books: The Development of Pornography in Eighteenth-Century England* (New York: Palgrave Macmillan, 2003), 130.

55. Christopher Grasso, *A Speaking Aristocracy: Transforming Public Discourse in Eighteenth-Century Connecticut* (Chapel Hill: University of North Carolina Press, 1999).

56. Kristeva, *Powers of Horror*, 127.

57. See Nancy Ruttenburg's account of George Whitefield's "irrational practice of compulsive public utterance" in *Democratic Personality: Popular Voice and the Trial of American Authorship* (Stanford, CA: Stanford University Press, 1998), 3; Jeffrey Hammond, *Sinful Self, Saintly Self: The Puritan Experience of Poetry* (Athens: University of Georgia Press, 1993), 23; and Michael Warner's forthcoming *The Evangelical Public Sphere in Eighteenth-Century America* (University of Pennsylvania Press).

58. Jürgen Habermas, *Structural Transformation of the Public Sphere*, trans. Thomas Burger and Frederick Lawrence (1962; repr., Cambridge, MA: MIT Press, 1989), 94–95.

59. As Chapter 4 considers in greater detail, one of Richard von Krafft-Ebing's patient-correspondent's writes, "The general relation desired" by masochists is "not that in which a woman stands to a man, but that of the slave to the master." Richard von Krafft-Ebing, *Psychopathia Sexualis*, trans. Franklin S. Klaf (New York: Arcade, 1998), 99.

60. Edmund Burke, *A Philosophical Enquiry into the Origin of Our Ideas of the Sublime and Beautiful*, 4th ed. (London: R. and J. Dodsley, 1764), 54.

61. Halttunen, "Humanitarianism and the Pornography of Pain in Anglo-American Culture," 309 n. 17.

62. Burke, *A Philosophical Enquiry into the Origin of Our Ideas of the Sublime and Beautiful*, 59.

63. Peter Cosgrove, "Edmund Burke, Gilles Deleuze, and the Subversive Masochism of the Image," *English Literary History* 66.2 (1999): 405–37; Jacques Khalip, *Anonymous Life: Romanticism and Dispossession* (Stanford, CA: Stanford University Press, 2009).

64. Marcus Wood, *Slavery, Empathy, and Pornography* (New York: Oxford University Press, 2002), 150, 157–63; Edmund Burke, "Two Letters Addressed to a Member of the Present Parliament, on the Proposals for Peace with the Regicide Directory of France by the Right Honourable Edmund Burke," in *Select Works*, ed. E. J. Payne, 3 vols. (Oxford: Clarendon, 1874–78), 3:89, 3:112.

65. Burke, *A Philosophical Enquiry into the Origin of Our Ideas of the Sublime and Beautiful*, 216.

66. Frances Ferguson, *Solitude and the Sublime: Romanticism and the Aesthetics of Individuation* (New York: Routledge, 1992), 52.

67. Edmund Burke, *Reflections on the Revolution in France*, 2nd ed. (London: J. Dodsley, 1790), 106.

68. Ibid. Burke's infamous description of blackness, and black people in particular, as intrinsically evoking sublime terror suggests his disdain for abolitionist pity.

69. Ibid. Charles Brockwell to the Secretary of the Society for the Propagation of the Gospel, February 18, 1742, cited in Juster, *Disorderly Women*, 30.

70. Habermas primarily credited Edmund Burke, *A Letter from Edmund Burke, Esq; One of the Representatives in Parliament for the City of Bristol, to John Farr and John Harris, Esqrs, Sherrifs of that City, on the Affairs of America* (London: J. Dodsley, 1777). See Habermas, *Structural Transformation of the Public Sphere*, 94–95. On American studies, see Sandra Gustafson, "American Literature and the Public Sphere," *American Literary History* 20.3 (2008): 465–78.

71. Carl Schmitt, *Political Theology: Four Chapters on the Concept of Sovereignty*, trans. George Schwab (Chicago: University of Chicago Press, 2005); Carl Schmitt, *Crisis of Parliamentary Democracy*, trans. Ellen Kennedy (Cambridge, MA: MIT Press, 1988); Walter Lippman, *The Phantom Public* (New York: Harcourt, Brace, 1925).

72. Antonio Gramsci, *Prison Notebooks*, 3 vols., trans. and ed. Joseph Buttigieg and Antonio Callari (New York: Columbia University Press, 2006), 1:137–57. See developments in, e.g., Giorgio Agamben, *The Kingdom and the Glory: For a Theological Genealogy of Economy and Government*, trans. Lorenzo Chiesa (Stanford, CA: Stanford University Press, 2011); Louis Althusser, "Ideology and Ideological State Apparatuses (Notes Towards an Investigation)," in *Lenin and Philosophy and Other Essays*, trans. Ben Brewster (New York: Monthly Review Press, 1971), 127–88; Ernesto Laclau and Chantal Mouffe, *Hegemony and Socialist Strategy: Towards a Radical Democratic Politics* (New York: Verso, 2001).

73. Habermas, *Structural Transformation of the Public Sphere*, xix; Habermas, *Struk-turwandel der Öffentlichkeit: Untersuchungen zu einer Kategorie der bürgerlichen Gesellschaft*, 2nd ed. (Neuwied am Rhein and Berlin: Luchterhand, 1965), 8.

74. Habermas's premises are visible in, e.g., his focus on print and the procedural norms of eighteenth-century bourgeois male sociability. For these and other criticisms, see Craig Calhoun, ed., *Habermas and the Public Sphere* (Cambridge, MA: MIT Press, 1992). Oskar Negt and Alexander Kluge's critique also has applications for my project, as it describes the proletarian public as the bourgeois public's abjected other, operating in "the forbidden zones of fantasy beneath the surface of taboos" and filled with "stereotypes of a proletarian context." However, this notion of a "beneath" or "behind" for the bourgeois public may develop Habermas's claims without substantially modifying them. Oskar Negt and Alexander Kluge, *Public Sphere and Experience: Toward an Analysis of the Bourgeois and Proletarian Public Sphere*, trans. Peter Labanyi et al. (1972; repr., Minneapolis: University of Minnesota Press, 1993), 57.

75. Orlando Patterson, *Slavery and Social Death: A Comparative Study* (Cambridge, MA: Harvard University Press, 1982).

76. E.g., rational-critical publicity is described as incidentally revealing, like a fossil mold, traces of subaltern or infamous speech. See Gayatri Chakravorty Spivak, "Can the Subaltern Speak?" in *A Critique of Postcolonial Reason: Toward a History of the Vanishing Present* (Boston: Harvard University Press, 1999), 283–84. Also see Michel Foucault, "Lives of Infamous Men," in *Power*, ed. James D. Faubion (New York: New Press, 1994), 157–75. Similarly, Paul Gilroy shows us how eighteenth-century black Atlantic "counter-culture[s] of modernity" give the lie to Enlightenment Habermasian norms as preconditions of their existence. Paul Gilroy, *The Black Atlantic: Modernity and Double Consciousness* (Cambridge, MA: Harvard University Press, 1993), 37–38. Much queer theory, too, is understood to propose an inherent resistance to public norms. As Kevin Floyd summarizes, "The framing of so much . . . work in queer studies by the discourse of the public sphere indicates the extent to which queer negotiations of the public . . . by definition perform a critique of the privatization of sexual intimacy [that] capital has persistently both normalized and disrupted." Kevin Floyd, *The Reification of Desire: Toward a Queer Marxism* (Minneapolis: University of Minnesota Press, 2009), 198. This will-to-oppositionality showcases the way that debates about the ground of the debate—i.e., what constitutes a public, or what constitutes print—are vital to ideological attempts to "fight it out." The opposition is rarely absolute, however. Michael Warner's earlier notion of the counterpublic, sometimes taken to concern distinctive performances of "expressive corporeality" that cannot be assimilated into a dominant public, is actually more qualified: Warner notes that such performances can be assimilated at the risk of "humiliat[ion]" and that "there are contradictions and perversities inherent in the organization of all publics, tensions that are not captured by critiques of the dominant public's exclusions or ideological limitations." Michael Warner, *Publics and Counterpublics* (New York: Zone Books, 2002), 103, 113.

77. Hortense J. Spillers, "Mama's Baby, Papa's Maybe: An American Grammar Book," *Diacritics* 17.2 (1987): 64–81.

78. Spillers, 67.

79. My commitment to wedding historical and theoretical approaches to abjection can be navigated, in part, by Spivak's handling of sadomasochism in her development of the subaltern. The subaltern and the abject have important differences, especially around access to publicity (the subaltern can "speak" only in the most negative fashion), but subalternality is valuable as it makes use of and historicizes psychoanalytic theories of suffering as part of an elaboration of an antiracist, antinationalist strategy. As Spivak notes, the opposition of theory to positivism takes each side too much at its word, underestimating the theoretical investments of positivism and the development of theoretical models from within specific historical modes of writing, reading, and circulation. At the same time, we should have a corollary mistrust of the literary-critical iteration of Freud's "wild" psychoanalysis, which erroneously reads a text as presenting "a *collective* fantasy symptomatic of a *collective* itinerary of sadomasochistic repression in a *collective* imperialist enterprise." Spivak's negative formulation is useful because it insists we read texts as historically grounded and individuated. Voices or expressions of abjection that may appear to be "sadomasochistic repression" cannot be subsumed within that larger intellectual narrative or teleology. Spivak, "Can the Subaltern Speak?" 283–84.

80. Designed to effect Jefferson's "pedagogic ambitions," Monticello's vestibule was something like the first presidential library, with an entirely unidirectional intellectual circulation. Duncan Faherty, *Remodeling the Nation: The Architecture of American Identity, 1776–1858* (Hanover, NH: University Press of New England, 2007), 31–32, and private correspondence.

81. Jack McLaughlin, *Jefferson and Monticello: The Biography of a Builder* (New York: Henry Holt, 1988), 256.

82. Lucia C. Stanton, *"Those who Labor for My Happiness": Slavery at Thomas Jefferson's Monticello* (Charlottesville: University of Virginia Press, 2012); Peter F. Fossett, "Once the Slave of Thomas Jefferson," New York *Sunday World* (January 30, 1898), rptd. in Kevin J. Hayes, ed., *Jefferson in His Own Time: A Biographical Chronicle of His Life, Drawn from Recollections, Interviews, and Memoirs by Family, Friends and Associates* (Iowa City: University of Iowa Press, 2012), 187–193.

83. Suggestively, Spillers later uses the term "vestibular" to connote something like Lacan's Imaginary, which provides structure by virtue of its absence. Hortense J. Spillers, "'All the Things You Could Be by Now, If Sigmund Freud's Wife Was Your Mother': Psychoanalysis and Race," *boundary* 2 23.3 (1996): 124.

84. On the "performative commons," see Elizabeth Maddox Dillon, *New World Drama: The Performative Commons in the Atlantic World, 1649–1849* (Durham, NC: Duke University Press, 2014), 1–31. On "disavowal," see Sibylle Fischer, *Modernity Disavowed: Haiti and the Cultures of Slavery in the Age of Revolution* (Durham, NC: Duke University Press, 2004), 37–38.

85. Theodor W. Adorno and Max Horkheimer, *Dialectic of Enlightenment* (New York: Verso, 1972), 119; Jürgen Habermas, "The Entwinement of Myth and Enlightenment," in *The Philosophical Discourse of Modernity*, trans. Fredrick Lawrence (Cambridge, MA: MIT Press, 1987), 120–30.

86. See Janet Lyon, *Manifestoes: Provocations of the Modern* (Ithaca, NY: Cornell University Press, 1999), 76; Susan Maslan, *Revolutionary Acts: Theater, Democracy, and the French Revolution* (Baltimore: Johns Hopkins University Press, 2005), 29.

87. Habermas, *Structural Transformation of the Public Sphere*, 168.

88. Zaret, 31–32.

89. Candy Gunther Brown, *The Word in the World: Evangelical Writing, Publishing, and Reading in America, 1789–1880* (Chapel Hill: University of North Carolina Press, 2004).

90. E.g., late seventeenth-century sectarian discussions of toleration pursued rational debate and engaged various "republics of letters"; Quaker and other dissenting circles were hothouses for early Enlightenment thought, and while many Enlightenment writers condemned some religious beliefs and rituals as "irrational," they almost always did so as part of an attempt to buttress other forms of faith. See, e.g., John Marshall, *John Locke, Toleration and Early Enlightenment Culture: Religious Toleration and Arguments for Religious Toleration in Early Modern and Early Enlightenment Europe* (Cambridge: Cambridge University Press, 2006); William Gibson, *Religion and the Enlightenment 1600–1800: Conflict and the Rise of Civic Humanism in Taunton* (Oxford: Peter Lang, 2007). On Habermas's evolving treatment of religion, see Michele Dillon, *Catholic Identity: Balancing Reason, Faith, and Power* (New York: Cambridge University Press, 1999); Don Browning and Francis Schüssler Fiorenza, eds., *Habermas, Modernity and Public Theology* (New York: Crossroad, 1992). What Habermas describes, in *Theory of Communicative Action*, as a decentered or desacralized worldview marked by a mechanistic universe, natural rights, and cultural spheres autonomous from governing institutions is one strain of this religious Enlightenment development. Habermas, *The Theory of Communicative Action, Vol. 2: Lifeworld and System: A Critique of Functionalist Reason*, trans. Thomas McCarthy (Boston: Beacon, 1989), 145–98, 224. Here, too, Habermas mirrors those eighteenth-century critics of religion by warning that positivistic reason creates potentially dangerous moral and emotional aporia incapable of being filled, in Arnoldian fashion, by literary or other aesthetic practice. Even more recently, Habermas's position on religion in his dialogue with Joseph Ratzinger seems to allow religion a greater role in determining moral reason and hence in grounding social critique. Joseph Ratzinger and Jürgen Habermas, *The Dialectics of Secularization: On Reason and Religion*, ed. Florian Schuller, trans. Brian McNeil (San Francisco: Ignatius, 2006). Though Habermas assumes a process of secularization and a disenchanted rational worldview, he presents reason as dependent on religion for its initial achievement of its claims to universality (e.g., through the "linguistification of the sacred"). Habermas, *The Theory of Communicative Action*, 77.

91. See Houston Baker, "Critical Memory and the Black Public Sphere," *Public Culture* 7.1 (1994): 3–33; Joanna Brooks, "The Early American Public Sphere and the Emergence of a Black Print Counterpublic," *William and Mary Quarterly* 62.1 (2005): 67–92; Bruce Burgett, *Sentimental Bodies: Sex, Gender, and Citizenship in the Early Republic* (Princeton, NJ: Princeton University Press, 1998), 42–48; Rita Felski, *Beyond Feminist Aesthetics: Feminist Literature and Social Change* (Cambridge, MA: Harvard University Press, 1989); Sandra Gustafson, *Eloquence Is Power: Oratory and Performance in Early America* (Chapel Hill: University of North Carolina Press, 2000); Glenn Hendler, *Public Sentiments: Structures of Feeling in Nineteenth-Century American Literature* (Chapel Hill: University of North Carolina Press, 2001), 47–52; Frank Lambert, *"Pedlar in Divinity": George Whitefield and the Transatlantic Revivals, 1737–1770* (Princeton, NJ: Princeton University Press, 2002); Susan Juster, *Doomsayers: Anglo-American Prophecy in the Age of Revolution* (Philadelphia: University of Pennsylvania Press, 2003), 51–54; Christopher Looby, *Voicing America: Language, Literary Form, and the Origins of the United States* (Chicago: University of Chicago Press, 1996).

92. Habermas, "Further Reflections on the Public Sphere," in *Habermas and the Public Sphere*, 427; Jürgen Habermas, "Vorwort zur Neuauflage, 1990," in *Strukturwandel der Öffentlichkeit: Untersuchungen zu einer Kategorie der bürgerlichen Gesellschaft* (Frankfurt am Main: Suhrkamp Verlag, 1990), 16.

93. Hobsbawm's placement of Methodist organizing hand in glove with labor organizing is more attractive, but Thompson's attention to publicity allows him to address structuring elements of Methodist rhetoric that more sanguine critics downplay. Eric Hobsbawm, *Laboring Men: Studies in the History of Labour* (London: Weidenfeld and Nicolson, 1964), 23–33; Eric Hobsbawm, "Methodism and the Threat of Revolution in Britain," *History Today* 7 (1957): 115–24. Also see Gauri Viswanathan, *Outside the Fold: Conversion, Modernity, and Belief* (Princeton, NJ: Princeton University Press, 1998), 51.

94. E. P. Thompson, *The Making of the English Working Class* (New York: Random House, 1964), 40–41, 371.

95. I.e., prevailing narratives of a secular, rational Enlightenment overcoming religion and emotion offer accounts of a public sphere opposed to religious influence and deflect attention from religion's positive role in shaping Enlightenment developments of sex, race, and eroticism. In the Marxist tradition, this problem has taken shape through the analysis of ideology, crystallized in Thompson's condemnation of Methodist revivalism as pathological ideology.

96. More recent historians have turned psychoanalytic tables on Thompson, reading the passages as his working out of his relationship with his father's Wesleyanism and commitment to Indian colonial reform. Bryan Palmer, *E. P. Thompson: Objections and Oppositions* (New York: Verso, 1994), 30–22. It is possible, of course, that Thompson's terms are less normalizing and more simply descriptive or even subversive endorsements. The subversive reading of Thompson's psychoanalytic language is appealing as a prelude to his richer picture of eighteenth-century dissent in his late *Witness Against the*

Beast: William Blake and the Moral Law (Cambridge: Cambridge University Press, 1993). Also see David Hempton, *The Religion of the People: Methodism and Popular Religion c. 1750–1900* (New York: Routledge, 1996), 196–97. Nevertheless, this reading seems to mirror the sort of wishful thinking that, in the 1960s and 1970s, made Thompson's friends and critics alike wish away his language as an embarrassing misstep into the "merely cultural." Judith Butler, "Merely Cultural," *Social Text* 52/53 (1997): 265–77.

97. See Marshall, *John Locke, Toleration and Early Enlightenment Culture*, 302–11.

98. Phyllis Mack, *Heart Religion in the British Enlightenment: Gender and Emotion in Early Methodism* (Cambridge: Cambridge University Press, 2008), 2–9.

99. Mack, *Heart Religion*, 36; also see Misty G. Anderson, *Imagining Methodism in Eighteenth-Century Britain: Enthusiasm, Belief, and the Borders of the Self* (Baltimore: Johns Hopkins University Press, 2012), 121–26; Anna M. Lawrence, *One Family Under God: Love, Belonging, and Authority in Early Transatlantic Methodism* (Philadelphia: University of Pennsylvania Press, 2011), 96–132; Jon F. Sensbach, *A Separate Canaan: The Making of an Afro-Moravian World in North Carolina* (Chapel Hill: University of North Carolina Press, 1998).

100. Mack, *Heart Religion*, 42–45.

Chapter 1

An earlier version of Chapter 1 was originally published in *GLQ: A Journal of Lesbian and Gay Studies* 18.4 (2012): 565–94.

1. *The Works of Jonathan Edwards*, 25 vols., ed. Perry Miller (New Haven, CT: Yale University Press, 1957–2006), 16:801; hereafter cited as *WJE*.

2. J. G. Barker-Benfield, *The Culture of Sensibility: Sex and Society in Eighteenth-Century Britain* (Chicago: University of Chicago Press, 1992), 273.

3. Some itinerant revivalist practice may have been primarily oral and performative, intersecting with writing and print only occasionally. Such performances were incorporated into revivalist ministers' writing, which was then, in turn, imbricated in multiple moments of ministerial and lay reading, writing, and performance, including letter writing, note taking, prayer meetings and small group worship, exhortation, or (most troubling for Edwards) lay preaching in church, fields, or private homes. On print circulation, see Jennifer Snead, "Print, Predestination, and the Public Sphere: Transatlantic Evangelical Periodicals, 1740–1745," *Early American Literature* 45.1 (2010): 93–118. Whitefield and his supporters stand out for their innovative connections between oration, publication, and social reform. On the contested notion of publics, see Calhoun, *Habermas and the Public Sphere*; Gustafson, "American Literature and the Public Sphere"; Gustafson, *Eloquence Is Power*; Warner, *The Evangelical Public Sphere in Eighteenth-Century America*.

4. Michael Warner, "Tongues Untied," in *Curiouser: On the Queerness of Children*,

ed. Steven Bruhm and Natasha Hurley (Minneapolis: University of Minnesota Press, 2004), 219.

5. Warner, "The Preacher's Footing," in *This Is Enlightenment*, ed. Clifford Siskin and William Warner (Chicago: University of Chicago Press, 2010), 368–83.

6. Norman Fiering, *Jonathan Edwards's Moral Thought and Its British Context* (Chapel Hill: University of North Carolina Press, 1981), 14.

7. Abram van Engen, *Sympathetic Puritans: Calvinist Fellow Feeling in Early New England* (New York: Oxford University Press, 2015), 118–43; Matthew Brown, *The Pilgrim and the Bee: Reading Rituals and Book Culture in Early New England* (Philadelphia: University of Pennsylvania Press, 2007); Michelle Burnham, *Captivity and Sentiment: Cultural Exchange in American Literature, 1682–1861* (Hanover, NH: University Press of New England, 1997); Janice Knight, *Orthodoxies in Massachusetts: Rereading American Puritanism* (Cambridge, MA: Harvard University Press, 1994)

8. Charles Cohen, *God's Caress: The Psychology of Puritan Religious Experience* (New York: Oxford University Press, 1986); Charles Hambrick-Stowe, *The Practice of Piety: Puritan Devotional Disciplines in Seventeenth-Century New England* (Chapel Hill: University of North Carolina Press, 1986); Philip Gura, *A Glimpse of Sion's Glory: Puritan Radicalism in New England, 1620–1660* (Middletown, CT: Wesleyan University Press, 1984); Philip Gura, *Jonathan Edwards: America's Evangelical* (New York: Hill and Wang, 2005); David Leverenz, *The Language of Puritan Feeling: An Exploration in Literature, Psychology, and Social History* (New Brunswick, NJ: Rutgers University Press, 1980); Anne Taves, *Fits, Trances, and Visions: Experiencing Religion and Explaining Experience from Wesley to James* (Princeton, NJ: Princeton University Press, 1999).

9. On liberal subjectivity and new modes of autobiography see Stephen Carl Arch, *After Franklin: The Emergence of Autobiography in Post-Revolutionary America, 1780–1830* (Hanover, NH: University Press of New England, 2001); Ann Fabian, *The Unvarnished Truth: Personal Narratives in Nineteenth-Century America* (Berkeley: University of California Press, 2000).

10. David Laurence, "Jonathan Edwards, Solomon Stoddard, and the Preparationist Model of Conversion," *Harvard Theological Review* 72.3/4 (1979): 267–83.

11. Susannah Brietz Monta, *Martyrdom and Literature in Early Modern England* (New York: Cambridge University Press, 2005), 117–57.

12. Ibid., 135–37; Richard Rambuss, "Pleasure and Devotion: The Body of Jesus and Seventeenth-Century Religious Lyric," in *Queering the Renaissance*, ed. Jonathan Goldberg (Durham, NC: Duke University Press, 1994), 253–79.

13. Sandra Gustafson, "Jonathan Edwards and the Reconstruction of 'Feminine' Speech," *American Literary History* 6.2 (1994): 185–212; Jessica Benjamin, "Master and Slave: The Fantasy of Erotic Domination," in *Powers of Desire: The Politics of Sexuality*, ed. Ann Snitow, Christine Stansell, and Sharon Thompson (New York: Monthly Review Press, 1983), 281.

14. Burke, *A Philosophical Enquiry into the Origin of Our Ideas of the Sublime and Beautiful*, 54, 59; Kristeva, *Powers of Horror*, 127.

15. Revivals in English colonial North America, somewhat misleadingly named a single "Great Awakening," were predominantly Calvinist, reflecting their origins in mid-Atlantic Pietism (led by Scottish, Dutch Reformed, and other European clergy), established Puritan revival traditions in New England, and the profound influence of George Whitefield throughout. In New England, after a period of acceptance, the revivals exacerbated existing divisions within the established church. Self-styled New Light ministers and their lay supporters confronted an anti-revivalist coalition of theologically conservative Old Light ministers and more theologically liberal ministers of wealthier urban congregations who had adopted witty, aristocratic modes suitable to their social circumstances. Converts were ripe for the picking by dissenting churches, but ministers who could ride the wave of revival were buoyed up. In England, established Anglicans were largely united against the revivals, leaving the field to Anglican Methodist innovators or nonconformists. With the notable exception of Whitefield, prominent revivalists in England usually preached some sort of Arminianism, then an umbrella term covering a range of liberal Christian humanist beliefs in action and will for salvation, with distinct Arminian and Calvinist evangelical factions emerging in the early 1740s. W. R. Ward, *The Protestant Evangelical Awakening* (Cambridge: Cambridge University Press, 1992), 241–92. On the revivals' construction of "a community of language," see Juster, *Disorderly Women*; Susan O'Brien, "A Transatlantic Community of Saints: The Great Awakening and the First Evangelical Network, 1735–1755," *American Historical Review* 91 (October 1986): 811–32; Frank Lambert, *Inventing the "Great Awakening"* (Princeton, NJ: Princeton University Press, 1999); Jennifer Snead, "Print, Predestination, and the Public Sphere: Transatlantic Evangelical Periodicals, 1740–1745," *Early American Literature* 45.1 (2010): 93–118.

16. Jonathan Beecher Field, *Errands into the Metropolis: New England Dissidents in Revolutionary London* (Hanover, NH: University Press of New England, 2009); Alison Searle, " 'Though I am a Stranger to You by Face, yet in Neere Bonds by Faith': A Transatlantic Puritan Republic of Letters," *Early American Literature* 43.2 (2008): 277–30.

17. E.g., in 1732, anti-revivalist Rev. Mather Byles delivered a sermon entitled "A Discourse on the Present Vileness of the Body and Its Future Glorious Change by Christ" that demonstrates some of the common theological ground and stylistic difference between revivalists and their critics. On melancholy, see Carla Freccero, *Queer/Early/Modern* (Durham, NC: Duke University Press, 2006); Angus Gowland, "The Problem of Early Modern Melancholy," *Past & Present* 191.1 (2006): 77–120; George Marsden, *Jonathan Edwards: A Life* (New Haven, CT: Yale University Press, 2003), 170–73.

18. Edwards's father and grandfather, both ministers, oversaw several "stirs" or "harvests." In the mid-Atlantic colonies, revivals led by the Tennent family and other pietistic Scots-Irish Presbyterians coincided with the Northampton revival, but these were not incorporated into a larger movement until later in the decade.

19. "The Scheming Triumvirate," engraving, published by G. Gibbs (c. 1760); William Hogarth, "Credulity, Superstition, and Fanaticism," 1762; on Hooper, see Lisa Forman Cody, *Birthing the Nation: Sex, Science, and the Conception of Eighteenth-Century Britain* (Oxford: Oxford University Press, 2005), 212.

20. Harry S. Stout, *The Divine Dramatist: George Whitefield and the Rise of Modern Evangelicalism* (Grand Rapids, MI: Eerdmans, 1991), 242–48.

21. Ralph Jephson, *Methodism and Enthusiasm Fully Display'd* (1740), second expanded edition published as *The Expounder Expounded* (London: M. Cooper, 1743), 40–41. Thompson, *The Making of the Working Class*, 40, 368–69; Samuel Foote's 1760 character "Dr. Squintum" may have had similar connotations. Also see G. J. Barker-Benfield, *The Culture of Sensibility*, 76–78; Brian D. Carroll, "'I Indulged My Desire Too Freely': Sexuality, Spirituality, and the Sin of Self-Pollution in the Diary of Joseph Moody, 1720–1724," *William and Mary Quarterly* 60.1 (2003): 155–70.

22. Her ornate facial tattoos, they supposed, would soon become popular among Methodist women in London. "Histories of the Tête-à-Tête annexed. Dr. Squintum and Parrawankaw (No. 37, 38)" in *The Town and Country Magazine*, 1769 supp., ed. Archibald Hamilton (London: A. Hamilton, 1769), 672–77. Also see Jon Butler, *Awash in a Sea of Faith: Christianizing the American People* (Cambridge, MA: Harvard University Press, 1990), 188.

23. In addition to Jephson's obscene pamphlet, Henry Fielding placed Whitefield's conversion narrative on Shamela's bookshelf to signal her impetuous, impulsive female nature, and Anglican clergymen mocked the presumption of a man lacking the education, experience, or rank to justify his publication. Henry Abelove. *The Evangelist of Desire: John Wesley and the Methodists* (Stanford, Calif.: Stanford University Press, 1990), 49–73; Karen Harvey, *Reading Sex in the Eighteenth Century: Bodies and Gender in English Erotic Culture* (Cambridge: Cambridge University Press, 2004), 204–5.

24. A wealthy Massachusetts merchant-farmer bemoaned established ministers who confused the "Trances & Transports" of the poor for the "Spiret of God" and allowed those of "the meanest Capacity" to enter the most sacred space of public performance. "[W]omen & even Common negroes," he wrote, "Extort their Betters even in the pulpit, before large assemblies." Nathan Bowen, "Extracts from Interleaved Almanacs of Nathan Bowen, Marblehead, 1742–1799," *Essex Institute Historical Collections* 91 (1955): 169. William Dillon Piersen, *Black Yankees: The Development of an Afro-American Subculture in Eighteenth-Century New England* (Amherst: University of Massachusetts Press, 1988), 71. Promiscuous associations of women, men, Indians, blacks, and slaves were ready figures for revival disorder. In Salem, an Anglican representative of the Society for the Propagation of the Gospel complained that ministers mistook revivalists' "groans, cries, screams, and agonies" for spiritual enlightenment until, in a frenzy, "Men, Women, Children, Servants, and Nigros . . . become (as they phrase it) Exhorters." Charles Brockwell to the Secretary of the Society of the Propagation of the Gospel, Salem, February 18, 1742, cited in Charles C. Goen, *Revivalism and Separatism in New*

England, 1740–1800 (New Haven, CT: Yale University Press, 1962), 30. Many tales of revivalist error were spread by Boston's arch anti-revivalist, the established Congregational minister Charles Chauncey. He directly contributed to the vituperative flood of publication in the watershed year of 1743, likening revivalist affect with female embodiment and openness to divine or satanic influence in his insistence that "the Unsafe Tenets of the present Day" bore close "Resemblance" to Anne Hutchinson's Antinomian dissent. Charles Chauncey, *Seasonable Thoughts on the State of Religion in New England* (Boston: Rogers and Fowle, 1743), viii. Later that year, Edwards's former classmate, Rev. Isaac Stiles, denounced itinerant revivalist preaching as "loudly threaten[ing] a subversion to all peaceable Order in a Government." Condemning itinerants' "barefac'd Contempt" for civil and ecclesiastical authority, Stiles uses a commonplace troping of shame as bodily display to emphasize the embodied, material nature of revivalism's threat. Isaac Stiles, *A Looking-Glass for Changelings: A Seasonable Caveat Against Meddling with Them That Are Given to Change* (New London, CT, 1743), cited in Grasso, *A Speaking Aristocracy*, 1.

25. *Gentleman's Magazine* 11 (June 1741): 320, in Abelove, *Evangelist of Desire*, 64.

26. Paul Goring, *Rhetoric of Sensibility in Eighteenth-Century Culture* (Cambridge: Cambridge University Press, 2005), 74–90; Timothy D. Hall, *Contested Boundaries: Itinerancy and the Reshaping of the Colonial American Religious World* (Durham, NC: Duke University Press, 1994), 41; Albert M. Lyles, *Methodism Mocked: The Satiric Reaction to Methodism in the Eighteenth Century* (London: Epworth Press, 1960), 90–93.

27. For example, churches in seventeenth-century New England seated African and Indian congregants in the back or gallery with English children and servants; by the 1750s, people of color were often segregated in separate galleries or pews. See John Wood Sweet, *Bodies Politic: Negotiating Race in the American North, 1730–1830* (Baltimore, MD: Johns Hopkins University Press, 2003), 110–11. Similarly, in mid-Atlantic and Southern colonies, slaves converted on a perhaps unprecedented scale and brought many new traditions into the fold, but Whitefield and most other prominent English revivalists insisted Christianity did not bring freedom as it once had and as some still thought it would. See Anne Dutton's *A Letter to the Negroes Lately Converted to Christ in America* (1743), in *Selected Spiritual Writings of Anne Dutton*, ed. Joann Ford Watson (Macon, GA: Mercer University Press, 2007), 5:363–79. As New England urbanized, politicians increasingly followed their English compatriots in valuing religion, which had been the driving force behind generations of conflict, for its ability to effect moral improvement or social control. Revivalists in New England, though sharing the established churches' Calvinism, tended to lay more stress on the inefficacy of good works for salvation and introduced new, highly mobile models of selfhood, communication, and social organization that did not map easily onto expectations for a steady moral life. The revivals' models of identity, communication, and social organization destabilized and, in the decades after 1740, restabilized social order and identity. As part of a longer articulation of power along lines of race, class, and gender in a more republican cultural and

material terrain, the revivals broadened New England's "speaking aristocracy" by allowing a larger portion of white men, including merchants, lawyers, and other professionals, to speak and publish with authority on social, political, and theological issues, thereby contributing to the rise of a new republican liberal subject. Christopher Grasso, *A Speaking Aristocracy: Transforming Public Discourse in Eighteenth-Century Connecticut* (Chapel Hill: University of North Carolina Press, 1999), 485.

28. Revivalists in the colonies, following English and German Pietist examples, established some of the earliest colonial charitable institutions of disciplinary reform, such as Moor's Indian School, Bethesda Orphanage, and other schools directed at Native Americans, African Americans, and the poor. See Philip S. Gorski, *The Disciplinary Revolution: Calvinism and the Rise of the State in Early Modern Europe* (Chicago: University of Chicago Press, 2003).

29. Historians have also identified the late seventeenth and early eighteenth centuries as a transitional moment or pivot point away from hierarchies of rank and toward popular notions of racial and gender difference in New England. John D'Emilio and Estelle B. Freedman, *Intimate Matters: A History of Sexuality in America* (New York: Harper and Row, 1988), 40.

30. Despite anti-revivalists' derision of their oration and publication as the "mimicry" of an "admiring Vulgar," these "other" revivalists were important agents. The revivals did not oversee the widespread admission of the colonial dispossessed into the public sphere, but in England, New England, and New York, black and Native converts such as Samuel Ashpo, Samson Occom, James Gronniosaw, Jupiter Hammon, John Marrant, Phillis Wheatley, and Olaudah Equiano used revivalist rhetoric, oration, and publication networks to create or expand oppositional black and Indian identities in local communities and larger oral and print publics. Whitefield and his patron, the Countess of Huntington, frequently served as touchstones for the publicity of the colonial dispossessed. See, e.g., Olaudah Equiano, *The Interesting Narrative of the Life of Olaudah Equiano or Gustavus Vassa, the African*, 9th ed. (London: For the Author, 1794), 183–84. In Narragansett, for example, Samuel Niles established a tribally diverse church with its own distinct practices after being ejected from the local Congregational church for exhorting; the Narragansett's assigned Congregational pastor condemned Niles's church for embracing "*Feelings, Impressions, Visions, Appearances*, and *Directions* of Angels and of Christ himself in a Visionary Way.*" Brooks, *American Lazarus*, 58. Sarah Osborn and other white women in Congregational and Presbyterian churches often worked with and through their ministers to foster a culture of female religious speech and publication that confirmed critics' worst fears. Catherine Brekus, *Strangers and Pilgrims: Female Preaching in America, 1740–1845* (Chapel Hill: University of North Carolina Press, 1998); Aaron Spencer Fogleman, *Jesus Is Female: Moravians and the Challenge of Radical Religion in Early America* (Philadelphia: University of Pennsylvania Press, 2007), 34–72; Charles E. Hambrick-Stowe, "The Spiritual Pilgrimage of Sarah Osborne (1714–1796)," *Church History* 61 (1992): 408–21. Even "admiring" converts who

did not preach or publish had substantial influence on revival publicity. Poorer converts swelled field meetings, encouraging itinerant revivalists' support of universal literacy, periodical advertisement, and distribution of free or inexpensive religious books. Joanna Brooks, *American Lazarus: Religion and the Rise of African-American and Native American Literatures* (New York: Oxford University Press, 2003), 21–50; Frank Lambert, "'I Saw the Book Talk': Slave Readings of the First Great Awakening," *Journal of Negro History* 77.4 (1992): 185–98; Erik R. Seeman, "'Justise Must Take Plase': Three African Americans Speak of Religion in Eighteenth-Century New England," *William and Mary Quarterly* 56 (1999): 393–414.

31. On Christian "divine transitivism" and "masochism," see Terry Eagleton, *Trouble with Strangers: A Study of Ethics* (Malden, MA: Wiley-Blackwell, 2008), 323.

32. Marsden, 170.

33. Thomas S. Kidd, *The Great Awakening: A Brief History with Documents* (Boston: Bedford/St. Martin's, 2008), 22–23.

34. Kenneth P. Minkema, "Old Age and Religion in the Writings and Life of Jonathan Edwards," *Church History* 70.4 (2001): 674–704.

35. Edwards, "A Faithful Narrative," in *A Jonathan Edwards Reader*, ed. John E. Smith, Harry S. Stout, and Kenneth P. Minkema (New Haven, CT: Yale University Press, 1995), 57; "The Monthly Catalogue for October 1737," in *The History of the Works of the Learned* (London: T. Cooper, 1737), 2:220; "The Monthly Catalogue for October, 1737," in *The London Magazine: and Monthly Chronologer* (London: C. Ackers, 1737), 14:580. On publication history see *WJE* 4:32–46; Lambert, *Inventing the "Great Awakening,"* 69–81. On Edwards, the public sphere, and the market, see Mark Valeri, "Jonathan Edwards, the Edwardsians, and the Sacred Cause of Free Trade," in *Jonathan Edwards at Home and Abroad*, ed. David William Kling and Douglas A. Sweeney (Columbia: University of South Carolina Press, 2003), 85–100.

36. *WJE* 4:32–45.

37. *WJE* 4:188, 108, 106, 199, 207.

38. *WJE* 17:412.

39. *A Faithful Narrative* maintained his preaching of predestination was vindicated by the 1734–35 revival, which occurred just as he was about to suffer "a very open abuse" for his Calvinism; his "corrections" for a 1738 Boston edition strengthen the possibility of immediate conversion as a result of an embodied sense of divinity.

40. Jennifer L. Leader, "'In Love with the Image': Transitive Being and Typological Desire in Jonathan Edwards," *Early American Literature* 42.2 (2006): 153–81.

41. On the broader colonial ministerial attempt to manage the affective "sense" of God, see Hall, *Contested Boundaries*, 93.

42. *WJE* 4:189.

43. Gustafson, *Eloquence Is Power*, 74.

44. See Hilary Hinds, *God's Englishwomen: Seventeenth-Century Radical Sectarian Writing and Feminist Criticism* (Manchester: Manchester University Press, 1996), 51–79;

Patricia Crawford, *Women and Religion in England 1500–1720* (New York: Routledge, 1993), 206.

45. Abelove, *The Evangelist of Desire*, 41.

46. Lambert, *Inventing the "Great Awakening,"* 83–180; D. Bruce Hindmarsh, *The Evangelical Conversion Narrative: Spiritual Autobiography in Early Modern England* (New York: Oxford University Press, 2005), 68–72; Hall, *Contested Boundaries*, 78–108.

47. English prejudice and revivalists' need to establish divine origins for such behavior also recommended against the recognition of cultural contributions as such. See Erik R. Seeman, *Pious Persuasions: Laity and Clergy in Eighteenth-Century New England. Early America: History, Context, Culture* (Baltimore: Johns Hopkins University Press, 1999), 139–46. On the revivals' idealization of "emotionalism, sensuality, and above all [a] porous sense of self" as less "distinctly female" than common to "marginal" converts, see Amy Schrager Lang, *Prophetic Woman: Anne Hutchinson and the Problem of Dissent in the Literature of New England* (Berkeley: University of California Press, 1987), 105–6. Rather than understanding these many converts as "more women," however, these forms of marginality helped produce new notions of gender, class, faith, and race that are mutually dependent. Juster, *Disorderly Women*, 4, 30–32. On co-development of race, gender, and class in England and its colonies see Anne McClintock, *Imperial Leather: Race, Gender and Sexuality in the Colonial Conquest* (New York: Routledge, 1995); Felicity Nussbaum, *Torrid Zones: Maternity, Sexuality, and Empire in Eighteenth-Century English Narratives* (Baltimore: Johns Hopkins University Press, 1995); Wheeler, *The Complexion of Race*.

48. Hindmarsh, 48–49; Edmund S. Morgan, *Visible Saints: The History of a Puritan Idea* (1963; repr., Ithaca, NY: Cornell University Press, 1965), 65–66. On New England Puritan conversion, also see Patricia Caldwell, *The Puritan Conversion Narrative: The Beginnings of American Expression* (1983; repr., New York: Cambridge University Press 1985); Norman Pettit, *The Heart Prepared: Grace and Conversion in Puritan Spiritual Life* (New Haven, CT: Yale University Press, 1966); Daniel Shea Jr., *Spiritual Autobiography in Early America* (Princeton, NJ: Princeton University Press, 1968); William K. B. Stoever, *"A Faire and Easie Way to Heaven": Covenant Theology and Antinomianism in Early Massachusetts* (Middletown, CT: Wesleyan University Press, 1978); Hambrick-Stowe, *The Practice of Piety*; Cohen, *God's Caress*; Hall, *Worlds of Wonder*; Delbanco, *The Puritan Ordeal*; Knight, *Orthodoxies in Massachusetts*.

49. See, e.g., Richard Baxter, Theodosia Alleine, and George Newton, *The Life and Death of Mr. Joseph Alleine, Late Teacher of the Church at Taunton, in Somersetshire, Assistant to Mr. Newton* (London: J. Darby, 1672), and Richard Baxter, *A Breviate of the Life of Margaret, the Daughter of Francis Charlton . . . and wife of Richard Baxter* (London: B. Simmons and Brabazon Aylmer, 1681).

50. On Puritan ministerial uses of femininity up to the 1730s, see Ruth H. Bloch, "Changing Conceptions of Sexuality and Romance in Eighteenth-Century America," *William and Mary Quarterly* 60.1 (2003): 13–42; Margaret W. Masson, "The Typology of

the Female as a Model for the Regenerate: Puritan Preaching, 1690–1730," *Signs* 2.2 (1976): 304–15; Laurel Thatcher Ulrich, "Vertuous Women Found: New England Ministerial Literature, 1668–1735," *American Quarterly* 28 (Spring 1976): 20–40; Michael P. Winship, "Behold the Bridegroom Cometh!: Marital Imagery in Massachusetts Preaching, 1630–1730," *Early American Literature* 27.3 (1992): 170–84; Amanda Porterfield, *Female Piety in Puritan New England: The Emergence of Religious Humanism* (New York: Oxford University Press, 1992), 133–37; Ann Kibbey, *The Interpretation of Material Shapes in Puritanism: A Study of Rhetoric, Prejudice, and Violence* (New York: Cambridge University Press, 1986); William Haller, *The Rise of Puritanism* (New York: Columbia University Press, 1938).

51. Shepard, in Michael McGiffert, ed., *God's Plot: The Paradoxes of Puritan Piety* (Amherst, MA: University of Massachusetts Press, 1972), 132, 134, 47.

52. Thomas Laqueur, *Making Sex: Body and Gender from the Greeks to Freud* (Cambridge, MA: Harvard University Press, 1990); for qualifications, see Harvey, *Reading Sex in the Eighteenth Century*, 79–81; Elizabeth Maddock Dillon, "Nursing Fathers and Brides of Christ: The Feminized Body of the Puritan Convert," in *A Centre of Wonders: The Body in Early America*, ed. Janet Moore Lindman and Michele Lise (Ithaca, NY: Cornell University Press, 2001), 29–43.

53. Masson, "The Typology of the Female as a Model for the Regenerate," 304–15.

54. Porterfield, *Female Piety in Puritan New England*, 9–10. For trends and recommendations in seventeenth- and eighteenth-century sermonizing, see Philip Doddridge, *Lectures on Preaching and the Several Branches of the Ministerial Office* (Boston: Manning and Loring, 1808).

55. For example, Solomon Stoddard, Edwards's grandfather and predecessor in the Northampton pulpit, authored *A Guide to Christ* (1714), a meticulous, numbered ministerial manual for managing conversion that emphasized "the work of humiliation" and focused on emotional distress; Increase Mather, in his introduction, assured readers that "the children of godly parents," carefully raised, might have an "easy" time. The *Guide* allowed for a variety of routes to conversion while demanding some "preparation." Stoddard recommends "the work of humiliation" (40): in Stoddard's guiding metaphor of the minister as physician, the minister must terrify the sinner to encourage a "searching [of] the wound," before "apply[ing] the remedy." For another account of the one-sex body and divine impregnation in the New England revivals, see Susan M. Stabile, "A 'Doctrine of Signatures': The Epistolary Physicks of Esther Burr's Journal," in *A Centre of Wonders*, 109–28.

56. Porterfield, *Female Piety in Puritan New England*, 9.

57. In New England's established churches, membership had traditionally given propertied European creole and immigrant men access to the civil vote, creating a tension between the church's roles as an instituted way to grace and a gathered congregation of the faithful. The 1662 Half-Way Covenant addressed this tension by allowing children of church members to receive communion and civil privileges without offering

an account of conversion, a separation subsequently reinforced by the Crown's attempts to centralize New England's colonial governments and strengthen Massachusetts Anglicanism. Voting in the church remained limited to full members but was implemented in a new way: English creole and immigrant female members largely retained church votes while African and Indian members' votes were regularly challenged and frequently denied. *WJE* 12:1.

58. Community standards began to grant greater sexual privacy for European creole and immigrant men in encounters with women outside of marriage, thereby increasing the relative public importance of women's sexual practices and other male sexual practices. See D'Emilio and Freedman, *Intimate Matters*, 40; Ava Chamberlain, "Bad Books and Bad Boys: The Transformation of Gender in Eighteenth-Century Northampton, Massachusetts," *New England Quarterly* 75.2 (2002): 179–203; Thomas A. Foster, *Sex and the Eighteenth-Century Man: Massachusetts and the History of Sexuality in America* (Boston: Beacon Press, 2006).

59. *WJE* 4:147–210.

60. Marsden, 184.

61. Pettit, *The Heart Prepared*, 6–13.

62. By substituting affective religious practice for illicit sexuality, revivalism prevents illicit sexual practices from becoming habitual. This would make youths more likely to channel sexual practice into marriage, a traditional focus of New England Puritan sexual management, but during the revivals, marriage was far less important than affective communal religious practice and individual affective experiences with God.

63. *WJE* 4:176.

64. As Edwards wrote in 1743, after the most fractious period of revivalism, converts placed too much emphasis on the "show and appearance" of "great religious affections" while their "temper and conversation" became worse, until they were "running wild" with accusations, slanders, and attacks on their neighbors. Marsden, 211–12, 233–38.

65. See Warner's account of "disembodied address" in his *Evangelical Public Sphere*. On Edwards's covert but more public response to Whitefield, see Ava Chamberlain, "The Grand Sower of the Seed: Jonathan Edwards's Critique of George Whitefield," *New England Quarterly* 70.3 (1997): 368–85.

66. Myra Jehlen and Michael Warner, eds., *The English Literatures of America, 1500–1800* (New York: Routledge, 1997), 605.

67. *WJE* 16:747; Daniel Shea, "The Art and Instruction of *Jonathan Edwards's Personal Narrative*," *American Literature* 37.1 (1965): 17–32. On this category of advice literature, see Jeremy Gregory, "*Homo Religiosus*: Masculinity and Religion in the Long Eighteenth Century," in *English Masculinities, 1660–1800*, ed. Tim Hitchcock and Michèle Cohen (New York: Longman, 1999), 85–110; Mark E. Kann, *A Republic of Men: The American Founders, Gendered Language, and Patriarchal Politics* (New York: New York University Press, 1998).

68. *WJE* 16:799.

69. Ibid., 799–801. Also see Brooks, *American Lazarus*, 39.

70. Kidd, 7. Edwards's metaphors closely resemble Stoddard's insistence, in *A Guide to Christ*, that the convert must be "wholly broken off from his own righteousness and sufficiency" (127) and "emptied of himself" before he can receive a "new heart" or "new nature" (145).

71. Samson Occom, "Temperance Hannabal" (1754), in *The Collected Writings of Samson Occom, Mohegan: Leadership and Literature in Eighteenth-Century Native America*, ed. Joanna Brooks (New York: Oxford University Press, 2006), 44.

72. Heaton, in Juster, *Disorderly Women*, 60–63.

73. Douglas L. Winiarski, "Souls Filled with Ravishing Transport: Heavenly Visions and the Radical Awakening in New England," *William and Mary Quarterly* 61 (2004): 3–46. Jonathan Edwards, "The Narrative of Sarah Pierpont Edwards," in *The Works of President Edwards: With a Memoir of His Life*, ed. Sereno Dwight (New York: G. & C. & H. Carvill, 1830), 1:171–86.

74. Lambert, " 'I Saw the Book Talk,' " 12.

75. *WJE* 16:94.

76. Whitefield ingeniously conceded the phrasing was impolitic but only because his conversion, like St. Augustine's, had been inspired entirely by God, without the benefit of doctrinal conversation and reading. See *A Letter from the Reverend Mr. Whitefield, to Some Church Members of the Presbyterian Persuasion: In Answer to Certain Scruples and Queries Relating to Some Passages in His Printed Sermons and Other Writings, To which is Added, Two Letters from Nathanael Love-Truth, to the Rev. Mr. Whitefield, Containing Some Exceptions to His 'foresaid Letter*, 3rd ed. (Philadelphia; repr., Charlestown, SC: Peter Timothy, 1741).

77. Henry Scougal, *Vital Christianity: A Brief Essay on the Life of God, in the Soul of Man* (London: printed for Charles Smith and William Jacob, 1677). On Scougal's colonial publication history see J. C. D. Clark, *The Language of Liberty 1660–1832: Political Discourse and Social Dynamics in the Anglo-American World, 1660–1832* (Cambridge: Cambridge University Press, 1994), 28 n. 106.

78. Rodger M. Payne, *The Self and the Sacred: Conversion and Autobiography in Early American Protestantism* (Knoxville: University of Tennessee Press, 1998), 9; William James, *Varieties of Religious Experience* (New York: Longmans, Green, 1905), 189. Also see Gauri Viswanathan, *Outside the Fold: Conversion, Modernity, and Belief* (Princeton, NJ: Princeton University Press, 1998), 83–89.

79. Franklin subsequently printed Tennent's 1739 sermon as Gilbert Tennent, *The Danger of an Unconverted Ministry, Considered in a Sermon on Mark Vi. 34. Preached at Nottingham, in Pennsylvania, March 8, Anno 1739, 40* (Philadelphia: Benjamin Franklin, 1740). For another situation of Edwards's tears in a history of affective masculinity, see Evan Carton, "What Feels an American? Evident Selves and Alienable Emotions in the New Man's World," in *Boys Don't Cry?: Rethinking Narratives of Masculinity and*

Emotion in the U.S., ed. Milette Shamir and Jennifer Travis (New York: Columbia University Press, 2002), 23–43.

80. Kenneth P. Minkema, "A Great Awakening Conversion: The Relation of Samuel Belcher," *William and Mary Quarterly* 44 (1987): 121–26.

81. Juster, *Disorderly Women*, 61, 68–74.

82. Whitefield authorized ten editions, with various titles, sizes, and prices, in London, Edinburgh, Boston, and Philadelphia, including 3,000 copies printed by one Boston publisher alone. Frank Lambert, *"Pedlar in Divinity": George Whitefield and the Transatlantic Revivals* (Princeton, NJ: Princeton University Press, 1994), 14.

83. Whitefield, *A Brief and General Account of the First Part of the Life of the Rev. Mr. George Whitefield from his Birth to his Entering into Holy-Orders* (Boston: J. Draper for Henchman, 1740), 21.

84. Ibid., 51, 12, 47, 36.

85. Ruttenburg, 118.

86. Edwards's contestation of Whitefield's model may also be illustrated by comparing his narrative to the famously eloquent Whitefield's only account of a lapse into silence. George Whitefield, *Journal of a Voyage from London to Savannah* (London: Hunt and Clarke, n.d.), 205.

87. *WJE* 16:801, my emphasis.

88. Cohen, *God's Caress*, 233.

89. Paul David Johnson, "Jonathan Edwards's 'Sweet Conjunction,'" *Early American Literature* 16.3 (1981/1982): 278.

90. For a semiotic/psychoanalytic analysis of the Romantic development of the latter, "negative" form of sublimity as an aesthetic struggle of identification, see Thomas Weiskel, *The Romantic Sublime: Studies in the Structure of Transcendence* (Baltimore: Johns Hopkins University Press, 1976).

91. Gilles Deleuze, "Coldness and Cruelty," in *Masochism: Coldness and Cruelty and Venus in Furs*, trans. Jean McNeil (New York: Zone Books, 1991), 82–84.

92. Deleuze, 84.

93. Immanuel Kant, *The Conflict of the Faculties*, trans. Mary J. Gregor (1798; repr., Lincoln: University of Nebraska Press, 1992), 115.

94. Anthony Ashley Cooper Shaftesbury, *A Letter Concerning Enthusiasm* (London: J. Morphew, 1708), 82.

95. Peter Cosgrove, "Edmund Burke, Gilles Deleuze, and the Subversive Masochism of the Image," *English Literary History* 66.2 (1999): 405–37.

96. Burke, 68.

97. Shaftesbury, 83.

98. Tom Furniss, *Edmund Burke's Aesthetic Ideology: Language, Gender, and Political Economy in Revolution* (Cambridge: Cambridge University Press, 1993), 30. On the politics and aesthetics of sublimity, see Peter de Bolla, *The Discourse of the*

Sublime: Readings in History, Aesthetics and the Subject (New York: Basil Blackwell, 1989), and Terry Eagleton, *The Ideology of the Aesthetic* (New York: Basil Blackwell, 1990).

99. Burke, 135; *The State of Religion in New-England: Since the Reverend Mr. George Whitefield's Arrival There, In a Letter from a Gentleman in New-England to His Friend in Glasgow, To which is Subjoined an Appendix, Containing Attestations of the Principal Facts in the Letter* (Glasgow: Robert Foulis, 1742), available in Kidd, *The Great Awakening: A Brief History with Documents*, 97–98; *WJE* 4:86–87.

100. Ava Chamberlain, "The Theology of Cruelty: A New Look at the Rise of Arminianism in Eighteenth-Century New England," *Harvard Theological Review* 85.3 (1992): 335–56.

101. Anthony Cascardi, *Consequences of Enlightenment* (Cambridge: Cambridge University Press, 1999).

102. Marianne Noble, *The Masochistic Pleasures of Sentimental Literature* (Princeton, NJ: Princeton University Press, 2000), 67.

103. Gustafson, 185–87.

104. A. O. Aldridge, "The Pleasures of Pity," *English Literary History* 16.1 (1949): 76–87; Fiering, 201.

105. Richardson's connections to Sade, in addition to Sade's own proclamations, are traced in R. F. Brissenden, *Virtue in Distress: Studies in the Novel of Sentiment from Richardson to Sade* (New York: Barnes & Noble, 1974), and Laura Hinton, *The Perverse Gaze of Sympathy: Sadomasochistic Sentiments from* Clarissa *to* Rescue 911 (Albany: State University of New York Press, 1999).

106. Halttunen, "Humanitarianism and the Pornography of Pain in Anglo-American Culture," 303–34.

107. On Locke and Edwards, see Leon Chai, *Jonathan Edwards and the Limits of Enlightenment Philosophy* (New York: Oxford University Press, 1998), 2–38; Alan Heimert, *Religion and the American Mind from the Great Awakening to the Revolution.* (Cambridge, MA: Harvard University Press, 1966); Bruce Kuklick, *Churchmen and Philosophers: From Jonathan Edwards to John Dewey* (New Haven, CT: Yale University Press, 1987), 29–30; Perry Miller, "From the Covenant to the Revival," in his *Nature's Nation* (Cambridge, MA: Harvard University Press, 1967), 90–120.

108. Ivy Schweitzer, *The Work of Self-Representation: Lyric Poetry in Colonial New England* (Chapel Hill: University of North Carolina Press, 1991), 32–34.

109. *WJE* 2:89.

110. Gayatri Chakravorty Spivak, "The Politics of Interpretations," *Critical Inquiry* 9.1 (1982): 259–78.

111. Kristeva, 127.

112. Ibid., 4.

113. Ibid., 127.

114. Sigmund Freud, "The Economic Problem of Masochism," in *Essential Papers on*

Masochism, ed. Margaret Ann Fitzpatrick Hanly (New York: New York University Press, 1995), 282–83.

115. Bersani, 90; Judith Butler, *The Psychic Life of Power: Theories of Subjection* (Stanford, CA: Stanford University Press, 1997), 62.

116. Judith Butler, *Bodies That Matter: On the Discursive Limits of "Sex"* (New York: Routledge, 1993), 60.

117. Bersani, 89–90.

118. Adam Phillips describes this broad notion of self-shattering as the "capacity to desire the ultimately overwhelming intensities of feeling that we are subject to." See Leo Bersani and Adam Phillips, *Intimacies* (Chicago: University of Chicago Press, 2008), 93.

119. By attempting to manage the connection between affective performance, religious expression, and community formation, Edwards foreshadowed the eighteenth-century U.S. formation of liberal individual rights, social contract, and public-sphere norms of disembodied abstraction around the exclusion of women, Native Americans, African Americans, and other people of color. At the same time, Calvinist principles of divine providence and disinterested benevolence, developed by Edwards and popularized Huntingtonians, Samuel Hopkins, and others of Edwards's students, were taken up by black and native Calvinist revivalists and helped form the basis of late eighteenth-century abolitionist thought. See Joanna Brooks, *Religion and the Rise of African-American and Native American Literatures* (New York: Oxford University Press, 2003), 87–113, 171–73; Joanna Brooks and John Saillant, eds., *"Face Zion Forward": First Writers of the Black Atlantic, 1785–1798* (Boston: Northeastern University Press, 2002); Charles Hambrick-Stowe, "All Things Were New and Astonishing: Edwardsian Piety, the New Divinity, and Race," in *Jonathan Edwards at Home and Abroad: Historical Memories, Cultural Movements, Global Horizons*, ed. David W. Kling and Douglas A. Sweeney (Columbia: University of South Carolina Press, 2003), 121–36; John Saillant, "Antiguan Methodism and Antislavery Activity: Anne and Elizabeth Hart in the Eighteenth-Century Black Atlantic," *Church History* 69 (2000): 86–115.

120. Robert H. Abzug, *Cosmos Crumbling: American Reform and the Religious Imagination* (New York: Oxford University Press, 1994).

Chapter 2

An earlier version of Chapter 2 was originally published in *Journal of the Early Republic*, 30.2 (2010): 225–51. Copyright 2010 Society for Historians of the Early American Republic.

1. On Apess at Mashpee, see Drew Lopenzina, *Red Ink: Native Americans Picking Up the Pen in the Colonial Period* (Albany: SUNY University Press, 2012), 3, and Lopenzia's forthcoming biography of Apess. On Apess and abolition, see Barry O'Connell, ed., *On Our Own Ground: The Complete Writings of William Apess, a Pequot* (Amherst: University of Massachusetts Press, 1992), 226; Maureen Konkle, "Indian Literacy, U.S.

Colonialism, and Literary Criticism," *American Literature* 69.3 (1997): 473–74. On sectarian and public-sphere organizing, see Robert H. Abzug, *Cosmos Crumbling: American Reform and the Religious Imagination* (New York: Oxford University Press, 1994). On Apess and Methodism, see Laura Donaldson, "Making a Joyful Noise: William Apess and the Search for Postcolonial Method(ism)," in *Messy Beginnings: Postcoloniality and Early American Studies*, ed. Malini Johar Schueller and Edward Watts (New Brunswick, NJ: Rutgers University Press, 2003), 29–44; Sandra Gustafson, "Nations of Israelites: Prophecy and Cultural Autonomy in the Writings of William Apess," *Religion and Literature* 26.1 (1994): 33 and passim; Carolyn Haynes, *Divine Destiny: Gender and Race in Nineteenth-Century Protestantism* (Jackson: University Press of Mississippi, 1998), 28–46; Arnold Krupat, *Red Matters: Native American Studies* (Philadelphia: University of Pennsylvania Press, 2002), 15–16; O'Connell, "Introduction," i–lxxvii; Karim M. Tiro, "Denominated 'SAVAGE': Methodism, Writing, and Identity in the Works of William Apess, A Pequot," *American Quarterly* 48 (1996): 653–79; Cheryl Walker, *Indian Nation: Native American Literature and Nineteenth-Century Nationalisms* (Durham, NC: Duke University Press, 1997), 41–59; Robert Warrior, "William Apess: A Pequot and Methodist Under the Sign of Modernity," in *Liberation Theologies, Postmodernity, and the Americas*, ed. David B. Batstone et al. (New York: Routledge, 1997): 188–204; Hilary Wyss, *Writing Indians: Literacy, Christianity, and Native Community in Early America* (Amherst: University of Massachusetts Press, 2000), 154–66; Bernd Peyer, *The Tutor'd Mind: Indian Missionary-Writers in Antebellum America* (Amherst: University of Massachusetts Press, 1997), 117–65.

2. *A Son of the Forest*, in *The American Monthly Review*, vol. 2 (Cambridge, MA: Brown, Shattuck; Boston: Hillard, Gray, 1832), 149. Samuel Gardner Drake, *Indian Biography: Containing the Lives of More Than Two Hundred Indian Chiefs* (Boston: Josiah Drake, 1832), 268.

3. Eileen Razzari Elrod, *Piety and Dissent: Race, Gender and Biblical Rhetoric in Early American Autobiography* (Amherst: University of Massachusetts Press, 2008).

4. On Occom, see Dana D. Nelson, "'I Speak Like a Fool but I Am Constrained': Samson Occom's Short Narrative and Economies of the Racial Self," in *Early Native American Writing: New Critical Essays*, ed. Helen Jaskoski (New York: Cambridge University Press, 1996), 46–65; Wyss, *Writing Indians*, 135.

5. William Apess, *A Son of the Forest: The Experience of William Apes, A Native of the Forest* (New York: By the Author, 1829), 114. On the mouth as a longstanding site of Indian resistance to colonialism, see Olivia Bloechl, *Native American Song at the Frontiers of Early Modern Music* (Cambridge: Cambridge University Press, 2008), 58–80. On speech as an extension of the mouth and breath, see Kathleen M. Brown, *Foul Bodies: Cleanliness in Early America* (New Haven, CT: Yale University Press, 2014), 137. On the U.S. political valence of biblical troping of mouths, see Sandra Gustafson, *Imagining Deliberative Democracy in the Early American Republic* (Chicago: University of Chicago Press, 2011), 18–19.

6. On instrumentality in Awakening and nineteenth-century African American female oratory, see Ruttenburg, 96; Joycelyn Moody, *Sentimental Confessions: Spiritual Narratives of Nineteenth-Century African American Women* (Athens: University of Georgia Press, 2003), 38–42.

7. "Notice," *New York Evangelist*, June 26, 1830, 51. Summersides's likely companions were Ruth Watkins and Thomas Morris. See John Petty, *The History of the Primitive Methodist Connexion* (London: Primitive Methodist Book Committee, 1860), 309; Julia Werner, *The Primitive Methodist Connexion: Its Background and Early History* (Madison: University of Wisconsin Press, 1984); Deborah Valenze, "Pilgrims and Progress in Nineteenth-Century England," in *Culture, Ideology and Politics: Essays for Eric Hobsbawm*, ed. Raphael Samuel and Gareth Jones (London: Routledge, 1982), 116; Sean Wilentz, *Chants Democratic: New York City and the Rise of the American Working Class, 1788–1850* (New York: Oxford University Press, 1984), 158–62, 165–67, 177–211.

8. Apess charged fifty cents at a September lecture in Hartford and a year later in Salem. "Notice," *Christian Secretary* (Hartford, CT), September 25, 1830, 143; *A Son of the Forest*, *Salem Gazette*, October 11, 1831, 3.

9. Apess, *A Son of the Forest*, 48, 115.

10. Sandra Gustafson, "American Literature and the Public Sphere," *American Literary History* 20.3 (2008): 473; Apess, *A Son of the Forest* (1829), 18. The reformist Methodist public may be understood in light of recent scholarship on late eighteenth- and nineteenth-century feminist, black, abolitionist, temperance, and labor publics with whom it shared its strategies and, sometimes, its membership. This scholarship develops Habermas's description of the modern liberal public sphere as both a pillar of bourgeois hegemony and a norm whose nonexistence allows for counterhegemonic critique. It describes a public sphere constituted by multiple competing publics and using various discursive modes, including oral address, idiom, affect, print, and bodily performance. We might identify these nonrational techniques as what Michael Warner calls a public style or, in a religious context, an aesthetics of the sacred, which helps establish and contest norms of religious behavior. See Warner, *Publics and Counterpublics*, 128.

11. Dee Andrews, *The Methodists and Revolutionary America, 1760–1800: The Shaping of an Evangelical Culture* (Princeton, NJ: Princeton University Press, 2000); Sylvia Frey, " 'The Year of Jubilee Is Come': Black Christianity in the Plantation South in Post-Revolutionary America," in *Religion in a Revolutionary Age*, ed. Ronald Hoffman and Peter J. Albert (Charlottesville: University Press of Virginia, 1994), 87–124; Will Gravely, "African Methodisms and the Rise of Black Denominationalism," in *Reimagining Denominationalism: Interpretive Essays*, ed. Robert Bruce Mullin and Russell E. Richey (New York: Oxford University Press, 1994), 239–63; Phillip N. Mulder, *A Controversial Spirit: Evangelical Awakenings in the South* (New York: Oxford University Press, 2002), 66–88; John H. Wigger, *Taking Heaven by Storm: Methodism and the Rise of Popular Christianity in America* (New York: Oxford University Press, 1998), 127–30.

12. Susan Juster, "Mystical Pregnancy and Holy Bleeding: Visionary Experience in

Early Modern Britain and America," *William and Mary Quarterly* 57.2 (2000): 249–88; Juster, *Doomsayers*, 84–85.

13. Wigger, *Taking Heaven by Storm*, 87.

14. Juster, *Doomsayers*, 83–84. For a similar development of scientific community in opposition to sentimental domestic moral agency, see Dana Nelson, "'No Cold or Empty Heart': Polygenesis, Scientific Professionalization, and the Unfinished Business of Male Sentimentalism," *differences: A Journal of Feminist Cultural Studies* 11.3 (1999): 39.

15. Alexander M'Caine, *The History and Mystery of Methodist Episcopacy* (Baltimore: Richard J. Matchett, 1827).

16. "Substance of the Semi-centennial Sermon Before the New-York Annual Conference, at its Session, May 1826. By the Rev. Freeborn Garrettson," *Methodist Magazine* 10 (1827): 357, 397–98.

17. *Mutual Rights of the Ministers and Members of the Methodist Episcopal Church* (Baltimore: John D. Toy, 1824–28), continued as *Mutual Rights and Christian Intelligencer* (Baltimore: D. B. Dorsey, 1828–30). On the AME and African American identity, see Frances Foster, "A Narrative of the Interesting Origins and (Somewhat) Surprising Developments of African-American Print Culture," *American Literary History* 17.4 (2005): 714–40; Hortense J. Spillers, "Moving On Down the Line," *American Quarterly* 40.1 (1988): 93. On AME Zion and the Methodist Society, see Richard Carwardine, "Charles Sellers's 'Antinomians' and 'Arminians': Methodists and the Market Revolution," in *God and Mammon: Protestants, Money, and the Market, 1790–1860*, ed. Mark A. Noll (New York: Oxford University Press, 2001), 79; Leslie M. Harris, *In the Shadow of Slavery: African Americans in New York City, 1626–1863* (Chicago: University of Chicago Press, 2003), 84; Nathan Hatch, *The Democratization of American Christianity* (New Haven, CT: Yale University Press, 1989), 125–46; David Hempton, *Methodism: Empire of the Spirit* (New Haven, CT: Yale University Press, 2006), 86–108; John Jamison Moore, *History of the A.M.E. Zion Church* (York, PA: Teachers' Journal Office, 1884), 15–33; Samuel Stilwell, *Historical Sketches of the Rise and Progress of the Methodist Society* (New York: W. M. Stilwell & William Bates, 1821), 12–17; Mulder, 8; William Sutton, *Journeymen for Jesus: Evangelical Artisans Confront Capitalism in Jacksonian Baltimore* (University Park: Pennsylvania State University Press, 1998), 69–130; William Sutton, "To Extract Poison from the Blessings of God's Providence': Producerist Respectability and Methodist Suspicions of Capitalist Change in the Early Republic," in *Methodism and the Shaping of American Culture*, ed. Nathan Hatch and John Wigger (Nashville, TN: Abingdon, 2001), 223–56; Ronald Schultz, *The Republic of Labor: Philadelphia Artisans and the Politics of Class, 1720–1830* (New York: Oxford University Press, 1993), 205–7; Wilentz, 80–85, 277–300; Michael Zuckerman, "Holy Wars, Civil Wars: Religion and Economics in Nineteenth-Century America," *Prospects* 16 (1991): 205–40.

18. "Address of the Editors," *Methodist Magazine* 1.1 (1818): 3; Andrews, 230; Candy Gunther Brown, *The Word in the World: Evangelical Writing, Publishing, and Reading in*

America, 1789–1880 (Chapel Hill: University of North Carolina Press, 2004), 200–208; Hatch, *Democratization*, 204; Mulder, 149–67; Wigger, 189.

19. William Hamilton, *An Oration Delivered in the African Zion Church on the 4th of July, 1827* (New York: Gray & Bunce, 1827); *Constitution of the N.Y. Baptist Missionary Society* (New York: Gray & Bunce, 1829). Also see Sidney F. Huttner and Elizabeth Stege Huttner, *A Register of Artists, Engravers, Booksellers, Bookbinders, Printers & Publishers in New York City, 1821–42* (New York: Bibliographical Society of America, 1993), 42, 100.

20. "Lecture in Boylston Hall," *Christian Register* (Boston), May 5, 1832, 71.

21. An advertisement for his 1830 lecture in Hartford, Connecticut, trumpeted him as a "descendent of the celebrated King Philip, of the Pequot tribe." "Notice," *Christian Secretary* (Hartford, CT), September 25, 1830, 143.

22. On Paradise, see Andrews, 336 n. 48.

23. Donald Yacovone, "The Transformation of the Black Temperance Movement, 1827–1854: An Interpretation," *Journal of the Early Republic* 8.3 (1988): 281–97; Robert S. Levine, "'Whiskey, Blacking, and All': Temperance and Race in William Wells Brown's *Clotel,*" in *The Serpent in the Cup: Temperance in American Literature*, ed. David Reynolds and Debra Rosenthal (Amherst: University of Massachusetts Press, 1997), 93–114; Glenn Hendler, *Public Sentiments: Structures of Feeling in Nineteenth-Century American Literature* (Chapel Hill: University of North Carolina Press, 2001), 47–48.

24. James Fenimore Cooper, *The Pioneers* (New York: Oxford University Press, 1999), 185; "The Unhappy Effects of Intemperance," *Piscataqua Evangelical Magazine* 1.4 (1805): 145; "On Intemperance in Drinking," *Moral and Religious Cabinet* 1.14 (1808): 221; "On the Ruinous Effects of Ardent Spirits," *Panoplist, and Missionary Magazine* 5.9 (1813): 415–18; 5.10 (1813): 442–46; 5.12 (1813): 536–538; *Adviser or, Vermont Evangelical Magazine* 5.5 (1813): 147–51; 5.7 (1813): 212–15; *Utica Christian Magazine* 1.1 (1813): 11–19; 1.8 (1814): 298–304; 1.9 (1814): 326–30; *Vehicle or, New York Northwestern Christian Magazine* 1.3 (1814): 139–43. On romantic treatments of the drunken Indian, see Jill Lepore, *Name of War: King Philip's War and the Origins of American Identity* (New York: Vintage, 1999); Lora Romero, "Vanishing Americans: Gender, Empire, and New Historicism," *American Literature* 63.3 (1991): 385–404; William J. Rorabaugh, *The Alcoholic Republic: An American Tradition* (New York: Oxford University Press, 1979), 233; Dan McKanan, *Identifying the Image of God: Radical Christians and Nonviolent Power in the Antebellum United States* (New York: Oxford University Press, 2002), 108; Susan Scheckel, *The Insistence of the Indian: Race and Nationalism in Nineteenth-Century American Culture* (Princeton, NJ: Princeton University Press, 1998), 40–64, 107–26, 215–20; Nicholas Warner, *Spirits of America: Intoxication in Nineteenth-Century American Literature* (Norman: University of Oklahoma Press, 1997), 94–123. On English missionary anxiety, see Anna Johnston, *Missionary Writing and Empire, 1800–1860* (New York: Cambridge University Press, 2003).

25. Richard Allen, *The Life, Experience, and Gospel Labours of the Rt. Rev. Richard Allen* (Philadelphia: Martin & Boden, 1833), 11.

26. Stephen Hum, "'When We Were No People, Then We Were a People': Evangelical Language and the Free Blacks of Philadelphia in the Early Republic," in *A Mighty Baptism: Race, Gender, and the Creation of American Protestantism*, ed. Susan Juster and Lisa MacFarlane (Ithaca, NY: Cornell University Press, 1996), 235–58.

27. "On Christian Temperance," *Mutual Rights* 1.7 (February 1825): 257; Betsy Erkkila, "Franklin and the Revolutionary Body," *English Literary History* 67.3 (2000): 718.

28. "Introduction," *Wesleyan Repository* 1.1 (1821): 3; Samuel Jennings, "Editorial Address," *Mutual Rights* 1.1 (1824): 1–2; William Stilwell, "Prospectus," *Friendly Visitor* 1.1 (1825): 1.

29. Nicholas Snethen, "Lectures on Missions to American Indians," *Wesleyan Repository* 3.6 (1823): 213. On race and sensation, see Bruce Dain, *A Hideous Monster of the Mind: American Race Theory in the Early Republic* (Cambridge, MA: Harvard University Press, 2002); Wheeler, *The Complexion of Race*; Jared Gardner, *Master Plots: Race and the Founding of an American Literature, 1787–1845* (Baltimore: Johns Hopkins University Press, 1998), 1–24; Hendler, 36–43.

30. Cornelius Blatchly, *Essay on Common Wealths* (New York: Society for Promoting Communities, 1822) 4, 24–25.

31. Apess, *A Son of the Forest* (1829), 15; Franklin, cited in Erkkila, 717. On Apess and republican masculinity, see Haynes, 28–46.

32. Apess, *A Son of the Forest* (1829), 14; Dana Nelson, *National Manhood: Capitalist Citizenship and the Imagined Fraternity of White Men* (Durham, NC: Duke University Press, 1998), 26, 67.

33. Apess, *A Son of the Forest* (1829), 81, 54. On gender and conversion, see Haynes, 28–46.

34. Apess, *A Son of the Forest* (1829), 99, 78, 100; Joshua R. Greenberg, "'Powerful—Very Powerful Is the Parental Feeling': Fatherhood, Domestic Politics, and the New York City Working Men's Party," *Early American Studies* 2.1 (2004): 192–227.

35. Apess, *A Son of the Forest* (1829), 99.

36. Anonymous (J.S.), "An address to master Mechanics, whom it may concern," *Friendly Visitor* 1.21 (May 21, 1825): 164–65.

37. Apess, *A Son of the Forest* (1829), 99–100.

38. Ibid., 99–100; O'Connell, 204.

39. Apess, *A Son of the Forest* (1829), 76–80. On race and indenture, see Ruth Wallis Herndon, "'Proper' Magistrates and Masters: Binding Out Poor Children in Southern New England, 1720–1820," in *Children Bound to Labor: The Pauper Apprentice System in Early America*, ed. Ruth Wallis Herndon and John E. Murray (Ithaca, NY: Cornell University Press, 2009), 39–51.

40. Andrews, 235; James E. Kirby et al., *The Methodists* (Westport, CT: Greenwood, 1996), 352; Sutton, *Journeymen for Jesus*, 63, 106–17; James R. Williams, *History of the Methodist Protestant Church* (Baltimore: Book Committee of the Methodist Protestant Church, 1843), 284–87.

41. "A Son of the Forest," *Baltimore Patriot* 37.71 (March 24, 1831): 1; O'Connell, 312, 3.

42. O'Connell, 316–17, 8, 5–7. On sentiment in Apess's 1831 edition, see Laura Mielke, *Moving Encounters: Sympathy and the Indian Question in Antebellum Literature* (Amherst: University of Massachusetts Press, 2008), 70–78.

43. Apess, *A Son of the Forest* (1829), 14, 28, 78, 70; compare to O'Connell, 316, 318, 319, 33.

44. Thomas W. Laqueur, "Bodies, Details and the Humanitarian Narrative," in *The New Cultural History*, ed. Lynn Hunt (Berkeley: University of California Press, 1989), 176–204; Elizabeth Barnes, *States of Sympathy: Seduction and Democracy in the American Novel* (New York: Columbia University Press, 1997); Lauren Berlant, *The Female Complaint: The Unfinished Business of Sentimentality in American Culture* (Chapel Hill: Duke University Press, 2008), 36–37; Peter Coviello, *Intimacy in America: Dreams of Affiliation in Antebellum Literature* (Minneapolis: University of Minnesota Press, 2005); Julie Ellison, *Cato's Tears and the Making of Anglo-American Emotion* (Chicago: University of Chicago Press, 1999); Saidiya Hartman, *Scenes of Subjection: Terror, Slavery, and Self-Making in Nineteenth-Century America* (New York: Oxford University Press, 1997); Christine Levecq, *Slavery and Sentiment: The Politics of Feeling in Black Atlantic Antislavery Writing, 1770–1850* (Hanover, NH: University Press of New England, 2008); Julia Stern, *The Plight of Feeling: Sympathy and Dissent in the Early American Novel* (Chicago: University of Chicago Press, 1997).

Chapter 3

1. "Capt. Walker," *New York Tribune*, in "Capt. Jonathan Walker," *Prisoner's Friend*, 1.17 (July 23, 1845): 67.

2. Sophia L. Little, *The Branded Hand* (Pawtucket, RI: RW Potter, 1845).

3. Jonathan Walker, *Trial and Imprisonment of Jonathan Walker* (Boston: Dow & Jackson for the Boston Anti-Slavery Office, 1845); "Branded Hand of Captain Jonathan Walker," daguerreotype, Southworth and Hawes, August 1845.

4. "That Hand," Boston *Emancipator and Republican* 10.16 (August 13, 1845): 63.

5. Russ Castronovo, *Necro Citizenship: Death, Eroticism, and the Public Sphere in the Nineteenth-Century United States* (Durham, NC: Duke University Press, 2001), 224.

6. On evolving abolitionist conceptions of racial identity see James Brewer Stewart, "The Emergence of Racial Modernity and the Rise of the White North, 1790–1840," *Journal of the Early Republic* 18 (Summer 1998): 181–217.

7. "The Branded Hand," *Niles' National Register* 18.25 (August 23, 1845): 395.

8. "The Branded Hand," *Philadelphia Public Ledger* (January 21, 1845): 1; "The Branded Hand," *Liberator* 15.2 (January 10, 1845): 7.

9. Deborah Van Broekhoven, *"The Devotion of These Women": Rhode Island in the Antislavery Network* (Amherst: University of Massachusetts Press, 2002); Lee

Chambers-Schiller, "'A Good Work Among the People': The Political Culture of the Boston Antislavery Fair," in *Abolitionist Sisterhood*, ed. Jean Fagan Yellin and John Van Horne (Ithaca, NY: Cornell University Press, 1994), 249–74; Beverly Gordon, *Bazaars and Fair Ladies: The History of the American Fundraising Fair* (Knoxville: University of Tennessee Press, 1988); W. Caleb McDaniel, "The Fourth and the First: Abolitionist Holidays, Respectability, and Radical Interracial Reform," *American Quarterly* 57.1 (2005): 129–51; Augusta Rohrbach, "'Truth Stronger and Stranger Than Fiction': Reexamining William Lloyd Garrison's *Liberator*," *American Literature* 73.4 (2001): 727–55.

10. Joanna Brooks, "The Early American Public Sphere and the Emergence of a Black Print Counterpublic," *William and Mary Quarterly* 62.1 (2005): 67–92; Frances Smith Foster, "A Narrative of the Interesting Origins and (Somewhat) Surprising Developments of African-American Print Culture," *American Literary History* 17 (Winter 2005): 714–40; James O. Horton and Lois E. Horton, *In Hope of Liberty: Culture, Community and Protest and North Free Blacks, 1700–1860* (New York: Oxford University Press, 1997); Stephen Hum, "'When We Were No People, Then We Were a People': Evangelical Language and the Free Blacks of Philadelphia in the Early Republic," in *A Mighty Baptism: Race, Gender, and the Creation of American Protestantism*, ed. Susan Juster and Lisa MacFarlane (Ithaca, NY: Cornell University Press, 1996), 235–58; Patrick Rael, *Black Identity and Black Protest in the Antebellum North* (Chapel Hill: University of North Carolina Press, 2002); James Sidbury, *Becoming African in America: Race and Nation in the Early Black Atlantic* (New York: Oxford University Press, 2007).

11. David Grimsted, *American Mobbing, 1828–1865: Toward Civil War* (New York: Oxford University Press, 1998).

12. Wood, *Blind Memory*, 246–50.

13. "The Branded Hand," Worcester *Christian Citizen*, in the Boston *Emancipator and Republican* 10.16 (August 13 1845): 63.

14. John Greenleaf Whittier, "The Branded Hand," in *Poems* (Boston: Benjamin B. Mussey, 1849), 199–200. The poem was published in, among other places, the Salem, Massachusetts, *Gazette*, September 16, 1845; Boston *Christian Reflector* 8.33 (August 14, 1845): 132; Boston *Liberator* 15.33 (August 15, 1845): 132; Boston *Zion's Herald and Wesleyan Journal* 16.34 (August 20, 1845): 1; Hartford *Christian Secretary* 24.33 (October 24, 1845): 3; Boston *Emancipator and Republican* 10.15 (October 6, 1845): 59.

15. Whittier, 199–200.

16. Katie Stevenson, "Contesting Chivalry: James II and the Control of Chivalric Culture in the 1450s," *Journal of Medieval History* 33.2 (2007): 197–214.

17. Saidiya V. Hartman, *Scenes of Subjection: Terror, Slavery, and Self-Making in Nineteenth-Century America* (New York: Oxford University Press, 1997), 19.

18. Jonathan Walker, *Trial and Imprisonment of Jonathan Walker* (Boston: Anti-Slavery Society, 1845), 28.

19. Ibid., 38.

20. Ibid., 42.

21. Frederick Douglass, *Narrative of the Life of Frederick Douglass, An American Slave, Written by Himself* (Boston: Published at the Anti-Slavery Office, 1845), 5.

22. Christopher Castiglia, *Interior States: Institutional Consciousness and the Inner Life of Democracy in the Antebellum United States* (Durham, NC: Duke University Press, 2008), 101–35.

23. Denise Ferreira da Silva, *Toward a Global Idea of Race* (Minneapolis: University of Minnesota Press, 2007); Hartman, *Scenes of Subjection*; Eric Lott, *Love and Theft: Blackface Minstrelsy and the American Working Class* (New York: Oxford University Press, 1993); Barnes, *States of Sympathy;* Coviello, *Intimacy in America;* Stern, *The Plight of Feeling.*

24. Houston Baker, "Critical Memory and the Black Public Sphere," *Public Culture* 7.1 (1994): 3–33; Brooks, "The Early American Public Sphere and the Emergence of a Black Print Counterpublic"; Bruce Burgett, *Sentimental Bodies: Sex, Gender, and Citizenship in the Early Republic* (Princeton, NJ: Princeton University Press, 1998), 42–48; Rita Felski, *Beyond Feminist Aesthetics: Feminist Literature and Social Change* (Cambridge, MA: Harvard University Press, 1989); Jay Fliegelman, *Declaring Independence: Jefferson, Natural Language, and the Culture of Performance* (Stanford, CA: Stanford University Press, 1993); Calhoun, *Habermas and the Public Sphere;* Looby, *Voicing America.*

25. For some modern analogues, see David Cook, *Martyrdom in Islam* (New York: Cambridge University Press, 2007); Talal Asad, *On Suicide Bombing* (New York: Columbia University Press, 2007); Charles Kurzman, *The Missing Martyrs: Why There Are So Few Muslim Terrorists* (New York: Oxford University Press, 2011).

26. Robert H. Abzug, *Cosmos Crumbling: American Reform and the Religious Imagination* (New York: Oxford University Press, 1994).

27. On Quaker martyrology, see John Knott, "Joseph Besse and the Quaker Culture of Suffering," in *The Emergence of Quaker Writing: Dissenting Literature in Seventeenth-Century England,* ed. Thomas N. Corns and David Loewenstein (Portland, OR: Frank Cass, 1995), 126–41; Phyllis Mack, *Visionary Women: Ecstatic Prophecy in Seventeenth-Century England* (Berkeley: University of California Press, 1992); Anne G. Myles, "From Monster to Martyr: Re-Presenting Mary Dyer," *Early American Literature* 36.1 (2001): 1–30; Julie Sievers, "Awakening the Inner Light: Elizabeth Ashbridge and the Transformation of Quaker Community," *Early American Literature* 36 (2001): 235–61.

28. Michael Meranze, "Materializing Conscience: Embodiment, Speech, and the Experience of Sympathetic Identification," *Early American Literature* 36.1 (2002): 71–88.

29. Thomas D. Hamm, *The Quakers in America* (New York: Columbia University Press, 2003), 44.

30. Merton L. Dillon, *Benjamin Lundy and the Struggle for Negro Freedom* (Urbana: University of Illinois Press, 1966), 156.

31. Quakers also used public-sphere organizing in, e.g., the 1843 establishment of the radical Quaker Anti-Slavery Friends.

32. "The Libel Suit," *Genius of Universal Emancipation* 2.1 (May 1830): 17–18; "The Libel Suit—Again," *Genius of Universal Emancipation* 3.1 (June 1830); "Garrison's Second Trial," *Genius of Universal Emancipation* 7.1 (October 1830): 97–101.

33. William Lloyd Garrison, *A Brief Sketch of the Trial of William Lloyd Garrison* (Boston: Garrison and Knapp, 1834), 15.

34. Garrison in Wendell P. and Francis J. Garrison, *William Lloyd Garrison, 1805–1879: The Story of His Life Told by His Children*, 2 vols. (New York: Century, 1885), 1:351.

35. Castiglia, *Interior States*, 130.

36. Other Lovejoy martyrologies include Amos Blanchard, *A Sermon in Reference to the State of the Times* (Concord, NH: Printed at the *Observer* Press, 1838); Henry Tanner, *History of the Rise and Progress of the Alton Riots* (Buffalo, NY: James D. Warren, 1878); Fred Tracy, *A Sermon Occasioned by the Alton Outrage* (Newburyport, MA: Charles Whipple, 1838); John Trow, *Alton Trials: of Winthrop S. Gillman* (New York: J. F. Trow, 1838); Leonard Worcester, *A Discourse on the Alton Outrage* (Concord, NH: Asa McFarland, 1838).

37. Jonathan Blanchard, "The Voice of Blood," in *Voices of the True-Hearted* (Philadelphia: Merrihew & Thompson, 1846), 277.

38. R. Laurence Moore, "Spiritualism and Science: Reflections on the First Decade of the Spirit Rappings," *American Quarterly* 24.4 (1972): 474–500; Daphne Brooks, *Bodies in Dissent: Spectacular Performances of Race and Freedom* (Durham, NC: Duke University Press, 2006), 17, 124–25; John J. Kucich, *Ghostly Communion: Cross-Cultural Spiritualism in Nineteenth-Century American Literature* (Hanover, NH: University Press of New England, 2004), 54–55.

39. On the post-Reconstruction evolution of this threat, see Susan Kay Gillman, *Blood Talk: American Race Melodrama and the Culture of the Occult* (Chicago: University of Chicago Press, 2003).

40. Phillips also relies on the emotional resonance of oblique references to the famous dead, such as "Warren lies dead upon the field," to cement his sentimental appeal. Wendell Phillips, "The Murder of Lovejoy," in *Speeches, Lectures and Letters* (Boston: J. Redpath, 1863), 7, 3.

41. Dana Nelson, *National Manhood: Capitalist Citizenship and the Imagined Fraternity of White Men* (Durham, NC: Duke University Press, 1998), 15.

42. Edward Beecher, for example, describes Lovejoy as the "first martyr in America to the great principles of the freedom of speech and of the press." See Edward Beecher, *Narrative of Riots at Alton: In Connection with the Death of Rev. Elijah P. Lovejoy* (Alton, IL: G. Holton, 1838), 5. Similarly, *The Memoir of the Rev. Elijah P. Lovejoy*, commissioned by the American Anti-Slave Society and compiled by Lovejoy's brothers, describes Lovejoy as "a martyr to the holy cause of right, and truth, and freedom," "a martyr to the great and inestimable rights of the freedom of the press," and "the first martyr to the

cause of humanity." See Joseph and Owen Lovejoy, *Memoir of the Rev. Elijah P. Lovejoy who was Murdered in Defence of the Liberty of the Press* (New York: John S. Taylor, 1838), 317–18, 326.

43. Robert Fanuzzi, *Abolition's Public Sphere* (Minneapolis: University of Minnesota Press, 2003), xv–xxx.

44. Beriah Green, *The Martyr* (New York: American Anti-Slavery Society, 1838), 12, 14.

45. Ibid., 12.

46. "Petition of Peter Bestes, Sambo Freeman, Felix Holbrook, and Chester Joie," April 20, 1773, in *Early Negro Writing, 1760–1837*, ed. Dorothy Porter (Baltimore: Black Classic Press, 1995), 245.

47. Eric Slauter, "Neoclassical Culture in a Society with Slaves: Race and Rights in the Age of Wheatley," *Early American Studies* 2.1 (2004): 81–122.

48. "A Venerable Document," from the Boston *Commonwealth*, cited in Philadelphia *Friends' Review* 4.51 (September 1851): 822–23.

49. Green, 12, 15.

50. Karen Halttunen, *Murder Most Foul: The Killer and the American Gothic Imagination* (Cambridge, MA: Harvard University Press, 1998), 68–69.

51. Beecher, 106.

52. Green, 16–17.

53. Ibid., 17

54. Beecher, 89–90.

55. Ibid., 102.

56. These notions would soon be popularized in John O'Sullivan's Jacksonian *United States Magazine and Democratic Review*. Specifically, Beecher anticipates O'Sullivan's 1839 editorial, "A Divine Destiny for America," which first distilled, in explicitly Christian terms, what he would later recast as a more secular "manifest destiny." See Robert D. Sampson, *John L. O'Sullivan and His Times* (Kent, OH: Kent State University Press, 2003).

57. Thomas T. Stone, *The Martyr of Freedom* (Boston: Isaac Knapp, 1838), 21.

58. Ibid., 21–22.

59. On Jefferson's Anglo-Saxonism, see Reginald Horsman, *Race and Manifest Destiny* (Cambridge, MA: Harvard University Press, 1981), 18–23; Allen J. Frantzen, *Desire for Origins* (New Brunswick, NJ: Rutgers University Press, 1990), 203–7.

60. The *Democratic Review* links Turner's Anglo-Saxonism with literary developments of race and American empire by following their review of Turner with a review of James Fenimore Cooper's *The Deer-Slayer* (*United States Democratic Review* 9.40 [1841]: 404). Sharon Turner, *The History of the Anglo-Saxons*, 3 vols. (1799–1805; repr., Paris: W. Galignani, 1840), 1:10.

61. Green, 17.

62. Ibid., 15.

63. Douglass, *Narrative*, 5.

64. Robert Reid-Pharr, *Conjugal Union: The Body, the House, and the Black American* (New York: Oxford University Press, 1999), 35. For a compelling alternate reading of Douglass's disembodiment, see Robyn Wiegman, *American Anatomies: Theorizing Race and Gender* (Durham, NC: Duke University Press, 1995), 70–78.

65. Paul Gilroy, *The Black Atlantic: Modernity and Double Consciousness* (Cambridge, MA: Harvard University Press, 1995), 19.

66. On Douglass and masculinity, see Weigman and Richard Yarborough, "Race, Violence, and Manhood: The Masculine Ideal in Frederick Douglass's 'The Heroic Slave,'" in *Frederick Douglass: New Literary and Historical Essays*, ed. Eric Sundquist (New York: Cambridge University Press, 1990), 166–83.

67. The exchange between white and black abolitionists was, of course, robust. Douglass's narrative was prefaced by Garrison's authenticating account of Douglass's orations and Wendell Phillips's affectionate review, as well as shaped with the expectations of white abolitionist spectators and readers in mind. Douglass's description of his "sense of [his] own manhood" came in for special notice by Phillips, who was "glad to learn . . . how early the most neglected of God's children waken to a sense of their rights." See "Letter from Wendell Phillips, Esq.," in Douglass, *Narrative*, xxi.

68. Stone, 6.

69. Ibid., 6–7, 19.

70. Joan Landes, *Women and the Public Sphere in the Age of the French Revolution* (Ithaca, NY: Cornell University Press, 1988).

71. Ibid., 22.

72. Julie Ellison, *Cato's Tears and the Making of Anglo-American Emotion* (Chicago: University of Chicago Press, 1999).

73. Harriet Martineau, "The Martyr Age of the United States," *London and Westminster Review* 62 (December 1838): 1–32.

74. On Martineau and transatlantic abolition, see Clare Midgley, *Women Against Slavery: The British Campaigns, 1780–1870* (New York: Routledge, 1992), 130–40.

75. Harriet Martineau, *Writings on Slavery and the American Civil War*, ed. Deborah Anna Logan (DeKalb: Northern Illinois University Press, 2002), 96.

76. "Miss Martineau on America," *American Quarterly Review* 63 (September 1837): 25, 26, 28, 22; Chapman, cited in G. J. Barker-Benfield and Catherine Clinton, *Portraits of American Women: From Settlement to the Present* (New York: Oxford University Press, 1998), 150.

77. Martineau, *Writings*, 59–61.

78. Chapman, n.d., 1855, cited in Barker-Benfield and Clinton.

79. Martineau, *Writings*, 60.

80. On abolition and female publicity, see Lori Ginzberg, *Women and the Work of Benevolence: Morality, Politics, and Class in the Nineteenth-Century United States* (New Haven, CT: Yale University Press, 1990); Debra Gold Hansen, *Strained Sisterhood:*

Gender and Class in Boston Female Anti-Slavery Society (Amherst: University of Massachusetts Press, 1993); Julie Roy Jeffrey, *The Great Silent Army of Abolitionism: Ordinary Women in the Antislavery Movement* (Chapel Hill: University of North Carolina Press, 1998); Shirley Yee, *Black Woman Abolitionists: A Study in Activism, 1828–1860* (Knoxville: University of Tennessee Press, 1992); Jean Fagan Yellin, *Women and Sisters: The Anti-Slavery Feminists in American Culture* (New Haven, CT: Yale University Press, 1989).

81. On other uses of McIntosh's burning, see Castronovo, *Fathering the Nation: American Genealogies of Slavery and Freedom* (Berkeley: University of California Press, 1995), 1–5.

82. Joseph and Owen Lovejoy, 364.

83. Martineau, *Writings*, 64.

84. See Elisa Tamarkin, "Black Anglophilia; or, The Sociability of Antislavery," *American Literary History* 14.3 (2002): 466.

85. Harriet Beecher Stowe, *A Key to Uncle Tom's Cabin* (Boston: John P. Jewett & Co., 1853), 226, 224.

86. Ibid., 227.

87. Ibid., 228. The passage, in Hebrews, grants Abel an enduring voice in contrast to the silenced Cain, whose "mark" nineteenth-century advocates of slavery associated with blackness (11:4).

88. Ibid., 228.

89. Stowe, *Uncle Tom's Cabin* (New York: Oxford University Press, 1998), 370, 388.

90. Stowe, *Key*, 65.

91. *Blackwood's Edinburgh Magazine* 74 (October 1853): 399. Also see Sarah Meer, *Uncle Tom Mania: Slavery, Minstrelsy, and Transatlantic Culture in the 1850s* (Athens: University of Georgia Press, 2005), 30–50.

92. *Blackwood's Edinburgh Magazine*, 398.

93. Stowe, *Uncle Tom's Cabin*, 77–79.

94. Ibid., 48.

95. Ibid., 82.

96. Ibid., 81–82.

97. See Glenda Carpio, *Laughing Fit to Kill: Black Humor in the Fictions of Slavery* (Oxford: Oxford University Press, 2008), 29–71.

98. Stowe, *Uncle Tom's Cabin*, 177, 251.

99. Mark Maslan makes this comparison in *Whitman Possessed: Poetry, Sexuality, and Popular Authority* (Baltimore: Johns Hopkins University Press, 2001), 205 n. 14.

100. Lora Romero, *Home Fronts: Domesticity and Its Critics in the Antebellum United States* (Durham, NC: Duke University Press, 1997), 84.

101. Stowe, *Uncle Tom's Cabin*, 384.

102. Wood, *Blind Memory*, 250–52; David Luis-Brown, "An 1848 for the Americas: The Black Atlantic, 'El negro mártir,' and Cuban Exile Anticolonialism in New York

City," *American Literary History* 21.3 (2009): 431–63. On Gordon and Bogle, see Henry Bleby, *The Reign of Terror* (London: William Nichols, 1868), 94–95; "The Jamaica Insurrection," Philadelphia *Friends' Review* 19 (December 30, 1865): 282–83; and David King, "A Sketch of the Late Mr. G. W. Gordon," Edinburgh *United Presbyterian Magazine* 10 (May 1866): 195. On Placido, see Robert S. Levine, *Martin Delany, Frederick Douglass, and the Politics of Representative Identity* (Chapel Hill: University of North Carolina Press, 1997), 204–5.

103. Franklin Benjamin Sanborn, *Life and Letters of John Brown* (Boston: Roberts Brothers, 1885), 1. Also see Franny Nudelman, *John Brown's Body: Slavery, Violence, and the Culture of War* (Chapel Hill: University of North Carolina Press, 2004), 42; Stephen B. Oates, *To Purge This Land with Blood: A Biography of John Brown* (New York: Harper & Row, 1972), 41–42.

104. August H. Nimtz, *Marx, Tocqueville and Race in America: The "Absolute Democracy" or "Defiled Republic"* (Lanham, MD: Lexington Books, 2003), 70; Benjamin Quarles, *Black Abolitionists* (New York: Oxford University Press, 1969), 242–43; Victor B. Howard, *Conscience and Slavery: The Evangelic Calvinist Domestic Missions, 1837–1861* (Kent, OH: Kent State University Press, 1990), 172–75; James Redpath, *Echoes of Harper's Ferry* (Boston: Thayer and Eldridge, 1860), 8.

105. Susan M. Ryan, "Charity Begins at Home: Stowe's Antislavery Novels and the Forms of Benevolent Citizenship," *American Literature* 72.4 (2000): 751–82.

106. Stowe, *Uncle Tom's Cabin*, 440–43, 117–18.

107. As Stowe's metonymic "good steamer Cincinnati" indicates, *Uncle Tom's Cabin* presents Cincinnati and, by extension, the American West as a temporary transitional space to educate slaves. For Stowe's location of African Americans in the national body, see Karen Sánchez-Eppler, *Touching Liberty: Abolition, Feminism, and the Politics of the Body* (Berkeley: University of California Press, 1993), 47–48; Michelle Burnham, *Captivity and Sentiment: Cultural Exchange in American Literature, 1682–1861* (Hanover, NH: University Press of New England, 1997), 146.

108. Stowe, *Uncle Tom's Cabin*, 442.

109. Nancy Bentley, "White Slaves: The Mulatto Hero in Antebellum Fiction," *American Literature* 65.3 (1993): 502.

110. Jean Fagan Yellin, "Doing It Herself: Uncle Tom's Cabin and Woman's Role in the Slavery Crisis," in *New Essays on* Uncle Tom's Cabin, ed. Eric Sundquist (Cambridge: Cambridge University Press, 1986), 85–106.

Chapter 4

1. Harry Oosterhuis, *Stepchildren of Nature: Krafft-Ebing, Psychiatry, and the Making of Sexual Identity* (Chicago: University of Chicago Press, 2000), 146–91, 202, 223–37; "Krafft-Ebing: Neue Forschungen auf dem Gebiet der Psychopathia sexualis," *Centralblatt für Nervenheilkunde und Psychiatrie* 15 (July 1892): 335; Wladimir Russalkow,

Grausamkeit und Verbrechen im Sexuellen Leben: Historisch-psychologische Studien (Budapest: For the Author): 57.

2. See, e.g., Freud and Jung's *Jahrbuch für Psychoanalytische und Psychopathologische Forschungen* 5 (1913): 468–69, 497. For earlier generations of critics, the presence of *Uncle Tom's Cabin* in sexological and psychoanalytic accounts of masochism was, at best, a curiosity. It signaled, if anything, the way in which a novel's worldwide popularity made it available to all sorts of misreading. But, as we have already seen, humanitarian abolition helped structure desirable erotic suffering by proliferating scenes of slave suffering that developed deterministic notions of racial difference as "deep," internal, and affective. Critics have argued that the novel's popularity among white men depended precisely on its ability to evoke fears of social humiliation, displace them on to black men, and shift those fears from an economic framework into a spiritual one. The masochist, in this reading, exposes the logic of sadomasochism underlying both Stowe's work and nineteenth-century U.S. white male life. See, e.g., David Leverenz, *Manhood and the American Renaissance* (Ithaca, NY: Cornell University Press, 1989), 200; Walter Benn Michaels, *The Gold Standard and the Logic of Naturalism: American Literature at the Turn of the Century* (Berkeley: University of California Press, 1987), 115–16. On *Uncle Tom's Cabin* in sexological and early psychoanalytic literature, see Halttunen, "Humanitarianism and the Pornography of Pain in Anglo-American Culture," 331; Marianne Noble, "The Ecstasies of Sentimental Wounding in *Uncle Tom's Cabin*," *Yale Journal of Criticism* 10.2 (1997): 295–96; Noble, *The Masochistic Pleasures of Sentimental Literature* (Princeton, NJ: Princeton University Press, 2000), 126–27; Wood, *Blind Memory*, 184–85, 260–63.

3. Noble, *Masochistic Pleasures*, 128–29.

4. This specificity may also be reinforced by the enduring popularity of *Uncle Tom's Cabin* as a childhood "classic," as modern Anglophone critics implicitly or explicitly embed their interpretations in their own youthful reading experiences of standardized U.S. and U.K. editions. See, e.g., Laura Wexler's personal account in *Tender Violence: Domestic Visions in an Age of U.S. Imperialism* (Chapel Hill: University of North Carolina Press, 2000), 98.

5. "Dass ein Mensch den andern besitzen, verkaufen, prügeln könne, regte mich ungemein auf, und bei der Lektüre von 'Onkel Tom's Hütte' (welches Werk ich etwa zur Zeit den eintretenden Pubertät las), hatte ich Erectionen." Richard von Krafft-Ebing, *Psychopathia Sexualis*, 10th ed. (Stuttgart: Ferdinand Enke Verlag, 1892), 106; Richard von Krafft-Ebing, *Psychopathia Sexualis, with Especial Reference to Contrary Sexual Instinct: A Medico-Legal Study*, 7th ed., trans. Gilbert Chaddock (Philadelphia: F. A. Davis, 1894), 105.

6. Though my focus here is on early masochism's political valence, the plurality of early masochisms bears out the commonsense suggestion, in recent queer and critical race studies, that masochism and "ethical" antisocial acts or performances such as "self-shattering" can hold radically different political potentials for differently situated subjects.

7. Edward Said, "Traveling Theory," in *The World, the Text, and the Critic* (Cambridge, MA: Harvard University Press, 1983), 226–30; Edward Said, "Travelling Theory Reconsidered," in *Reflections on Exile and Other Essays* (Cambridge, MA: Harvard University Press, 2000). On abolitionist contestations of geographic stability, see Martha Schoolman, *Abolitionist Geographies* (Minneapolis: University of Minnesota Press, 2014).

8. "Extract from a Letter from the late Thomas Watts, Esq., Librarian of the British Museum, to Professor Stowe," in Harriet Beecher Stowe, *The Writings of Harriet Beecher Stowe*, 2 vols. (Boston: Houghton, Mifflin and Co., 1896), 2:456–76; the letter was also published in Kate Brannon Knight, *History of the Work of Connecticut Women at the World's Columbian Exposition, Chicago, 1893* (Hartford, CT: Hartford Press, 1898), 93–123. On the U.S. publication history of *Uncle Tom's Cabin*, see Michael Winship, "The Library of Congress in 1892: Ainsworth Spofford, Houghton, Mifflin and Company, and *Uncle Tom's Cabin*," *Libraries & the Cultural Record* 45.1 (2010): 85–91. On dramatic and other popular interpretations of Stowe's novel, see Stephen A. Hirsch, "Uncle Tomitudes: The Popular Reaction to *Uncle Tom's Cabin*," in *Studies in the American Renaissance*, ed. Joel Meyerson (Boston: Twayne, 1978), 303–30; Bluford Adams, *E Pluribus Barnum: The Great Showman and the Making of U.S. Popular Culture* (Minneapolis: University of Minnesota Press, 1997), 130–63; Bruce McConachie, "Out of the Kitchen and into the Marketplace: Normalizing *Uncle Tom's Cabin* for the Antebellum Stage," *Journal of American Drama and Theatre* 1 (Winter 1991): 24; Bruce McConachie, *Melodramatic Formations: American Theatre and Society, 1820–1870* (Iowa City: University of Iowa Press, 1992); David Grimsted, "Uncle Tom from Page to Stage: Limitations of Nineteenth-Century Drama," *Quarterly Journal of Speech* 56 (October 1970): 235–44.

9. Sarah Meer, *Uncle Tom Mania: Slavery, Minstrelsy, and Transatlantic Culture in the 1850s* (Athens: University of Georgia Press, 2005); Audrey A. Fisch, *American Slaves in Victorian England: Abolitionist Politics in Popular Literature and Culture* (Cambridge: Cambridge University Press, 2000). On James, see Robin Bernstein's *Racial Innocence: Performing American Childhood from Slavery to Civil Rights* (New York: New York University Press, 2011), 99–100.

10. Heike Paul, "'Schwarze Sklaven, Weisse Sklaven': The German Reception of Harriet Beecher Stowe's *Uncle Tom's Cabin*," in *Amerikanische Populärkultur in Deutschland*, ed. Heike Paul and Katja Kanzler (Leipzig: Leipziger Universitätsverlag, 2002), 21–40.

11. Marion Wilson Starling, *The Slave Narrative: Its Place in American History* (Washington, DC: Howard University Press, 1988), 28–30.

12. On patients and their roles, see Oosterhuis, 129–208, especially 201.

13. Frederick Merk, *Manifest Destiny and Mission in American History: A Reinterpretation* (New York: Alfred A. Knopf, 1963), 195–201; Michael Paul Rogin, *Subversive Genealogy: The Politics and Art of Herman Melville* (New York: Alfred A. Knopf, 1983), 20–21; Larry J. Reynolds, *European Revolutions and the American Literary Renaissance*

(New Haven, CT: Yale University Press, 1988); Larry J. Reynolds, *Righteous Violence: Revolution, Slavery, and the American Renaissance* (Athens: University of Georgia Press, 2011), especially 38–55, Eric Sundquist, *To Wake the Nations: Race in the Making of American Literature* (Cambridge, MA: Belknap Press of Harvard University Press, 1993), 93–134.

14. The history of German and German American engagement with *Uncle Tom's Cabin* has been generally recognized since the early twentieth century and more recently developed by Heike Paul, but perhaps because many psychoanalytic readings isolate the erotic from the political, this history has not been considered a significant precedent for early masochism.

15. Late twentieth-century feminist and lesbian-feminist debates about contemporary masochism's staging of historical violence replicate this nineteenth-century dialogue between sentimental and parodic/imitative constructions of race and gender.

16. "Auch meine masochistischen Neigungen haben nichts, was weiblich oder weibisch zu nennen ware (?)." Krafft-Ebing, *Psychopathia Sexualis*, 10th ed., 96.

17. "Allerdings ist hierbei die Neigung vorherrschend, vom Weibe gesucht und begehrt zu werden, doch ist das allgemeine Verhältniss zur 'Herrin', wie es herbeigesehnt wird, nicht das, in welchem das Weib zum Manne steht, sondern das Verhältniss des Sklaven zum Herrn, das des Hausthieres zu seinem Besitzer." *Psychopathia Sexualis*, 10th ed., 96.

18. Sander L. Gilman, *Difference and Pathology: Stereotypes of Sexuality, Race, and Madness* (Ithaca, NY: Cornell University Press, 1985); Sander L. Gilman, "Black Bodies, White Bodies: Toward an Iconography of Female Sexuality in Late Nineteenth-Century Art, Medicine, and Literature," *Critical Inquiry* 12 (Autumn 1985): 204–38; Nancy Leys Stepan, "Race and Gender: The Role of Analogy in Science," *Isis* 77.2 (1986): 261–77; Nancy Leys Stepan and Sander L. Gilman, "Appropriating the Idioms of Science: The Rejection of Scientific Racism," in *The Bounds of Race: Perspectives on Hegemony and Resistance*, ed. Dominick LaCapra (Ithaca, NY: Cornell University Press, 1991), 72–103.

19. Joseph Roach, *Cities of the Dead: Circum-Atlantic Performance* (New York: Columbia University Press, 1996), 25–26.

20. Robert Reid-Pharr, *Conjugal Union: The Body, the House, and the Black American* (New York: Oxford University Press, 1999), 95–97.

21. Krafft-Ebing, *Psychopathia Sexualis*, 12th German ed., trans. Franklin Klaf (New York: Arcade, 1998), 87.

22. David Brion Davis, *The Problem of Slavery in Western Culture* (Ithaca, NY: Cornell University Press, 1966).

23. Even pets, since the rise of the Society for the Prevention of Cruelty to Animals and like-minded organizations, were increasingly covered by laws and social norms discouraging cruelty.

24. "Würde sie bis zu den alten Gesellschaften herunter gesetzt haben, in denen der Grundsatz galt, daß ein Mensch den andern besitzen konnte." Michel Chevalier, *Briefe*

über Nord-Amerika (Leipzig: Philipp Reclam Verlag, 1837), 4:175, originally Michel Chevalier, *Lettres sur L'Amerique du Nord* (1836). My translation from Michael Chevalier, *Society, Manners and Politics in the United States* (Boston: Weeks, Jordan and Co., 1839).

25. Gilles Deleuze, "Coldness and Cruelty," in *Masochism: Coldness and Cruelty and Venus in Furs*, trans. Jean McNeil (New York: Zone Books, 1989), 70.

26. Bertolt Brecht, *Brecht on Theatre: The Development of an Aesthetic*, ed. and trans. John Willett (New York: Hill & Wang, 1964), 91–99.

27. David Paul Nord, *Faith in Reading: Religious Publishing and the Birth of Mass Media in America* (New York: Oxford University Press, 2004), 83–89; John R. McKivigan, *The War Against Proslavery Religion: Abolitionism and the Northern Churches, 1830–1865* (Ithaca, NY: Cornell University Press, 1984); Bertram Wyatt-Brown, *Lewis Tappan and the Evangelical War against Slavery* (Baton Rouge: Louisiana State University Press, 1969).

28. Joan D. Hedrick, *Harriet Beecher Stowe: A Life* (New York: Oxford University Press, 1994), 334; Harriet Beecher Stowe, *Uncle Tom's Cabin, Illustrated Edition* (Boston: John P. Jewett, 1853).

29. William Hendry Stowell, "Uncle Tom's Cabin and Its Opponents," *Eclectic Review* 96.4 (1852): 720.

30. Harriet Beecher Stowe, "Préface de Madame Beecher Stowe pour Cette Nouvelle Traduction de Son Livre," *La Case de L'Oncle Tom*, trans. L. Sw. Belloc (Paris: Libraire-Éditeur, 1853), i–vi; Sherry Simon, *Gender in Translation: Cultural Identity and the Politics of Transmission* (New York: Routledge, 1996), 60. On Stowe's prefaces, also see Claire Parfait, *The Publishing History of Uncle Tom's Cabin, 1852–2002* (Burlington, VT: Ashgate, 2007), 64–66.

31. On Cruikshank, see Wood, *Blind Memory*, 182–205.

32. Stowe, *Uncle Tom's Cabin* (Paris: Baudry's European Library, 1853). On *Pictures of Slavery in the United States*, see Jo-Ann Morgan, *Uncle Tom's Cabin as Visual Culture* (Columbia: University of Missouri Press, 2007), 45.

33. In 1905, the Boston public library circulated Hamburg, Nürnberg, Pest, Leipzig, and Vienna editions from 1853 and later editions from Leipzig (1878) and Stuttgart (1881).

34. See Franz Hoffman, *Loango, eine Negergeschichte für de Jungend* (Stuttgart: Schmidt & Spring, 1845); Gerhard Anton von Halem, "Zimeo, eine Negergeschichte," *Geschichte und Politik* 9 (1802), rpt. *Der Sammler* 1 (1809): 317–19, 325–28. Thanks to Katherine Gaudet for pointing out that these stories resuscitated the "Loango" and "Ziamo" or "Zimeo" tales circulating in the late eighteenth century, including "Ziamo, The African" in *The Ladies Magazine and Musical Repository* (October 1801): 203; "The Death of Loango," *Massachusetts Magazine* III (February 1791): 115; "Zimeo: A Tale," *American Museum* VI (November 1789): 317–73. For some discussion of this tradition, see Mukhtar Ali Isani, "Far from 'Gambia's Golden Shore': The Black in the Late Eighteenth-Century American Imaginative Literature," *William and Mary Quarterly* 36.3 (1979): 353–72.

35. Grace Edith MacLean, *"Uncle Tom's Cabin" in Germany* (New York: D. Appleton & Co., 1910), 22; Heike Paul, *Kulturkontakt und Racial Presences: Afro-Amerikaner und die deutsche Amerika-Literatur, 1815–1914* (Heidelberg: C. Winter, 2005); Paul, "'Schwarze Sklaven, Weisse Sklaven,'" 30.

36. "The Effect of Uncle Tom in Europe," Brooklyn, May 7, 1853, excerpted from the *New York Herald*, http://utc.iath.virginia.edu/notices/noar107it.html.

37. See Philip J. Deloria, *Playing Indian* (New Haven, CT: Yale University Press, 1998).

38. On Stowe's millennialism, see Hedrick, 148–50.

39. E.g., her 1853 tour of Germany included a "pilgrimage" to Erfurt, culminating in what Charles Beecher, attempting to place Stowe firmly in a reformist tradition, described as her reverent handling of Luther's "pocket testament and inkstand" (Hedrick, 250).

40. For Stowe's investment in authorial character, see Susan M. Ryan, "Stowe, Byron, and the Art of Scandal," *American Literature* 83 (2011): 59–91; Gérard Genette, *Paratexts: Thresholds of Interpretation*, trans. Jane E. Lewin (Cambridge: Cambridge University Press, 1997), 196–236.

41. Stowe, *Uncle Tom's Cabin* (Boston: Houghton, Mifflin, 1890), xxi.

42. Stowe, "Preface to the European Edition," *Life of Harriet Beecher Stowe: Compiled from Her Letters and Journals*, ed. Charles Edwards Stowe (Boston: Houghton Mifflin. 1889), 192–95.

43. See *Onkel Tom's Hütte; oder, Negerleben in den Sklavenstaaten von Nord-Amerika, mit 40 Illustrationen* (Leipzig: J. J. Weber, 1853), vii–viii; *Onkel Tom's Hütte, oder, die Geschichte eines christlichen Sklaven*, trans. L. Du Bois (Stuttgart: Franck, 1853).

44. Donald Spencer, *Louis Kossuth and Young America: A Study of Sectionalism and Foreign Policy, 1848–1852* (Columbia: University of Missouri Press, 1977); Michael A. Morrison, "American Reaction to European Revolutions, 1848–1852: Sectionalism, Memory, and the Revolutionary Heritage," *Civil War History* 49 (2003): 111–32; Edwards Stone, "Kossuth's Hat: Foreign Militants and the American Muse," *ESQ: A Journal of the American Renaissance* 23 (1977): 36–40; "The End of Enthusiasm: Lajos Kossuth's American Descent," in *The Oxford Handbook of Transcendentalism*, ed. Joel Myerson et al. (New York: Oxford University Press, 2010), 81–82.

45. Mitch Kachun, "'Our Platform Is as Broad as Humanity': Transatlantic Freedom Movements and the Idea of Progress in Nineteenth-Century African American Thought and Activism," *Slavery and Abolition* 24.3 (2003): 1–23.

46. R. J. M. Blackett, *Building an Antislavery Wall: Black Americans in the Atlantic Abolitionist Movement, 1830–1860* (Baton Rouge: Louisiana State University Press, 1983), 10–12.

47. William Lloyd Garrison, *Letter to Louis Kossuth: Concerning Freedom and Slavery in the United States* (Boston: American Anti-Slavery Society, 1852), 7.

48. George Templeton Strong, *Diary: The Turbulent Fifties, 1850–1859* (New York:

Macmillan, 1952), 76. Alan Johnson, "Magyar-Mania in New York City: Louis Kossuth and American Politics," *New-York Historical Society Quarterly* 48 (1964): 237–49.

49. Susan M. Ryan, *The Grammar of Good Intentions: Race and the Antebellum Culture of Benevolence* (Ithaca, NY: Cornell University Press, 2003), 150–53.

50. Werner Sollors, *Neither Black nor White Yet Both: Thematic Explorations of Interracial Literature* (New York: Oxford University Press, 1997), 208–12.

51. On "mixed-race" fantasy in psychoanalytic literature, see Hiram Perez, "Two or Three Spectacular Mulatas and the Queer Pleasures of Overidentification," *Camera Obscura* 23.1 67 (2008): 120–21.

52. Richard Hildreth, *The White Slave: Another Picture of Slave Life in America* (London: George Routledge, 1852), 197.

53. Paul, "Schwartze Sklaven," 29–31.

54. Maclean, 23–24.

55. Hedrick, 119–23.

56. Harriet Beecher Stowe, *Onkel Tom's Hütte, oder: Leben unter den Verstossnen*, trans. Adolf Strodtmann (Philadelphia: F. W. Thomas Verlag, 1853). On Stowe's lawsuit, see Melissa J. Homestead, *American Women Authors and Literary Property, 1822–1869* (London: Cambridge University Press, 2005), 105–49, and Hedrick, 333.

57. Paul, "Schwartze Sklaven," 23–28.

58. Friedrich Wilhelm Hackländer, *Clara, or, Slave Life in Europe* (New York: Harper & Brothers, 1856), 56; Maclean, 61.

59. Diane Roberts, *The Myth of Aunt Jemima: Representations of Race and Region* (New York: Routledge, 1994), 228, 51–53.

60. On the development of abolitionist scenes of suffering alongside other nineteenth-century subgenres, see Colette Colligan, "Anti-Abolition Writes Obscenity: The English Vice, Transatlantic Slavery, and England's Obscene Print Culture," in *International Exposure: Perspectives on Modern European Pornography, 1800–2000*, ed. Lisa Z. Sigel (New Brunswick, NJ: Rutgers University Press, 2005), 67–99; Halttunen, *Murder Most Foul*, 68; J. V. Ridgely, "George Lippard's *The Quaker City*: The World of the American Porno-Gothic," *Studies in the Literary Imagination* 7 (Spring 1974): 77–94; Ian Gibson, *The English Vice, Beating, Sex and Shame in Victorian England and After* (London: Duckworth, 1978); Stephen Marcus, *The Other Victorians: A Study of Sexuality and Pornography in Mid-Nineteenth-Century England* (New York: Basic Books, 1966); Wood, *Blind Memory*, 44–45, 189–90; Glenda Carpio, *Laughing Fit to Kill: Black Humor in the Fictions of Slavery* (New York: Oxford University Press, 2008), 137.

61. Thomas Laqueur, "Bodies, Details and the Humanitarian Narrative," in *The New Cultural History* (Berkeley: University of California Press, 1989), 176–204.

62. Halttunen, "Humanitarianism and the Pornography of Pain in Anglo-American Culture," 304.

63. Ibid., 327.

64. Horace Moulton in Theodore Weld, *American Slavery as It Is: Testimony of a Thousand Witnesses* (New York: American Anti-Slavery Society, 1839), 20.

65. Laqueur, "Bodies, Details and the Humanitarian Narrative," 183; Halttunen, *Murder Most Foul*, 83.

66. Halttunen, "Humanitarianism and the Pornography of Pain in Anglo-American Culture," passim; Wood, *Slavery, Empathy, and Pornography*, 87–140; Wood, *Blind Memory*, 215–41; Mario Klarer, "Humanitarian Pornography: John Gabriel Stedman's Narrative of a Five Years Expedition Against the Revolting Negroes of Surinam (1796)," *New Literary History* 36.4 (2005): 559–87.

67. On colonial newspapers and slavery, see Robert E. Desrochers, Jr., "Slave-for-Sale Advertisements and Slavery in Massachusetts, 1704–1781," *William and Mary Quarterly* 59.3 (July 2002): 623–64.

68. See Halttunen, "Humanitarianism and the Pornography of Pain in Anglo-American Culture," 332.

69. Angelina Grimké, in Weld, *American Slavery as It Is*, 53.

70. Ibid., 327–30.

71. Weld, *American Slavery*, 7. On juridical metaphor in abolitionist writing, see Jeannine DeLombard, "'Eye-Witness to the Cruelty': Southern Violence and Northern Testimony in Frederick Douglass's 1845 *Narrative*," *American Literature* 73.2 (2001): 245–75.

72. Gilbert Hobbs Barnes, *The Antislavery Impulse, 1830–1844* (New York: Harcourt, 1964), 231.

73. On the mutual development of female debasement in urban Gothic fiction and slave narrative, see Jennifer Rae Greeson, "The 'Mysteries and Miseries' of North Carolina: New York City, Urban Gothic Fiction, and Incidents in the Life of a Slave Girl," *American Literature* 73.2 (2001): 277–309.

74. See Augusta Rohrbach, "'Truth Stronger and Stranger Than Fiction': Reexamining William Lloyd Garrison's *Liberator*," *American Literature* 73.4 (2001): 727–55.

75. Noble, *Masochistic Pleasures*, 128–29.

76. It is not incidental that this passage invoking the "real presence" culminates in Stowe's direct address of Southern white men as "brothers" whose "noble and generous hearts" should overcome "state interest." Among the most important readers Stowe could hope to transform were those Southern whites who would peremptorily reject sensational representations of slave suffering. Harriet Beecher Stowe, *Uncle Tom's Cabin* (New York: Oxford University Press, 1998), 94–95.

77. Christopher Castiglia, *Interior States: Institutional Consciousness and the Inner Life of Democracy in the Antebellum United States* (Durham, NC: Duke University Press, 2008), 101–35.

78. Elizabeth B. Clark, "'The Sacred Rights of the Weak': Pain, Sympathy, and the Culture of Individual Rights in Antebellum America," *Journal of American History* 82.2 (1995): 475.

79. Some passages offered increasingly detailed descriptions of the process of sympathetic feeling. Quaker Elizabeth Margaret Chandler presents an early representative example of this sort of instruction in her 1836 *Essays,* where she directs the reader to imaginatively "let the fetter lie with its weight upon their wrists" and feel "the successive strokes of the keen thong fall upon their shoulders till the flesh rises in long welts beneath it, and the spouting blood follows every blow." Other authors attempted to encourage readers to act against slavery by narrating characters' transformations from passive witness to active agent. See Elizabeth Margaret Chandler, *Essays, Philanthropic and Moral, Principally Relating to the Abolition of Slavery in America* (1836), 117–18, in Franny Nudleman, "'The Blood of Millions': John Brown's Body, Public Violence, and Political Community," *American Literary History* 13 (Winter 2001): 645.

80. On Stowe's plantation Gothic, see Leonard Cassuto, *The Inhuman Race: The Racial Grotesque in American Literature and Culture* (New York: Columbia University Press, 1997), 159–60.

81. See Susan Wolstenholme, *Gothic (Re)Visions: Writing Women as Readers* (Albany: State University of New York Press, 1993).

82. Stowe, *A Key to Uncle Tom's Cabin* (Boston: John P. Jewett & Co., 1853).

83. Noble, *Masochistic Pleasures,* 129–39. See Jean Laplanche, *Life and Death in Psychoanalysis* (Baltimore: Johns Hopkins University Press, 1976), and "Masochism and the General Theory of Seduction," *Essays on Otherness* (New York: Routledge, 1999), 197–213.

84. See Halttunen, "Humanitarianism and the Pornography of Pain in Anglo-American Culture," passim; Wood, *Blind Memory*; Mario Klarer, "Humanitarian Pornography: John Gabriel Stedman's *Narrative of a Five Years Expedition Against the Revolting Negroes of Surinam* (1796)," *New Literary History* 36.4 (2005): 559–87.

85. Saidiya Hartman, *Scenes of Subjection: Terror, Slavery, and Self-Making in Nineteenth-Century America* (New York: Oxford University Press, 1997), 27; Eric Lott, *Love and Theft: Blackface Minstrelsy and the American Working Class* (New York: Oxford University Press, 1993), especially 211–33; David R. Roediger, *The Wages of Whiteness: Race and the Making of the American Working Class* (New York: Verso Books, 1999), 123; Linda Williams, *Playing the Race Card: Melodramas of Black and White from Uncle Tom to O.J.* (Princeton, NJ: Princeton University Press, 2002).

86. Tavia Nyong'o, *The Amalgamation Waltz: Race, Performance, and the Ruses of Memory* (Minneapolis: University of Minnesota Press, 2009), 103–7.

87. On German song, see Thomas L. Riis, "The Music and Musicians in Nineteenth-Century Productions of *Uncle Tom's Cabin,*" *American Music* 4.3 (1986): 268–86.

88. Stowe, *Uncle Tom's Cabin,* 248–50. Stowe's wedding of "entertaining" black suffering with "high" sentiment serves, in Hartman's words, to "set the stage" for minstrel performances that "wed cruelty and festivity" (Hartman, 27).

89. Harriet Jacobs, *Incidents in the Life of a Slave Girl* (Boston: For the Author, 1861), 83–84.

90. Karen Sanchez-Eppler, *Touching Liberty: Abolition, Feminism, and the Politics of the Body* (Berkeley: University of California Press, 1993), 133–41.

91. "Uncle Tom's Cabin in England," *Frederick Douglass' Paper*, December 31, 1852.

Epilogue

1. On legal accounts of cabin boys and rape, see Jonathan Ned Katz, *Love Stories: Sex Between Men Before Homosexuality* (Chicago: University of Chicago Press, 2001), 70. On cabin boys, eroticism, and cannibalism, see Howard L. Malchow, *Gothic Images of Race in Nineteenth Century Britain* (Stanford, CA: Stanford University Press, 1996), 100–101.

2. Child's technique was honed in her editing of the influential children's magazine *Juvenile Miscellany* (1826–34).

3. Lydia Maria Child, *The Oasis* (Boston: Benjamin C. Bacon, 1834), 139.

4. For a broader picture of incestuous and other dangerous intimacies, see Brian Connolly, *Domestic Intimacies: Incest and the Liberal Subject in Nineteenth-Century America* (Philadelphia: University of Pennsylvania Press, 2014).

5. Amy Kaplan, *The Anarchy of Empire in the Making of U.S. Culture* (Cambridge, MA: Harvard University Press, 2002), 41–50. Also see Carolyn Karcher, "Rape, Murder and Revenge in 'Slavery's Pleasant Homes': Lydia Maria Child's Antislavery Fiction and the Limits of Genre," *Women's Studies International Forum* 9.4 (1986): 323–32; Joy Kasson, "Mind in Matter in History: Viewing The Greek Slave," *Yale Journal of Criticism* 11.1 (Spring 1998): 79–83.

6. Louise E. Robbins, *Elephant Slaves and Pampered Parrots: Exotic Animals in Eighteenth-Century Paris* (Baltimore: Johns Hopkins University Press, 2002), 190–205; Yi-Fu Tuan, *Dominance and Affection: The Making of Pets* (New Haven, CT: Yale University Press, 1984), 132–61.

7. Srinivas Aravamudan, *Tropicopolitans: Colonialism and Agency, 1688-1804* (Durham, NC: Duke University Press, 1999), 30–49.

8. Thomas Jefferson, "Notes on Virginia," in *The Writings of Thomas Jefferson*, ed. H. A. Washington (New York: Derby, 1861), 8:382. See Robin Bernstein, *Racial Innocence: Performing American Childhood from Slavery to Civil Rights* (New York: New York University Press, 2011), 50.

9. Jennifer Mason, *Civilized Creatures: Urban Animals, Sentimental Culture, and American Literature, 1850-1900* (Baltimore: Johns Hopkins University Press, 2005), 123–28, 212.

10. E.g., in *Typee*, missionary reform and, in *White-Jacket*, naval reform.

11. Pip is black in a different way from Dagoo, the African sailor, who is marked by his independence.

12. Boston *Daily Times* review of *Pierre*, cited in Hershel Parker, *Herman Melville: A Biography, Vol. 2, 1851-1891* (Baltimore: Johns Hopkins University Press, 2002), 632.

13. C. L. R. James, *Mariners, Renegades and Castaways: The Story of Herman Melville and the World We Live In* (1985; repr., Hanover, NH: Dartmouth College Press, 2001), 57.

14. John Stauffer, "Interracial Friendship," in *Frederick Douglass & Herman Melville: Essays in Relation*, ed. Robert Levine and Samuel Otter (Chapel Hill: University of North Carolina Press, 2008).

15. Herman Melville, *Moby-Dick, or The Whale*, ed. Harrison Hayford, Hershel Parker, and G. Thomas Tanselle (Evanston and Chicago: Northwestern University Press and Newberry Library, 1988), 522. On Ahab and Lear, see Lawrance Thompson, *Melville's Quarrel with God* (Princeton, NJ: Princeton University Press, 1952), 228; Merton M. Sealts, Jr., "Melville and the Platonic Tradition," in Sealts, *Pursuing Melville, 1940–1980: Chapters and Essays* (Madison: University of Wisconsin Press, 1982), 287; Julian Markels, *Melville and the Politics of Identity: From* King Lear *to* Moby-Dick (Urbana: University of Illinois Press, 1993), 62–65

16. Melville, *Moby-Dick,* 64.

17. Ibid., 534.

18. Roxann Wheeler, *The Complexion of Race: Categories of Difference in Eighteenth Century British Culture* (Philadelphia: University of Pennsylvania Press, 2000), 52; Toni Morrison, *Playing in the Dark: Whiteness and the Literary Imagination* (Cambridge, MA: Harvard University Press, 1992).

19. As Werner Sollors argued, nineteenth-century Indian plays such as Stone's *Metamora*, which depicted dying Indians' transmission of the land to sympathetic whites, developed a different form of willed or providential submission. For a discussion of late eighteenth- and early nineteenth-century uses of providential slavery in proslavery and emigrationist abolitionist writing, see John Saillant, "Slavery and Divine Providence in New England Calvinism: The New Divinity and a Black Protest, 1775–1805," *New England Quarterly* 68.4 (1995): 584–608.

20. Peter Hulme, *Colonial Encounters: Europe and the Native Caribbean, 1492–1797* (New York: Routledge, 1986), 205–16; George Boulukos, *The Grateful Slave: The Emergence of Race in Eighteenth-Century British and American Culture* (Cambridge: Cambridge University Press, 2012), 22–24.

21. Gardner, *Master Plots*, 51.

22. On Backus, see "The Hubbard Copy of *The Whale*," in Melville, *Moby-Dick,* 1012–13.

23. Melville, *Moby-Dick,* 414. On utopian potential, see Peter Coviello, *Intimacy in America: Dreams of Affiliation in Antebellum Literature* (Minneapolis: University of Minnesota Press, 2005), 114–15.

24. Melville, *Moby-Dick,* 522, 479.

25. Ibid., 414. For this reading of Melville and Kantian sublimity in a theological and philosophical context, see Richard Kearney, in *Questioning God*, ed. John D. Caputo (Bloomington: Indiana University Press, 2001), 166.

26. John Tchen, *New York Before Chinatown: Orientalism and the Shaping of American Culture, 1776–1882* (Baltimore: Johns Hopkins University Press, 1999).

27. James, *Mariners, Renegades and Castaways*, 56; Melville, *Moby-Dick*, 154. Black and white Americans both engaged in extensive Oriental imaginings, with white Orientalism responding to black claims about Egyptian cultural heritage. Eighteenth- and nineteenth-century "black Orientalism" includes affiliational Egyptology and Masonic ritual as well as moralistic condemnations of Chinese and Turkish sensuality and tyranny. See Helen H. Jun, "Black Orientalism: Nineteenth-Century Narratives of Race and U.S. Citizenship," *American Quarterly* 58.4 (2006), 1047–66; Scott Trafton, *Egypt Land: Race and Nineteenth-Century American Egyptomania* (Durham, NC: Duke University Press, 2004).

28. Ussama Makdisi, *Artillery of Heaven: American Missionaries and the Failed Conversion of the Middle East* (Ithaca, NY: Cornell University Press, 2007), 72–103.

29. In *Pierre*, Melville, with due irony, charts the outcome of this path for the eponymous hero, who moves away from reform and toward a novel that might "gospelize the world anew." See Priscilla Wald, "Hearing Narrative Voices in Melville's *Pierre*," *boundary 2* 17.1 (1990): 100–132.

30. James Baird, *Ishmael* (Baltimore: Johns Hopkins Press, 1956), xv; Jenny Franchot, "Melville's Traveling God," in *The Cambridge Companion to Herman Melville*, ed. Robert S. Levine (Cambridge: Cambridge University Press, 1998), 157–85. Also see Dorothée Finkelstein, *Melville's Orienda* (New Haven, CT: Yale University Press, 1961).

31. Ruth Frankenberg and Lata Mani, "Crosscurrents, Crosstalk: Race, 'Post-Coloniality,' and the Politics of Location," *Cultural Studies* 7.2 (1993): 292–310; Malini Johar Schueller, *U.S. Orientalisms: Race, Nation, and Gender in Literature, 1790–1890* (Ann Arbor: University of Michigan Press, 1998), 130.

32. Etienne Balibar, "Difference, Otherness, Exclusion," *parallax* 11.1 (2005): 19–34.

33. Carolyn Karchner, *Shadow over the Promised Land: Slavery, Race and Violence in Melville's America* (Baton Rouge: Louisiana State University Press, 1980), 69–91.

34. On the "disappearing Indian" and racial metaphor, see Wai-chee Dimock, *Empire for Liberty: Melville and the Poetics of Individualism* (Princeton, NJ: Princeton University Press, 1989), 117; Patrick Brantlinger, *Dark Vanishings: Discourse on the Extinction of Primitive Races, 1800–1930* (Ithaca, NY: Cornell University Press, 2003). On the different political potentialities of the analogy between slavery and white-Indian life, see Ezra Tawil, *The Making of Racial Sentiment: Slavery and the Birth of the Frontier Romance* (Cambridge: Cambridge University Press, 2006).

35. Ernest J. Wilson III, "Orientalism: A Black Perspective," in *Orientalism: A Reader*, ed. Alexander Lyon Macfie (New York: New York University Press, 2000), 239–48; Heike Raphael-Hernandez and Shannon Steen, eds., *AfroAsian Encounters: Culture, History, Politics* (New York: New York University Press, 2006); Bill Mullen, *Afro-Orientalism* (Minneapolis: University of Minnesota Press, 2004).

36. Felicity Nussbaum, "Between 'Oriental' and 'Blacks, So Called,' 1688–1788," in

The Postcolonial Enlightenment: Eighteenth-century Colonialism and Postcolonial Theory, ed. Daniel Carey and Lynn Festa (New York: Oxford University Press, 2009), 145. Also see "Blackening 'the Turk' in Roger Ascham's *A Report of Germany* (1553)," in *Re-reading the 'Black Legend': Racial and Religious Discourses in the Renaissance Empires*, ed. Margaret Greer, Walter Mignolo, and Maureen Quilligan (Chicago: University of Chicago Press, 2007), 270–92.

37. Richard Nash, *Wild Enlightenment: The Borders of Human Identity in the Eighteenth Century* (Charlottesville: University Press of Virginia, 2003), 55–58; also see Julia Douthwaite, "*Homo ferus*: Between Monster and Model," *Eighteenth-Century Life* 21.2 (1997): 176–202; Adriana S. Benzaquén, *Encounters with Wild Children: Temptation and Disappointment in the Study of Human Nature* (Montreal: McGill-Queen's University Press, 2006); Felicity A. Nussbaum, *The Limits of the Human: Fictions of Anomaly, Race, and Gender in the Long Eighteenth Century* (Cambridge: Cambridge University Press, 2003).

38. On portraiture, see David Dabydeen, *Hogarth's Blacks: Images of Blacks in Eighteenth Century English Art* (Manchester: Manchester University Press, 1987), 23, 127; Yi-Fu Tuan, 132–61.

39. Wood, *Blind Memory*, 154–59. Also see Beth Fowkes Tobin, *Picturing Imperial Power: Colonial Subjects in Eighteenth-Century British Painting* (Durham, NC: Duke University Press, 1999).

40. "S.F. to Frederick Douglass," *The North Star*, October 3, 1850.

41. Sterling Stuckey, *African Culture and Melville's Art: The Creative Process in* Benito Cereno *and* Moby-Dick (New York: Oxford University Press, 2009), 33; Robert C. Toll, *Blacking Up: The Minstrel Show in Nineteenth-Century America* (New York: Oxford University Press, 1974), 172–98.

42. See *Urlina, the African Princess*, and the 1895 London panorama *The Orient*. Marian Hannah Winter, "Juba and American Minstrelsy," in *Inside the Minstrel Mask: Readings in Nineteenth-Century Blackface Minstrelsy*, ed. Annemarie Bean, James V. Hatch, and Brooks McNamara (Hanover, NH: Wesleyan University Press, 1996), 232.

43. Edward Said, *Orientalism: Western Conceptions of the Orient* (New York: Penguin, 1995), 6.

44. Joseph A. Boone, "Vacation Cruises; Or, the Homoerotics of Orientalism," *PMLA* 110.1 (1995): 89–107; Joseph Massad, *Desiring Arabs* (Chicago: University of Chicago Press, 2007), 11.

45. Bruce Harvey, in his elaboration of Nina Baym's "The Erotic Motif in Melville's *Clarel*," points to Burton as "explicitly nam[ing]" those sins that *Clarel's* Dead Sea, as the remnant of Sodom and Gomorrah, exemplifies in its absence. Bruce A. Harvey, *American Geographics: U.S. National Narratives and the Representation of the Non-European World, 1830–1865* (Stanford, CA: Stanford University Press, 2001), 141–42.

46. Stephen O. Murray, "Some Nineteenth-Century Reports of Islamic Homosexualities," in *Islamic Homosexualities: Culture, History, and Literature*, ed. Stephen O. Murray and Will Roscoe (New York: New York University Press, 1997), 217.

47. Michel Foucault, *The History of Sexuality, Vol. 1: An Introduction*, trans. Robert Hurley (New York: Pantheon, 1980), 43. In a similar manner, the critical focus on the distinction between Christian and non-Christian depends on the existence of "climate" as a truth outside of ideology. But sexuality, religion, and climate were historically made together. Earlier eras understood religious difference as, in part, a product of geography and made geography a sacred endeavor.

48. Eugene Schuyler, *Turkistan: Notes of a Journey in Russian Turkistan, Khokand, Bukhara, and Kuldja*, 2 vols. (New York: Scribner, Armstrong & Co. 1877), 1:131.

49. Ibid., 1:134–36.

50. Ibid., 1:133.

51. Ibid., 1:137.

52. On Melville and German Romanticism, see Christopher S. Durer, *Herman Melville, Romantic and Prophet: A Study of His Romantic Sensibility and His Relationship to European Romantics* (Toronto: York Press, 1996), 107–10; Anna Hellén, "Melville and the Temple of Literature," in *Melville "Among the Nations,"* ed. Sanford E. Marovitz et al. (Kent, OH: Kent State University Press, 2001), 335–38.

53. On the play's early staging and debts to Shakespeare, see Alan Leidner, "Introduction," in *Sturm und Drang*, ed. Alan C. Leidner (New York: Continuum, 1992), xiii.

54. Sander L. Gilman, "The Figure of the Black in German Aesthetic Theory," *Eighteenth-Century Studies* 8.4 (1975), 373–91; Rashid Pegah, "Real and Imagined Africans in Court Divertissements," paper presented at the Black Diaspora and Germany Across the Centuries Conference, German Historical Institute, Washington, DC, March 19–21, 2009; Wendy-Lou Hilary Sutherland, *Staging Blackness: Race, Aesthetics and the Black Female in Two Eighteenth-Century German Dramas: Ernst Lorenz Rathlef's "Die Mohrinn zu Hamburg" (1775) and Karl Friedrich Wilhelm Ziegler's "Die Mohrinn" (1801)*, PhD dissertation (University of Pennsylvania, 2002).

55. Friedrich Klinger, *Sturm und Drang*, in *Sturm und Drang*, ed. Alan C. Leidner (New York: Continuum, 1992), 150–51.

56. Ibid., 169.

57. Ibid., 150.

58. Ibid., 179.

59. Ibid., 180.

60. Melville, *Moby-Dick*, 65.

61. Benjamin Rush, *Medical Inquiries and Observations upon the Diseases of the Mind* (Philadelphia: Kimber and Richardson, 1812), 41; Samuel A. Cartwright, "Diseases and Peculiarities of the Negro Race," *De Bow's Review of the Southern and Western States* 1 (1851): 64–69, 331–36; see also Cartwright to Daniel Webster, "How to Save the Republic, and the Position of the South in the Union," *De Bow's Review of the Southern and Western States* 1 (1851): 184–97. Cartwright faults white slaveowners who disregard the black body's "anatomical" tendency toward kneeling and submission.

62. For a psychoanalytic reading of this process, see Sharon Cameron, *The*

Corporeal Self: Allegories of the Body in Melville and Hawthorne (Baltimore: Johns Hopkins University Press, 1981), 582–83.

63. Harriet Jacobs, *Incidents in the Life of a Slave Girl* (Boston: For the Author, 1861), 175. For other uses of Crusoe, see Shawn Thomson, *The Fortress of American Solitude: Robinson Crusoe and Antebellum Culture* (Cranbury, NJ: Fairleigh Dickinson University Press, 2009). On Crusoe and *The Arabian Nights*, see Srinivas Aravmudan, "The Adventure Chronotope and the Oriental Xenotrope: Galland, Sheridan, and Joyce Domesticate *The Arabian Nights*," in *The Arabian Nights in Historical Context: Between East and West*, ed. Saree Makdisi and Felicity Nussbaum (New York: Oxford University Press, 2008), 235–64.

64. See Robert Levine and Samuel Otter, eds., *Frederick Douglass & Herman Melville: Essays in Relation* (Chapel Hill: University of North Carolina Press, 2008).

INDEX

Page numbers in italics followed by the letter *f* indicate images.

abolitionist martyrology (*cont.*)
    and Revolutionary War heroes, 98, 100,
    105–6; rhetorical strategies, 96–106, 109, 110;
    sensationalism and embodied female suffer-
    ing, 105–6; Stone, 85, 102–3, 105–6; Stone's
    sermon *The Martyr of Freedom*, 102–3;
    Stowe's parody of republican martyrology,
    85, 111–15; Stowe's sentimental account of
    Tom's death in *Uncle Tom's Cabin*, 85, 110–17,
    142; Stowe's *Uncle Tom's Cabin* and the "real
    presence" of emotional distress, 111–12, 118,
    121, 137, 140–42, 211n76; tears shed for white
    martyrs, 105–6; tensions in the gap between
    embodied/disembodied public subjects,
    97–98; visual tropes of abjection (tortures of
    slavery and perverse spectatorship), 89–92,
    89f, 90f, 91f; Walker's book and three cuts
    depicting white suffering, 88–92, *89f, 90f,
    91f*; Walker's branded hand (as icon), 12, 84,
    85–94; and white women's publicity/partici-
    pation in public-sphere speech, 107–12;
    white women's sympathetic emotional suf-
    fering, 106–17
African Methodist Episcopal (AME) church
    (New York), 63, 71
African Methodist reformers (New York),
    62–63, 66–70, 71–72. *See also* reformist
    Methodism in nineteenth-century New
    York
African Repository, 4
Allen, Richard, 71
Allen, William G., 132
American Anti-Slavery Society (AAAS), 95,
    99, 106, 200n42
American Monthly Review, 56
American Quarterly Review, 107
American Tract Society, 63–64
Anglicans, 29, 180n15, 181n24
Anthony, Susanna, 43
Apess, William, 3, 55–83, *68f*; autobiographical
    A Son of the Forest, 56–58, 59, 66, *67f, 68f, 69f*,
    72–79, 80–82; and conversion narrative
    genre, 76–78, 80–81; depictions of temperate
    labor, 77–79; early experiences with dissent-
    ing Methodist churches, 60–61; economic
    readings of temperance, 73–74, 78–79, 82;
    "Eulogy on King Philip" and image of Indian
    virtue, 55–56, 82; first oration at the Associate
    Methodist Church, 58–59, 64; *The Increase of
    the Kingdom of Christ: A Sermon*, 66; Indian

temperance discourse and creation of an
    Indian male subject, 57, 73–79, 81–82; indict-
    ment of U.S. imperial expansion for Indian
    mistreatment, 74–76, 81–82; itinerant preach-
    ing and peddling of religious books, 59; lec-
    ture "On the Principles of Civilization" in
    Boston's Boylston Hall, 66; and Mashpee
    sovereignty, 59, 78; metaphor of being the
    "mouth for God," 57; and Methodist liberal-
    rational style, 75, 80; narrative of ascetic self-
    control, 61; Pequot self-identification, 66, 81;
    reformist Methodist temperance discourse,
    55–58, 61, 66–79. *See also* reformist Method-
    ism's evangelical temperance discourse
Arminianism, 180n15
Associate Methodist Church (Manhattan),
    58–59, 64
Attucks, Crispus, 115, 116
Augsburg *Allgemeine Zeitung*, 134
Augustine, Saint, 36, 188n76
Austin, James, 98

Bailey, Gamaliel, Jr., 79–80, 81, 82, 125
Balibar, Etienne, 146, 154
Bangs, Nathan, 63–64
Barker-Benfield, J. G., 23
Beecher, Edward, 85, 100–102, 110, 200n42;
    Narrative of Riots at Alton, 101
Beecher, Henry Ward, 116
Belcher, Samuel, 43
Benezet, Anthony, 4
Bentley, Nancy, 117
Bersani, Leo, 52–53, 165–66n4
Besse, Joseph, 95; *Sufferings of the People
    Called Quakers*, 95
Billings, Hammatt, 125
blackface. *See* minstrelsy, blackface
Blanchard, Jonathan, 97
Blatchly, Cornelius, 74; "Essay on Common
    Wealth," 74
Bleby, Henry, 115
Bogle, Paul, 115
Boston Anti-Slavery Fair, 147
Boston *Commonwealth*, 100
Boston *Emancipator and Republican*, 84
Boston Female Anti-Slavery Society, 106, 108
Brainerd, David, 55
Brattle Street Congregational Church (Bos-
    ton), 30, 55
Brecht, Bertolt, 125

Brockwell, Charles, 15–16

Brown, Henry "Box," 97

Brown, John, 115–16

Brown, William Wells, 114, 135

Bunce, George F., 66

Burke, Edmund, 13–16, 24, 28, 173n68; account of aesthetics (sublimity) and political revolutions, 13–16, 47–48; account of black sublimity, 153, 162; *Enquiry into the Origins of the Sublime and Beautiful*, 13–14; *Reflections on the Revolution in France*, 15; on sublime pleasure/pain and beauty, 13–15, 48; on torture and the spectator's pleasure in sublime terror, 14–15

Burton, Richard, 157–58, 216n45

Butler, Judith, 52

Buxton, Thomas, 96

Byles, Rev. Mather, 180n17

cabin boys. *See* child pets (Oriental "dancing boys")

Calvinism: logic of salvation, 46; and New England revivalism, 46, 180n15, 182n27

Cartwright, Samuel A., 164, 217n61

Cassell, John, 127

Castiglia, Christopher, 141

Chandler, Elizabeth Margaret, 212n79

Chapman, Maria Weston, 85, 147; and French translation of *Uncle Tom's Cabin*, 127; *Right and Wrong in Boston*, 106; white female sympathy and emotional suffering in white abolitionist martyrology, 106–10

Chauncey, Charles, 181–82n24

Chesnutt, Charles, 114

Chevalier, Michel, 124

Child, Lydia Maria, 147–49; *The Oasis*, 147–49, *148f*

child pets (Oriental "dancing boys"), 146–54, *148f, 159f*; abolitionist critiques of, 146–50, *148f*, 154–57; "A Dancing Boy of Bengal," *159f*; as *ficelle*, 149–50, 154–55; gendered public performances of feminine grace, 158–61; "Little Scipio" in Child's *The Oasis*, 147–49, *148f*; Melville and abolitionist critiques of, 146, 150–54; Melville and trope of the "grateful slave," 151–53, 163–64; Orientalist rhetoric to explain sexual practice and personhood, 158–61; Oriental sexuality/eroticism (iconography of the turbaned pageboy), 155–57; Pip as Ahab's cabin boy (Melville's

Moby-Dick), 146, 150–54, 161, 163–64; Pip's hallucination in Ahab's cabin (Melville's *Moby-Dick*), 150–51; Powers's "Greek Slave" sculpture, 156; Schuyler's 1877 Turkistan travelogue account of *batchas*, 158–61; Wertmüller's "Danaë and the Shower of Gold," 156; "wild Peter" (the "wild boy of Hanover"), 154–55; the young Moor in Klinger's *Sturm und Drang*, 161–64. *See also* Orientalist discourse of racial difference, nineteenth-century

Christian republican martyrology, 99–106. *See also* abolitionist martyrology, white

Colman, Benjamin, 30–31, 36

colonial world, 9–10; colonial French martyrological accounts of suffering in New France, 10; colonial print culture and New England revivalism, 28, 30, 33, 178n3; Pietism and revivalism, 180n15, 180n18, 183n28; Protestant colonial Atlantic martyrology and Indian martyrdom, 9–11. *See also* revivalism, New England

colonization: early nineteenth-century white evangelical writers' rejection of scientific racism, 4; Stowe's treatment of, 116–17, 204n107

Concepción Valdés, "Plácido" Gabriel de la, 115

conversion. *See* revival conversion narratives, eighteenth-century Protestant evangelical

Conway, Moncure Daniel, 116

Cooper, James Fenimore, 70, 201n60

Craft, William and Ellen, 135

Crèvecour, J. Hector St. John de, 124–25

Cromwell, Thomas, 10, 171n46

Cruikshank, George, 127

Damiens, Robert, 14

"A Dancing Boy of Bengal" (1848), *159f*

Delany, Martin, 115

Deleuze, Gilles, 46, 124, 165n4

Democratic Review, 102, 201n60

Dillon, Elizabeth Maddox, 34

Donne, John, 27

Douglass, Frederick, 79, 114, 150, 164; and Apess, 56; creation of black public subject by abjecting female suffering, 92, 104–5; *Narrative of the Life of Frederick Douglass*, 92, 104–5, 202n67; and nineteenth-century U.S. Orientalist discourse, 153; *Slavery and Freedom*, 120

Germany: immigrants' interest in the "German
slave," 134–36, 143; readers of *Uncle Tom's
Cabin* in the aftermath of the failed 1848 revo-
lutions, 120–21, 127–28, 131–36, 143, 207n14
Gilroy, Paul, 104, 174n76
Gordon, George William, 115
Great Awakening, 11, 180n15. *See also* revival
conversion narratives, eighteenth-century
Protestant evangelical
Green, Beriah, 85; *The Martyr*, 99–100, 101,
103–4
Grimké, Angelina, 56, 95, 108, 139
Grimké, Sarah, 56, 95
Gronniosaw, James, 41, 183n30
Gustafson, Sandra, 49, 59–60
Guyse, John, 30–33

Habermas, Jürgen: critics of, 16–17, 19–20, 94,
174n74, 174n76; notion of the plebeian public
"stripped of its literary garb," 16–17, 19–20;
on the plebian public sphere, 16–17, 19–20,
62, 193n10; on religious dissent in the En-
lightenment, 19–20, 176n90; *Structural
Transformation of the Public Sphere*, 16–17,
19–20, 174n74, 174n76; *Theory of Communi-
cative Action*, 176n90
Hackländer, Friedrich Wilhelm, 136; *Clara,
oder Europäische Sclavenleben* (*Clara; or,
Slave-Life in Europe*), 136
Haitian Revolution, 14–15, 128
Hale, Nathan, 98
Half-Way Covenant (1662), 186n57
Halttunen, Karen, 139
Hannabal, Montauk Temperance, 40
Harper, Frances, 115
Harrod, John, 79–80, 81
Hartman, Saidiya, 88, 143, 144–45, 212n88
Hatheway, Deborah, 41–42
Heaton, Hannah, 40
Hegel, G. W. F., 162
Henson, Josiah, 120
Hildreth, Richard, 135; *White Slave*, 135
Hobsbawm, Eric, 58, 177n93
Hopkins, Samuel, 43, 191n119
Hungarian revolutionary independence move-
ment, 131–33
Hutcheson, Francis, 49

imperial expansion. *See* U.S. imperial
expansion

Indians (Native Americans): Apess's depictions
of temperate labor by, 77–79; Apess's "Eulogy on King Philip" and image of Indian
virtue, 55–56, 82; Apess's indictment of U.S.
imperial expansion for mistreatment of, 54,
74–76, 81–82; Apess's Pequot identity, 66, 81;
Apess's temperance discourse and creation
of an Indian male subject/identity, 57, 73–79,
81–82; Methodist reformers' temperance
tracts and images of Indian drunkenness
and brutishness/savagery, 70–71, 72–73, 75;
nineteenth-century Indian plays and trope
of submission, 214n19; and Protestant colonial Atlantic martyrology, 9–11; revival conversion narratives by, 40; and revivalism,
40–41, 183n28, 183n30
Jacobs, Harriet, 144–45, 164
James, C. L. R., 150, 153
James, Henry, 119
James, William, 42
Jefferson, Thomas: *Notes on the State of Virginia* and articulation of Enlightenment
freedoms, 3; scientific notions of racial difference, 3, 4; vestibule at Monticello, 17–18,
175n80
Jehlen, Myra, 38
Jewett, John, 125
John Street Methodist Episcopal Church (New
York), 62
Juster, Susan, 63

Kant, Immanuel: Edwards and masochism's
Kantian philosophical bases/foundations, 27,
46–54; reading of blackness, 153; the shift
from Platonic/Christian model to Kantian/
Oedipal model of the law, 46; sublime, 46–47
Kaplan, Amy, 149
Karchner, Carolyn, 154
Klinger, Friedrich, 161–64; *Sturm und Drang*,
161–64
Kluge, Alexander, 174n74
Kossuth, Lajos, 131–33
Krafft-Ebing, Richard von: on masochism, 118,
120, 121–25, 172n59; patient-correspondent's
nostalgia for the "general relation" of slave
to master, 122–25, 127, 172n59; on private
erotic novel reading, 118, 120; *Psychopathia
Sexualis*, 122–24, 172n59
Kristeva, Julia, 6, 27, 51–52

ACKNOWLEDGMENTS

This project began as a meditation on the literary history of miracles and suffering. The late Lynda Hart kindled my interest in religious representations of the desirability and pleasure of abjection. Her unyielding determination taught me to love the crooked paths. Phyllis Rackin helped me find some origins of my concerns in the early modern period; Nancy Bentley and Max Cavitch established the eighteenth- and early nineteenth-century Atlantic world as a crucible for modern accounts of race, desire, pleasure, and pain. Daniel Richter and the other members of the McNeil Center for Early American Studies offered the soundest of advice, to which Hester Blum, Mark Rifkin, Camille Robcis, and Martha Schoolman added valuable friendship. At other places and times Duncan Faherty, Elaine Freedgood, Nan Goodman, Philip Gura, Sandra Gustafson, Jerry Hogle, Amy Kaplan, David Kazanjian, Chris Looby, Sam Otter, Caleb Smith, Teresa Toulouse, Michael Warner, and Hilary Wyss galvanized my work and served as models of personal and professional integrity.

My colleagues in the English Department at Hunter College, CUNY, have provided invaluable support. The friendship and generosity of Tanya Agathocleous, Jeff Allred, Kelvin Black, Rebecca Connor, Chong Chon-Smith, Michael Dowdy, Jeremy Glick, Gavin Hollis, Candice Jenkins, Richard Kaye, Donna Masini, Angela Reyes, Amy Robbins, Dow Robbins, Neal Tolchin, Alan Vardy, and Barbara Webb have made my time at Hunter a pleasure. Special thanks to Sarah Chinn for her deep knowledge of abolitionism and race; to Ramesh Mallipeddi for revealing some paradoxical modes of resistance to enslavement; to Janet Neary for connecting abolitionists' narrative and visual grammar; and to Sonali Perera for her insights into liminality, publicity, and my own writerly habits. Finally, boundless thanks Cristina Alfar for seeing me through smooth seas and rough.

Robert Lockhart at the University of Pennsylvania Press has been a deft editor and true partner in the publication process. I also owe a debt of gratitude to the librarians at the Library of Congress, the New York Public Library's Rare Book Division, and the Schomburg Center for Research in Black Culture. Titus Kaphar kindly gave permission to use his artwork on my cover; Brianna Bakke at Roberts & Tilton and Justin DeDemko both helped facilitate the process. The PSC-CUNY Research Foundation and Hunter's Presidential Funds provided welcome support. Thanks to Duke University Press for permission to reprint portions of Chapter 1.

My parents, Leonard and Carolyn Miller, remain the cornerstones of all my endeavors. Finally, this book is impossible to imagine without the brilliance and prudence of Amy McFarlane, my partner and love, and the young wit of my daughters Karolina and Sylvia, who helped grace its pages.